ABORIGINAL DREAMING PATHS AND TRADING ROUTES

FIRST NATIONS and the colonial encounter

Series Editor: David Cahill, Professorial Fellow, School of History, University of New South Wales

Series titles in order of publication

ABORIGINAL DREAMING PATHS AND TRADING ROUTES

THE COLONISATION OF THE AUSTRALIAN ECONOMIC LANDSCAPE

DALE KERWIN

sussex
ACADEMIC
PRESS

Brighton • Chicago • Toronto

2 4 6 8 10 9 7 5 3

First published in hardcover 2010, reprinted in paperback 2012, in Great Britain by
SUSSEX ACADEMIC PRESS
PO Box 139
Eastbourne BN24 9BP

Distributed in North America by
SUSSEX ACADEMIC PRESS
Independent Publishers Group
814 N Franklin St, Chicago, IL 60610, USA

British Library Cataloguing in Publication Data
A CIP catalogue record for this book is available from the British Library.

Library of Congress Cataloging-in-Publication Data
Kerwin, Dale.
Aboriginal dreaming paths and trading routes : the colonisation of the Australian economic landscape / Dale Kerwin.
p. cm.
Includes bibliographical references and index.
ISBN 978-1-84519-338-6 (h/c : alk. paper)
ISBN 978-1-84519-529-8 (pbk. : alk. paper)
  1. Aboriginal Australians—Economic conditions. 2. Aboriginal Australians—Social life and customs. 3. Aboriginal Australians—Land tenure. 4. Aboriginal Australians—History. 5. Mythology, Aboriginal Australian. 6. Aboriginal Australians—First contact with Europeans. 7. Aboriginal Australians—Colonization. 8. Australia—Colonization—History. I. Title.
GN666.K48 2010
994'.0049915—dc22

2009049766

Typeset and designed by Sussex Academic Press, Brighton & Eastbourne.
Printed and bound by CPI Group (UK) Ltd, Croydon, CR0 4YY
This book is printed on acid-free paper.

Contents

Contents

List of Illustrations, Figures and Maps

Cover illustrations
FRONT: Scenic lookout, Macartney Range Kennedy Development Road near Middleton, Queensland. "The Dreamtime spirits talk to those who will listen." Photo: Dale Kerwin, 2002. The photograph of the Aboriginal man is an image produced by the 1911 *Sydney Mail* newspaper; reproduced by the kind permission of the State Library of New South Wales.
BACK: Painting of Two Boys Dreaming – Wangkangurru storyline (trade routes) of the Mura. On display in the Simpson Desert National Parks Office, Birdsville. The skeletal remains of 'Mungo Man', published with kind permission of Willandra Elders. Photo: copyright and courtesy of J.M. Bowler (see below under Figure 11). Drawing of a possum/kangaroo skin cloak. Cloaks were made and designed for trade rather than local use (see below under Figure 31). Reproduced by kind permission of the Museum Victoria, Melbourne.

Prelim illustration
The trading way, reproduced by kind permission of Laurie Nilsen.

Figures

control/Aboriginal presence, thus creating a cultural landscape. Photo: Dale Kerwin, 2004.

10 Scenic lookout, Macartney Range Kennedy Development Road near Middleton, Queensland. "The Dreamtime spirits talk to those who will listen." Photo: Dale Kerwin, 2002

11 In July 1968, the geomorphologist Jim Bowler discovered skeletal remains of what is now known as 'Mungo Lady'. Five years later he discovered new remains of 'Mungo Man'. The archaeological dig was excavated by Dr Thorne at Lake Mungo. In 1999 Allan Thorne undertook DNA sampling of the skeletal remains of 'Mungo Man' and approximated the date of 'Lake Mungo man at about 62,000 years'. Mungo Man was ritually buried between 56,000 to 68,000 years ago at Willandra Lakes in New South Wales. His hands were crossed over his pelvis and red ochre was ground into a powdery substance and sprinkled over his body. Published with kind permission of Willandra Elders. Photo: copyright and courtesy of J.M. Bowler.

12 A Dig Tree and Interpretative sign at Nappa Merrie Station. Burke and Wills were offered food by the local Aboriginal people, but refused it. As a consequence they died from hunger despite the availability of edible and sustaining food in their travel environment. Original photo by *the Sydney Mail* newspaper, 1911. Kind permission to use granted by the State Library of New South Wales.

13 A compass rose used by medieval navigators.

14 A Queensland State High school year 8 activity sheet for map reading. Children are taught how to read a map, what function maps serve, and what the symbols on maps represent.

15 The painting *Wangkangurru Dreaming* provides information of the dreaming tracks, lore and history of the Aborigines. In the Simpson Desert Rangers Office, Birdsville. Photo: Dale Kerwin, 2004.

16 Generic Aboriginal symbols used in Aboriginal art, in Peterson 1981:46.

17 Sand drawing of Honey-ant Dreaming, in Charles Mountford 1976:60.

18 Map of camps and routes of honey-ant totemic beings, in Charles Mountford 1976:60.

19 Cartography drawn on a shield, from Western Australia, in Cowan 1992:12.

20 Illustration of a cyclon. Aboriginal material culture, in Marji Hill 1981:95. Cylcons are Aboriginal title deeds, considered as sacred objects, often carved from stone or moulded from clay. Some were known to be fired and were cylindrical in shape. They are about 30 cm. in length, and about 7 cm. wide, and are incised with totemic emblems that represent movement across country.

21 A carved tree of the Wiraduri nation, in Mulvaney 1989:85.

22 A toa from Lake Gregory providing interpretative information through the use of symbols, in Jones and Sutton 1986:62.

23 A message stick from Boulia, Queensland, in Roth 1897:137–38.

24 A Bora ring at Bestman Road, Toorbal Point.

25 Painting of a dugout canoe from Prince of Wales Island coming along side the Monarch, as described by Gregory 1857:7–8, in Birman 1979:99. The Aborigines bartered several articles with the crew of the schooner.

26 A Pituri plant.

27 A Pituri bag on display. Reproduced by kind permission of the National Museum, Australia.

28 Painting of Two Boys Dreaming. On display in the Simpson Desert National Parks Office, Birdsville.

29 Wangkangurru storyline (trade routes) of the Mura. Painting on the wall of the Simpson Desert National Parks Office, Birdsville.

30 Engraved pearl shells. Reproduced by kind permission of the National Museum of Australia, Canberra.

31 Drawing of a possum/kangaroo skin cloak. Reproduced by kind permission of the Museum Victoria, Melbourne.

32 Gyndier Drive, Noosaville, Queensland, was used as a coach track. Photo: 1880.

33 John Jones, an Elder from the Dalongabarra nation, reclaiming an Aboriginal path that runs along side Gyndier Drive. He stated "that the path is of cultural heritage significance". The road is located in the Woori State Forest of Noosaville, Queensland. Photo: John Jones, 2002.

34 Aboriginal well along the Moonie Highway near St George, Queensland. There are a series of these water wells dotted through the landscape that are used by Aboriginal travellers. Today they are maintained by Aboriginal CDEP workers. Photo: Dale Kerwin, 2003.

35 Leichhardt blazed tree stump. Photo: Dale Kerwin.

36 Mitchell's memorial, St George, Queensland. Photo: Dale Kerwin, 2004.

37 Mitchell's memorial, St George, Queensland. Photo: Dale Kerwin, 2004.

38 The boab tree, 2 July 1855. Gregory's base camp at Victoria River, Timber Creek, Northern Territory which is also an Aboriginal sacred site.

39 A stock route positioned on an Aboriginal trading way. Located on the Moonie Highway and Bendee Road. Photo: Dale Kerwin, 2002.

40 An Aboriginal path that is now a stock route, located along the Diamantina Road near Winton. Photo: Dale Kerwin, 2002.

41 Burke and Wills' dig tree Nappa Murrie valorising their feats. But in actual fact their exploration trip was a disaster.

42 Water bore at Burketown Queensland, established in 1897. Original depth 2,304 feet. These water bores litter the landscape of the Channel Country. They are uncapped and millions of mega-litres a year flow into the sand of the desert country.

Maps

1 Second smallpox epidemic spread by the movement of infected people along the river systems in New South Wales and Queensland. Adapted from Noel Butlin's *Our Original Aggression: Aboriginal Populations of Southeast Australia 1788–1850* (Sydney: George Allen & Unwin, 1983).

2 An interpretation of the Dreaming tracks as told by Kado Muir and Noel Nannup. Kado Muir is an anthropologist and traditional owner from Leonora in Western Australia who represented the Greens at the Federal Election in 2004. His totem

is the Dingo. Noel Nannup, a Wajuk man from the Bibbulmun nation, he was awarded an Honorary Doctorate from Western Australian University.

3 An interpretation of Kado Muir and Noel Nannup's account of the trade routes, with the major highways and roads detailed.

4 An interpretation of Noel Nunnup's story of traditional trading routes in Western Australia. These routes later became the Canning Traditional trade routes.

5 The Two Dog Dreaming story has several Aboriginal Dreaming ancestors associated with this story line; it also involves the movement of cultural property such as pituri. For example, the Rainbow Serpent Dreaming story chasing the Nightjar is associated with the Two Dog Dreaming story. Also associated with the Two Dog story is the dreaming story line of the Emu, Kuringii, being chased by the Two Dingoes. Further across the central desert the mythical Kangaroo, revenging the death of the blue-tongued lizard Nintaka, chased the Ninjuri lizard-man. Two Dogs also incorporates the Two Boys story of the Wangkangurru people as well as the Pigeon Dreaming of the Gurindji people of the Victoria River region. These stories represent the movement of pituri across Australia, starting at the place of harvest in the Channel Country and radiating outwards along the Dreaming tracks. These Dreaming stories are found within oral histories collected by McCarthy, Roth, Tindale and Rose.

6 Map detailing movement of goods in the Arnhem Land region with Oenpelli, Northern Territory, as the trade centre.

7 Interpretation of information provided by Roth (1897), Aiston (1937), McConell (1976) and Rose (1985) detailing trading centres established along the Pituri Road.

8 The east coast route follows the national horse riding trail. Aboriginal people travelling to the Bunya Fest would follow this route, which is part of a chain of Bora rings/grounds along the Great Diving Range of the east coast.

9 Cape York to South Australia route.

10 Kimberley to Eyre Peninsula route.

11 Yarralin people's tracks of the Nanganarri and Pigeon Dreamings strings. Nanganarii Dreaming follows a track between Wickham River and Gordon Creek to Pigeon Hole. This Dreaming crosses both Wickham River and Gordon Creek. Pigeon Dreaming follows Victoria River. Gregory followed both of these Dreaming tracks on his survey of 1855–56. Reproduced by kind permission of Deborah Bird Rose.

12 Gregory's northern survey of 1855–56, in Birman and Bolton (1972). While surveying around Victoria River Gregory followed the Pigeon Dreaming track south along Victoria River where he encountered Wickham River which he followed and subsequently established a depot. At the point of the depot, Nanganarii Dreaming crosses the river and turns back to Victoria River to cross Gordon Creek. Gregory followed this Dreaming track during his survey

13 David Mowaliarlai's (1993) map of trade routes and storylines linking Aboriginal nations across Australia. From David Mowaljarlai and Jutta Malnic, *Yorro yorro everything standing up alive: spirit of the Kimberley* (Perth: Magabala Books). *Yorro*

Yorro is the story of the Wandjina creation spirits and their transformation into ancestor beings and eventually into human form. It is the story of Aboriginal creation and the renewal of nature and life. Reproduced by kind permission of Magabala books.

14 Aboriginal cultural sites in the Brisbane area, Queensland; this is a Eurocentric map and without a legend is largely meaningless. However the map can be interpreted using the few reference points that are indicated using local knowledge. Located on the map of North Brisbane at C17 is Bald Hills Creek, C6 is Sandgate Golf Club site at the end of the Sandgate railway line (Mosquito Creek), and HG7 is the mouth of Breakfast Creek. Notice the other railway line, which is the line north to the Sunshine Coast. Both of these lines follow the major Aboriginal throughways for travelling north and south along the 'Bunya and Bora Ground', highways of the south-eastern route highlighted in Map 9.

15 Aboriginal Roads, Sunshine Coast, Queensland, based on maps by Gaiarbau (W. MacKenzie) cited in J. Steele (1983). Indicated on the map is a major Aboriginal road that heads north through the Glasshouse mountains and on to Gympie. From Wells 2003:28.

16 Sunshine Coast, Queensland. Aboriginal paths with the Queensland railway line over the north–south path. In Steele (1984:5).

17 Gyndier Drive. Reproduced by kind permission of Robin Wells.

18 Colleen Wall's detailed map of Kabi Kabi paths and cultural sites with Aboriginal names for places of significance. The map was used for a Native Title application. Detailed on the map are major road systems of the Sunshine Coast region, and the National Horse Trail. Gympie is in direct alignment with Gimbee. Colleen Wall, a Kabi Kabi woman, was in 2004 the Manager of the Aboriginal and Torres Strait Islander Arts Programs in the Department of Arts Queensland, and a practising artist.

19 Adapted from Bob Munn's story. Gunnggari peoples' trading path following the Warrego Highway between the western townships of Charleville to Chinchilla, and Balonne Highway between Cunnamulla and St George. The Moonie Highway between St George and Moonie follows the trading way to the Bunya Mountains and the Black Butt Range. Bob Munn is a Gungari person from south-western Queensland who was chairperson of the Queensland Aboriginal Consultative Committee for Education, and a member of the Aboriginal and Torres Strait Islander Advisory Board to the Queensland Government in 2000.

20 Adapted from Hazel McKellar, *Matya – Mundu: A History of the Aboriginal People of the South West Queensland* (Cunnamulla Aboriginal Native Welfare Association, Cunnamulla, 1984), p. 13. Kunja peoples had well established paths which took that mob around the small townships, near Cunnamulla in south-western Queensland. Today the tracks are stock routes, and the major thoroughfares of the Mitchell Highway and Bulloo Development Road. Kunja peoples' paths also travel over the Queensland and New South Wales border.

21 Adapted from Hazel McKellar, *Matya – Mundu: A History of the Aboriginal People of the South West Queensland* (Cunnamulla Aboriginal Native Welfare Association,

Cunnamulla, 1984), p. 44. Budjari peoples' paths in south-western Queensland between Cunnamulla and Thargominda. Bulloo Developmental Road, the Paroo Highway, and several stock routes follow these paths.

22   Adapted from Hazel McKellar, *Matya – Mundu: A History of the Aboriginal People of the South West Queensland* (Cunnamulla Aboriginal Native Welfare Association, Cunnamulla, 1984), p. 56. The traditional paths of the Kooma people are located between the small townships of Coongoola and Bollon and travel south to Cubbie.

23   Adapted from Hazel McKellar, *Matya – Mundu: A History of the Aboriginal People of the South West Queensland* (Cunnamulla Aboriginal Native Welfare Association, Cunnamulla, 1984), p. 56. Pathways of the Killilla people of the south-western corner of Queensland. The township of Thargomindah and Bulloo Track and Bulloo Developmental Road follow the Killilla peoples' paths which were used to stay clear of European settlement and avoid conflict.

24   W.O. Hodgkinson's north-western 1876 survey of the Channel Country. As adapted from the Queensland Department of Natural Resources and Mines map of marine and inland explorers' routes.

Series Editor's Preface
by David Cahill

Recent decades have witnessed a rise in self-awareness and self-assertiveness of First Nations peoples across the globe. This has brought indigenous histories, cultures, identities and politics into the mainstream of public and intellectual life, often in controversial manner. First Nations peoples across the world are beginning to receive the attention their welfare, cultures, and histories merit. For many of these peoples, this has come after five centuries of contact with European powers and nation states. First Nations have varied histories that are partly the result of their autochthonous cultures, their particular colonial experiences, and increasing integration into the world economy. Notwithstanding this wide variation, however, many of the generic colonial processes they have undergone are similar in nature. Aspects such as land rights, labour systems, miscegenation, evangelization, and the undermining of traditional laws by introduced legal systems, are generic problems that have produced a wide variety of local responses across cultures. Similarly, First Nations have been transformed by profit–based economic systems with different values, by new gender and social roles, and new forms of education to wean indigenous children away from traditional values. In effect, new lifeways, a loss of autonomy, new judicial and fiscal systems, and bewildering multiple levels of government, have all posed immense obstacles to the social reproduction of indigenous communities and nations across the world.

First Nations peoples underwent conquest that involved both violence and negotiation. Their responses were many and varied. First, there was resistance, most manifest in all types of rebellion as well as passive resistance. Second, there were processes of accommodation by which they sought to realign traditional belief, value, and authority systems with those imposed upon them, forcefully or persuasively, by the colonial powers. Third, there was also considerable opportunism and initiative, by which indigenous communities turned colonialism back on itself by appropriating colonial institutions and legal processes so as to optimize their own colonial condition. Fourth, there were positive outcomes stemming from the initiative of First Nations, notably in the development of native literatures in which chirographic representations were often replaced by, or supplemented with, writing systems; in the same way introduced artistic expressions were often reinterpreted through an indigenous lens. That conquest and colonialism brought many deleterious consequences in its train is evident, but the 'fatal impact' approach to the impact of colonialism upon colonised peoples has always been far too simplistic, skimming over, as it does, the many positive and creative adaptations of indigenous peoples to new and daunting challenges.

Most regions of the world were inhabited by indigenous peoples at the beginning of European conquest and colonization, from the late fifteenth century onwards. The

Americas, both north and south, included urban civilizations as well as nomadic peoples, and even today indigenous peoples are not always fully incorporated into the modern world, e.g., Amazonian peoples, who nevertheless manage to make their voice heard, sometimes to great effect, as for example in the 2009 victory of Native Peoples from the tropical Peruvian eastern lowlands over governmental and private development interests. In Oceania, including Australasia, conquests were often seaborne and sometimes took longer to grip, such that even today in New Zealand and especially Australia the condition of indigenous communities is often parlous. Varied processes of conquest, colonization, and colonial control have taken place across Asia with a range of responses that often included major revitalization movements, as for example in Burma, Indonesia and the Philippines. Indigenous peoples of Africa experienced, even into the twentieth century, different types of colonial oppression. Still other, diverse experiences of colonial and nation state control have been experienced by peoples in the Central Asian republics and Mongolia, while even Europe has its own indigenous group in the Sami of Scandinavia.

Some indigenous peoples have largely disappeared either wholly, or at least as cohesive social groups, for example the Guanches of the Canary Islands, who were largely extinct by the late sixteenth century. However, many descendants of supposedly extinct native peoples vigorously oppose the very idea that their culture and identity were obliterated by colonial rule. The rise of DNA analysis as a mainstream medical diagnostic tool has sometimes given them reason to do so. The widespread public perception that Tasmanian aborigines became extinct in the nineteenth century has been proven wrong, though no serious scholar ever believed it. DNA analysis has similarly disproved the theory of the disappearance of the native peoples of California, long believed by academics and non-academics to have become extinct, also in the nineteenth century. Rather, it has been shown that some among them escaped a state-backed genocide, based on bounty hunting, by adopting western dress and passing themselves off as Mexicans. Now, thanks to the wonder of DNA, their story can be told (and compensation claims can be lodged). For many erstwhile colonies with large indigenous populations, the attainment of post-colonial independence—from the eighteenth century to even the present day—merely resulted in a substitution of European colonialism by internal colonialism, i.e., the continued (and sometimes worsened) exploitation of native by non-native peoples, exploitation that often had, and has, the explicit or tacit support of nation states. Colonialism didn't die away in post-colonial societies, it merely metamorphosed and mutated—same horse, different rider.

Scholars, politicians, journalists and activists of all kinds have interpreted First Nations' cultures, histories, and present-day social conditions in many different ways, sometimes notable for malice borne towards indigenous peoples. This is highly contested ground, with indigenous claim-making posing challenges to conventional interpretations of indigenous histories, especially in the treatment of the early colonial encounter itself. Indigenous groups have made demands for formal apologies by the State for the felt abuses of colonial rule, sometimes accompanied by a recasting of the indigenous past as a kind of Golden Age in which humankind lived in harmony with the natural environment. Not infrequently, this has restored an indigenous storyline to national histories from which they had been largely excluded. Simultaneously, indigenous stakeholders have pressed their case for compensation for their colonial suffering, sometimes viewed as an unbroken continuum to the present. This recompense has been sought in the form of financial payments to groups and individuals, as social and educational programs designed especially for indigenous claimants, and—most controversially—the return of lands alienated during the twin processes of conquest and colonization. Indigenous land claims have provoked sometimes fierce resistance among stakeholders, especially from those present-day, non-native owners of lands alleged to be "tribal" homelands, many of whom dispute indigenous titles or entitlements. Beyond the question of land tenure and right of access to ancestral hunting territories and even spiritual space, opponents of such historical rights exhibit a wider resistance, explicitly denying that colonialism was deleterious for indigenous peoples, and alleging that perceived post-colonial conditions among indigenous peoples were and are due to their own inability to take advantage of the civilising possibilities ushered in by colonial rule and later post-colonial, sovereign governments. Put another way, their problems are entirely their own fault.

This denialism is the bane of productive debate. It embraces a wide range of opinions, ranging from journalistic contrariness to, in its worst manifestations, a crude racism, but is not necessarily unsophisticated for all that. Of more moment are contested questions of national, collective and even individual identity. Such debates and conflicts also represent a battle over History, of who should control normative versions of national history, national memory, and essentialised national myths. For example, in Australia, those who deny indigenous sufferings accuse their opponents of creating a "black armband" version of history. The latter respond that their critics, and especially denialists of whatever ilk, seek to "whitewash" national history, editing out shameful episodes of deleterious white policies and actions from national history and nationalistic myth. Whether explicitly or implicitly, each camp accuses the other of falsification of the national history. This standoff is reminiscent of an earlier debate over Spanish conquest and colonization in the Americas, in which partisans of the "Black Legend" were pitched against those of a "White Legend". This historiographical debate, which commenced in the sixteenth century, only petered out in the 1960s. It was resolved after a fashion, but only after a plethora of monographic, empirical studies settled many of the issues involved, such that proponents of both "Legends" were forced to resile from their more extreme assertions. Quite clearly, resolution of heated debates over First Nations histories will depend, in the final analysis, on the harvesting of a significant weight of empirical studies as well as public debates entered into in good faith. A further avenue of progress through these questions lies in a comparative, cross-cultural treatment of the histories of First Nations peoples: debates over indigenous claim-making are usually restricted to national writings, such that an awareness of the historiography on indigenous peoples in other "culture areas" is usually absent from each national debate. The context for understanding First Nations everywhere is not just local and national, but international and global—and everywhere historical.

However, there is an abundant and rich empirical historiography, ethnologically informed, on indigenous peoples, above all those of Canada, the USA, and Latin

America. In the Asia-Pacific region, there are many New Zealand studies of Maori–Pakeha colonial relations that are variable in quality, but among which are superb analyses of warfare, religion and land tenure. There are also numerous studies of the colonial encounter elsewhere in Polynesia and Melanesia. The historiography on indigenous Australians is even more variable in quality, ranging from ill-informed journalism, through poorly researched essays, to a small cluster of first-rate empirical and analytical studies. In order to respond to the lack of comparative studies, there is an urgent need for a general series that would compare the indigenous histories across national boundaries. It is envisaged that each volume in this Sussex Academic Press series will be informed by rich first order research on First Nations peoples. The series will focus especially on native peoples of Canada and the USA, Mesoamerica and the Andes, Oceania and Asia.

The greatest challenge in writing the history of First Nations peoples is that of discerning the views and meanings that indigenous people attached to their colonial experiences, to distinguish the insider viewpoint from the interpretations of those outside the indigenous culture—the 'emic' from the 'etic', in the formulation of linguist Frederick Pike. In this regard, the best intentions of scholars to delineate the indigenous meanings and interpretations have often resulted in indigenous cultures being portrayed as the 'Other' (coined by Edward Said), often with the subtext that indigenous peoples are merely victims of colonialism or the post-colonial state. The range of responses of First Nations peoples included, then as now, many creative options as they came to perceive European cultures and colonialisms as fountainheads of opportunities to enhance the welfare of their nations and communities. Dale Kerwin's path-breaking, 'emic' study explicitly eschews this 'othering' of Australian Aboriginal societies. His book identifies a pan-Aboriginal culture while acknowledging the sheer variety of its cultures and languages, and provides a welcome focus on their relationship to the Australian environment. The dreaming paths of the nations were not only ceremonial pathways but trade routes that criss-crossed the continent and along which goods and knowledge flowed. This study, rejecting as it does the hunter-gatherer image of Aboriginal Australia, represents a fresh appreciation not only of their nations but also inscribes them, to a greater extent than hitherto, into the very body of Australian history.

David Cahill
University of New South Wales

Preface

The first peoples of Australia are recognised in Australian Law and legislative mechanisms, and are legally denominated as Aboriginal people and Torres Strait Islander people. However, inherent Aboriginal sovereignty is not recognised by Australian and International law. Historically, Australia is a settled colony that was uninhabited and discovered and colonised by English subjects. The laws of England were the birthright of every person and constituted the only law of the settled country. Upon settlement of Australia, the colonisers falsely determined that the First Peoples of Australia were not organised into independent, self-governing communities and therefore not recognised as domestic nations, such that their original and natural rights were *ipso facto* extinguished by law. The classification of "settled colony" rather than ceded or conquered is critical to how Aboriginal sovereignty is defined in Australia. From an Aboriginal Australian point of view, we have not conceded our rights to our own domestic nations (Aboriginal semantics "Country"). There has not been any treaties signed yet; as Aboriginal people, we have not surrendered our rights as sovereign nations to the invaders.

Aboriginal culture, spread across the continent of Australia, has its origins in the traditions of trade and ceremonial exchange, whereby tangible and intangible property linked people across enormous distances, thereby facilitating the construction of extensive social networks. Each Aboriginal nation had its own laws, religious beliefs, and history; there is no distinct or generic Aboriginal culture; rather, it is considerably varied as evidenced by the fact that there were 250 distinct languages in existence. This remains evident today, as Aboriginal people self-identify regionally as Bama, Nyungar, Yongu, Goorie, Murri, Koorie, and Nations. However, anthropological terminology determines Aboriginal societies as moieties, tribes, hordes, clans and family groups. To add to these identification terms, the Australian government has developed other classifications which are used in legislation: historic people, traditional owners and a minority group. Nevertheless, there are commonalities in Aboriginal culture across the continent of Australia and, generally, the Aboriginal preferred term for place of origin is 'country'.

My starting position is that the Australian environment afforded all sustenance for the development of Aboriginal societies, and they developed technologies to utilise the resources on their lands. As with all societies, technology, development, and land management systems were used to harness local environmental conditions so as to provide and enhance a way of life.

The economics of Aboriginal land management systems provided time for people to practise the arts and religious customs. Aboriginal land management entailed a symbolic recording system for mapping the country,* which contributed to the maintenance of

---

* "Country" is a generic term for Aboriginal places (countries) on the map of Australia, not Australia as a whole. Prior to colonisation there were over 250 Aboriginal nations (countries) each with their

sedentary lifestyles. Law, business, ceremony, and food procurement determined how people lived, and not everyone was engaged in these activities to the same degree. The collection of food resources by members of a community was sufficient to feed people who participated in political discussions, but to also meet daily needs and feed members who did not contribute to food production. Aboriginal societies produced religious leaders, artisans, specialised craft persons, and philosophers – this much can easily be ascertained from available sources. Indeed, the chapters to follow contradict much (or most) of what is 'known' about Aboriginal societies. Because popular and scientific 'knowledge' is so well entrenched and hermeneutic, considerable effort is spent in Chapter 1 – Common Sense and Common Nonsense – to resist it through the meticulous amassing of counter-evidence. The chapter questions and debunks several myths about Aboriginal societies and replaces them with a humanised view of Aboriginal society, providing a context for the broader study of Aboriginal trading ways through an historic interpretation of the contact period based on social science literature. Arguments are scrutinised about nomadic and primitive societies, as well as Romantic views of culture and affluence. These are juxtaposed with evidence that indicates that Aboriginal societies are substantially sedentary and highly developed, capable of functional differentiation and foresight. The hunter-gatherer image is positioned in direct opposition by providing evidence of crop cultivation and land management.

The Australian landscape was shaped by Aboriginal land management, which in turn made the country more accessible for Europeans as they moved around. In other words, European settlement and land use was premised on Aboriginal land use practices. Early European paths and roads for communication were built on Aboriginal lines of movement and distribution. In a sense, European colonisation of Australia owes much of its success to the deliberate process of Aboriginal land management practices. The more notable and successful explorers such as Matthew Flinders, Thomas Mitchell, and Edmond Kennedy engaged Aboriginal guides, whereas Burke and Wills had no Aboriginal people to guide them and are better known for their failure.

Chapter 2 – Coming of the Aliens – traces accounts of contact from the early European bridgehead in Sydney Cove to the engagement of Aboriginal people as diplomats, scouts, and guides (Reynolds 1978, 1990; Willey 1979); it develops the theme of travel and trade between Aboriginal people and the invaders. Discussion focuses on the concept of trade, and explores the introduction of smallpox, which requires a chain of humans to spread. The rapid spread of smallpox verifies the existence of a well-developed network of travel across the Australian continent. If Aboriginal people did not trade across the breadth of Australia then smallpox would not have travelled as far and would not have decimated as many Aboriginal people. The spread of this disease along Aboriginal paths is critical to our understanding of the trade, trade routes, and communication between Aboriginal people, and it can be mapped.

own sovereignty. When an Aboriginal person talks about their place they are referring to their place (country) of origin. The reader can Google "Map of Aboriginal Australia" to view, in colour, the regional splits of the Aboriginal nations. The annexation of Aboriginal ownership of the land continues to dominate Australian politics and society.

Chapter 2 is premised upon the notion that Australia was already a cultivated land-scape, and it examines the effect of the clash of cultures and the means the invaders used to create a landscape they could call their own. The discussion then focuses on the land-scape and how the invaders created a wilderness that suited their needs. The physical and symbolic remnants of meetings between Aboriginal and European explorers are important markers in Australian history (Mulvaney 1989). Historical accounts tend to either ignore these as incidental to the grand narrative of development, or misread them as manifestations of Europeans-in-place, rather than as symbols of Europeans-in-contact. In most cases, however, the routes along which such contact took place were already established and important for Aboriginal peoples, because they provided for the movement of goods and the exchange of cultural knowledge. They were the story places, songlines or songways.

Chapter 3 – Only The Learned Can Read – affirms the relevance and importance of Aboriginal knowledge of Dreaming paths and develops a sense of Aboriginal spatial history and chronology to show that there was a need to trade. It also deals with the regulation of goods and social structures in Aboriginal communities, and includes Aboriginal oral histories to deconstruct the common belief that Aboriginal people did not travel to trade.

Chapter 4 – Maps, Travel and Trade as Cultural Processes – considers the cultural processes of developing material for orientation purposes. Map making has a long history of development and is a good indicator of cultural processes. The stars and land-scape have been used throughout time to assist people on their travels. The chapter also considers regional variations in Aboriginal map making and the importance of this in terms of creating niche demands for a product. Attention is paid to the role of myth in mapping landscapes, as well as the various tangible and intangible devices that are used for orientation. The chapter develops the concept of travel, and maps the actual paths used by Aboriginal people to move around the continent. The idea of roads and routes is located within the discourse of cultural landscapes, and at the intersections of such roads or routes marketplaces and trading centres can be found. The routes along which goods were traded are examined and the many ways in which these routes were mapped are discussed.

Chapter 5 – To Travel is to Learn – describes Aboriginal trading paths in south-west Queensland and highlights their critical role in assisting explorers to open the country for settlement. The chapter connects the routes explorers and surveyors mapped with Aboriginal trading ways, and goes on to elucidate the assistance Aboriginal guides provided. The broad aim here is to establish that the common ways Aboriginal people used to navigate the physical face of the Australian continent in order to trade and communicate.

The focus is on south-west Queensland; it traces the settlement in the south-east through to the last outpost of Aboriginal held territory in the Channel Country, in the south-western corner. Discussion focuses on specific explorers and surveyors, namely Ludwig Leichhardt who travelled to Port Essington (1844–1847), Thomas Mitchell's foray into tropical Australia (1845). Edmund Kennedy's survey with Galmarra (Jacky Jacky) from Rockingham Bay, Cardwell, for the overland trip in North Queensland to

Cape York (1848); and the Gregory brothers' survey from the western coast of Northern Territory to central Queensland and from Darling Downs to Adelaide, 1855–1858. The chapter also considers the Jardine brothers' cattle drive from Rockhampton to the tip of Cape York Peninsula (1864), and W.O. Hodgkinsons' north-western expedition into Queensland (1876).

Since the earliest years of the colonising process, Europeans used Aboriginal guides who predictably travelled along the paths already carved in the Aboriginal landscape. Settlers and graziers subsequently followed these pathways with the result that Aboriginal trading paths became drover runs and coach ways. Aboriginal land management such as fire stick farming presented the colonisers with a landscape that was already sculptured by humans to suit their needs. Finally, Chapter 5 details the history of stock routes in Queensland along with some of the major stockmen. Spatial dimensions and geography of these routes are outlined. White drovers also utilised Aboriginal stockmen, and plugged into their knowledge to move beasts over Aboriginal paths with water reserves along their route. The stock routes are once again superimposed over Aboriginal paths.

The final chapter – Misrepresentation of the Grand Narrative : 'Walk Softly on the Landscape' – draws together the themes presented in earlier chapters and summarises European attitudes to the Australian landscape. Europeans felt at home in Australia once they had mapped it with their spatial metaphors; the 'landscape looked forward to be occupied by a civilised society' (Carter 1987:340). Since the historic Mabo High Court decision in 1992, when the doctrine of *terra nullius** was thoroughly discredited in law, there is no option for Australia but to accept and recognise Aboriginal Australia. This recognition entails an acknowledgment that Aboriginal nations had, and continue to have, proprietary rights to their territories and soils (Gardiner-Garden 1994). The Mabo decision relating to the land of the Murray Islanders in the Torres Straits marked an acceptance by jurisprudence of these rights based in common law. Yet a cultural version of *terra nullius* still exists – the denial of the prior existence of a fully-fledged and viable culture.

---

* In 1992 the High Court of Australia overturned the doctrine of '*terra nullius*' by recognising in a limited fashion Australian Aboriginal people as the traditional owners of land. This recognition of Native Title accords Aboriginal people rights to their property. This, of course, is providing that Aboriginal people can prove that customary law and ownership is recognised within their own community and is protected within their own laws.

Eddie Koiki Mabo was one of five plaintiffs from Murray (Mer) Island in the Torres Straits. He is a member of the Meriam people. In May 1992 he and four other Murray Islanders began an action in the High Court of Australia seeking confirmation of their traditional land rights.

The Wik and Thayorre peoples whose traditional lands are on the Western Cape York Peninsula Queensland tested the legal argument that graziers were only granted pasturage rights under pastoral leases and that pastoral leases did not extinguish the traditional rights of occupancy and use by Traditional Owners. On 23 December 1996 the High Court delivered a verdict in favour of the Wik and Thayorre peoples. The court found that pastoral leases did not give exclusive possession, and did not necessarily extinguish all native title rights. The court stated that pastoral leases and Native Title can co-exist.

Figure I An Aboriginal Sacred Sites Heritage sign, Timber Creek, Victoria River, Northern Territory. Photo: Dale Kerwin, 2004.

Australians now recognise Aboriginal people as the first people of Australia. This became evident when millions of Australian people marched in a mass demonstration of support for reconciliation with Aboriginal people in all the major cities in 2000. But Aboriginal cultural heritage is still not recognised as a legitimate part of Australian heritage to be protected and presented as an equal to European culture. For instance, the *Queensland Aboriginal Heritage Act 2004* is not about the protection of Aboriginal and Torres Strait Islander movable cultural property, and does not contain any Aboriginal and Torres Strait Islander heritage protection principles. Furthermore there is no national Aboriginal language legislation, and Aboriginal languages receive considerably lower levels of funding than other languages taught in Australian schools. Even legislation to protect religious rights does not have provisions for the recognition of Aboriginal religious practices and rites.

Australian political institutions are trying to come to terms with concepts of Aboriginality and Aboriginal rights, but continue to draft policy and legislation that is discriminatory. As a case in point, Aboriginal cultural heritage protection laws are now being redesigned after the Hindmarsh Island fiasco which gave ownership of Aboriginal cultural heritage to the Crown. Politicians promote a 'bones and stones' approach to Aboriginal cultural heritage, when what is needed is a humanised view of Aboriginal cultural heritage that takes into account: we are here, we have survived.

The Mabo High Court decision has forced the Australian political system to devise laws for Aboriginal claims to country. Government policy requires Aboriginal nations to make Native Title claims to country through connection reports based on anthropology, archaeology, and historical evidence. Just as Aboriginal claims to country now need to be documented for Native Title claims, this book uses historical accounts, pictures, and anecdotal and symbolic representations to reauthor country and put Aboriginal roads back on a map of Australia. Aboriginal accounts of these places and the knowledge of these storyways and storylines are ingrained in memory. They have withstood what J. Brennan in Mabo (2) called the tide of history [that] washed away any real knowledge of traditional law and any real observance of traditional customs (Gardiner-Garden 1994; Hunter 1996:16).

Research for this book involved examining explorer journals, museum exhibitions, pioneers and research by social scientists, and more importantly Aboriginal oral history in order to gather evidence for the existence of Aboriginal trading ways. The argument put forward has built on work already detailed by such notable authors and researchers as Roth, McCarthy, Tindale, Mulvaney, Hercus, McBryde, Low, Rose, and Barlow, whose work is analysed and commented on throughout. These authors provided pointers to regional variance and supply and demand economics of Aboriginal people.

In a sense, this book engages with contested meanings of place and contributes to cultural geography, but such an engagement necessarily trespasses on various disciplinary boundaries. History, archaeology, and anthropology contribute, and indeed such a collage of sources is equally evident in the work of anthropologist Deborah Bird Rose, or historian Peter Read, or pre-historian and historical archaeologist John Mulvaney. The broader research context cannot therefore be identified by the project's contribution to a particular discipline. It rests, rather, in its contribution to undermine colonised meanings of place, and to affirm the relevance of Aboriginal knowledge.

Throughout the book all personal communication with Aboriginal people has been faithfully recorded in original communication form and is recognised in Australia as Aboriginal English – a form of 'pidgin' English which mixes Aboriginal words and English words. It is also a form of broken English that does not conform to the standard use of English in the sense of using verbs or any of the other rules that apply to the conventions of oral English grammar. Aboriginal English is colloquial and its throughout the book provides an insight to the adaption of oral English grammar by Aboriginal people to meet their needs to communicate.

The dual usage of paths by Aboriginal people and European explorers form the basis of the arguments put forward here. Many early surveyors meticulously recorded these contact sites. Historical societies and local governments have erected monuments to the passage of these surveyors, and many of these monuments are more or less correctly positioned. Local Aboriginal Community organisations have written connection reports and recorded their trading ways based on local knowledge. To sum up in one sentence: Aboriginal Dreaming tracks became European trading ways in south-west Queensland, and beyond.

The retention of the recorded spelling of Aboriginal nations and any words spelled differently are mainly due to the processes of translation and transposition into English.

Acknowledgements

I dedicate this work to the memory of my Grandfather Charlie Leon, 20 June 1900–1972, who took a group of Aboriginal dancers around the state of New South Wales in 1928 and donated half their gate takings to hospitals at each town they performed.

Without the encouragement of the following people this book would not have been written. To Rosy Crisp, who fought her own battle with cancer and lost; she was my line manager while I was employed at the Department of Aboriginal and Torres Strait Islander Policy (DATSIP) and was an inspiration to me. She assisted me in gaining study leave from my full-time employment. A sincere thanks.

I would also like to thank the Australian Research Council for a Discovery Grant that assisted me to conduct my fieldwork into Aboriginal oral history of the trading ways. During the fieldwork I interviewed and filmed fifteen people. To these fifteen people I owe a debt of gratitude: Mick Leon, Noel Nannup, Uncle Bob Anderson, Kado Muir, Jim Wharton, Jim Crombie, Colleen Wall, Murrandoo Yanna, Robert Smith, Isabel Tarrago, Alf Nathan, Alice Parker, John Jones, Bob Weatherall, and Delma Barton. I am also indebted to the fourteen other Traditional Owners whom I interviewed and who provided me with information that assisted me in my research: Danny MacKillar, Linda Crombie, Brenda Shields, Burton Bunyan, Don and Lynn Rowlands; Park Managers at the Simpson Desert National Park; Shirly MacNarra, Colin Saltner and Brad Foster; Chief Officer of the Carpentaria Native Title Representative Body; and Brett Lee, Aboriginal Ranger, Katherine, Northern Territory. May their memories speak from the pages of this book.

To my wife Jane, and five children – Mathew, Nichole, Melissa, Gabrielle and Nathan – for their endurance and support over the long periods of research for this book. Also to the spirits of my forebears for their counsel during the wee hours of the morning when motivation to continue was waning, a heart-felt thank you. My primary thanks go to Dr Regina Ganter for her insight, invaluable advice, and her instruction on research approaches and methodology, which motivated me to produce the best possible study. Further thanks go to Dr Fiona Paisley, my second academic supervisor for the original thesis, who instructed me on context and structure. I thank both of you.

My academic career has been driven by the need for a proper conversation between the colonisers' history and the first Australians' history. I first began the journey when the doors of University were opened up to Aboriginal people in 1985. After taking a Diploma of Teaching I was given the opportunity to study for other degrees and was subsequently appointed Aboriginal Research Fellow in 2007 at Griffith University, where I currently lecture. Throughout this period I was continually taught by my Elders to engage with non-Aboriginal people with a view to continuing that conversation for the benefit of both communities. It is my earnest hope that this book brings forward meaningful dialogue between our two communities.

Art by Laurie Nilsen

CHAPTER ONE

Common Sense and Common Nonsense

The continent of Australia

Despite what Dorothea has said
about the sun scorched land,
 you've never really loved her
nor sought to make her grand
you pollute all the rivers
and litter every road
your barbaric graffiti
cut scars where tall trees grow
the beaches and the mountains
are covered with your shame
injustice rules supremely
despite your claims to fame
the mud polluted rivers
are fenced off from the gaze
of travellers and the thirsty
for foreign hooves to graze
a tyranny now rules your soul
to your own image blind
a callousness and uncouth ways
now hallmarks of your kind.

Australia oh Australia
you could stand proud and free
we weep in bitter anguish
at your hate and tyranny
the scarred black bodies writhing
humanity locked in chains
land theft and racial murders
you boast on of your gains
in woodchip and uranium
the anguished death you spread
will leave the children of the land
a heritage that's dead.

Australia oh Australia
you could stand tall and free
we weep in bitter anguish
at your hate and tyranny.
(Aboriginal poet Kevin Gilbert 1989. *The New True Anthem*)

The European image of Australia is one of a sunburnt country composed of wide-open spaces devoid of beauty: a living hell. Geoffrey Serle described this nationally-held negative view of the landscape in Australian literature in 1856:

> The countryside was too thin and lacking in tradition; there were 'no ancient churches, castles, ruins the memorials of generations departed' and hence there was no hope of a Scott or Balzac or 'a poetry which reflects past glories; Australian life is too lacking in tradition, and confused. (Serle 1973:103)

When the British arrived to plant themselves in the Australian environment, they came with a sense of limited space, as their homeland was small and surrounded by sea. For the colonisers Australia seemed endless, and this caused anxiety as well as exuberance.

I love a sunburnt country,
A land of sweeping plains,
Of rugged mountain ranges,
Of droughts and flooding rains;
I love her far horizons,
I love her jewel-sea,
Her beauty and her terror—
The wide brown land for me.

(*My Country* by Dorothea Mackellar)

But for Aboriginal people the land is a numen; it is personified in the metaphysical relationship between people and the land that is expressed through spiritual beliefs embodied in the topography (Cowan 1989:31–33). The environment also provided habitats where food could be cultivated and harvested.

For Aboriginal people the land was a metaphysical and physical given, whereas for Europeans it was an aspect of life that could be embraced in a number of optional ways, and it was either loved or hated. The acquisition of Aboriginal Australia by the British began with the naming of parts of the landscape with English names from their own lexicon. This naming of 'country' (as Aboriginal Australians call it) in English rendered the landscape more readable for them, so it became more like their home world (Carter 1987). Some examples include the Glasshouse Mountains and the Brisbane River, while others became reference points, such as the Great Dividing Range and the Darling Downs.

In addition, the nomination of Aboriginal cultural property with English words and taxonomies (such as the rare Lumholtz tree-kangaroo), rendered the unknown more identifiable to the European, but simultaneously rendered the Aboriginal an artefact. The process of naming made the transition from Aboriginal to European complete. The overlay of the landscape and material property with English words made them more visual and cognisant for Europeans, so they were able to be marked on a map or illustrated in a book.

> The use of the Aboriginal name of this river (Barwan or Darling) is indispensable amongst the squatters* along its banks, who do not appear to know it to be the 'Darling'. It is most desirable to restore to such rivers their proper names as early as possible after they have been ascertained, were it only to enable strangers thereby to avail themselves of the intelligence and assistance of the natives, in identifying the country by means of published maps. (Mitchell 1848:71)

If Aboriginal terms had been used, Europeans would have found it difficult to navigate, describe, and enjoy the country. The etching of the European over the Aboriginal simplified the processes of owning and occupation. Paul Carter makes the point that the use of English labels effectively denied Aboriginal people the possession of country (Carter 1987).

The process of shaping Australia into a truly European place continues today. In the political landscape, Aboriginal people are making Native Title claims to country, and most are forced to use English names to identify natural features in the landscape. Furthermore the European geographical place-names used for describing boundaries strengthens the idea of cultural *terra nullius*. Cultural *terra nullius* essentially denies Aboriginal people their position as the first peoples in the country. It is based on outdated concepts that negate the fact that Aboriginal people have a truly vibrant culture and a history that can contribute in meaningful ways to Australian culture; it precludes the use of Aboriginal culture to reference Australia.

There are however some Aboriginal nations that do not use European taxonomy for naming country. The peoples of the Arrernte Nation have designed their own maps, complete with geographical names for the landscape and the borders depicted. The people of central Australia have also listed a series of Arkaya Dreaming sites and the Kestrel Dreaming paths on the Register of the National Estate (RNE). Listing these sites on the RNE provides them with Australian heritage protection (Isabel Tarrago, personal communication 2004).

When Europeans first came to the Australian landmass, it was an old land. The first people of this country had given the land a history, a culture, and tradition – a full space complete with Aboriginal noise. But to the Europeans it appeared to be a blank

---

* Since the earliest days of the colony of Australia, people acquired rural land simply by 'squatting' on it, occupying it and claiming it as their own. Squatters in Australia were originally Ticket-of-Leave Convicts and emancipists who occupied land illegally (according to the Empire). Squatting originally was seen as the illegal possession of land beyond the authorized occupation areas of the colony.

space. Before describing the clash of cultures, and how the European means of mapping changed the face of Aboriginal Australia, it is important to represent the landscape as Aboriginal people knew it: how they perceived and used the trading ways over it. Australia is a landmass devoid of human form – it is effectively bare. This depiction paves the way for the research undertaken, and provides the rationale that guides the chapters to follow. Australia is a huge country, and presents many difficulties for people when they travel through the landscape. The following extract from *Australian Heritage* enables readers to comprehend the very size, distance, and conditions that Aboriginal people encounter when they are on 'walkabout' (in others words, trading and doing business):

> Australia is flat and very dry, a geographically isolated continent. As a continent, it is one and half times the size of Western Europe. It is also almost as large as the United States, not including Alaska. Australia is sixth in the ranking of nations for size, being larger than India but smaller than Brazil, the distance from the west coast to the east coast is approximately 4,000 kilometres and from south to north approximately

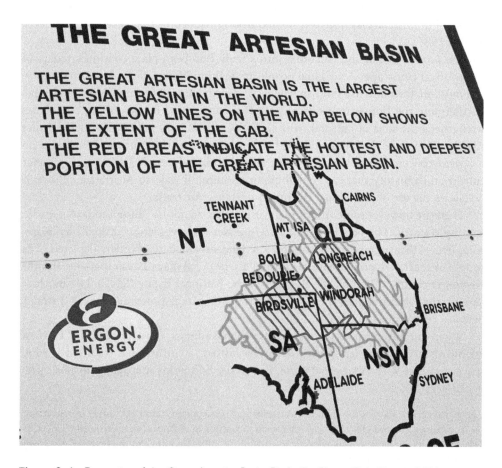

Figure 2 An Ergon sign of the Great Artesian Basin, Birdsville. Photo: Dale Kerwin 2004.

3,153 kilometres. As a low, flat land Australia has only about 6 percent of the land mass higher than 610 metres; the highest range is the Great Dividing Range, which is in fact a series of low plateaux. The Great Dividing Range separates the eastern and western river systems. (*Australia's Heritage*, vol. 1, 1989:31–35)

Gariwerd, the Aboriginal name for the Great Dividing Range, also known as the Eastern Highlands, stretches along the entire eastern coast from Victoria to the Cape York Peninsula in Queensland, with an average width of 240 kilometres. Its most northern peak is located on Thursday Island in the Torres Strait. This range is not high, but is extremely rocky and rugged, and weathering has carved gorges and escarpments in the sandstone. The narrow coastal strip that lies between the sea and the highlands receives a good annual rainfall (*Australia's Heritage*, vol. 1, 1989:31–35).

The Central Lowlands, encompassing the area from the Gulf of Carpentaria in the north to the Great Australian Bight in the south, has an average height of less than 153 metres above sea level. This area includes Millewa – Paaka, the Aboriginal name for the area known as the Murray–Darling Basin formed by the two most important river systems in Australia. The Murray River flows through New South Wales, Victoria and South Australia and is 2,589 kilometres long. The Darling River is the largest river in Australia: it flows for 2,740 kilometres and has as its source in several river systems from the Great Dividing Range and the Darling Downs in Queensland. The Darling River joins the Murray River at Wentworth in New South Wales (*Australia's Heritage*, vol. 1, 1989:31–35).

The Great Artesian Basin, also in the area of the Central Lowlands, is the largest artesian basin in Australia with a total area of 1,078,700 square kilometres expanding over parts of Queensland and New South Wales, the northern corner of South Australia and into the Northern Territory (see Figure 2). Much of the water that enters the Great Artesian Basin enters through the Flinders River and its tributaries, at Western Cape York, Queensland and through the Baroo, Nogoa, Warrego and Maranoa rivers. The Great Artesian Basin is mostly arid, reaching its lowest point of 11.9 metres below sea level at Lake Eyre in South Australia.

The Western Plateau is a vast dry, arid, flat land. The people of Warlpiri, Warumunga, Kaytetye, Alyawarre, Luritja, Pintupi, Pitjantjatjara, Yangkunytjatjara, Ngaanyatjarra, Pertame, Eastern and Western Arrernte live in this area. It covers two-thirds of Australia and has an average height of 610 metres, which is represented by widely separated hills like Tjukurpa (the Macdonnell Ranges) and Uluru (Ayers Rock). The Macdonnell Ranges is a band of rugged mountains in the Northern Territory with the highest peak being Mt Zeil at 1510 metres;

Figure 3 The Nullarbor Plains. Photo: Dale Kerwin, 2004.

Uluru is 335 metres high. Situated on the southern boundary of the Western Plateau is the Nullarbor Plain (*Australia's Heritage*, vol. 1, 1989:31–35).

The Nullarbor Plain runs along the southern coast and is occupied by Aboriginal people known as the Spinifix People the Mirnin and Wiranu people. The Nullarbor Plain is a dry limestone plateau that runs along the coast to Western Australia from the south-western corner of South Australia (see Figure 3). The Western Plateau is 2413 kilometres from north to south at its longest point and 1609 kilometres wide. Its coastline exceeds 4827 kilometres and its most striking feature is the absence of rivers at the southern end. For almost 1120 kilometres along the southern stretch of Western Australia there are no rivers or watercourses, but up along the western coastline rivers are more numerous with the largest being Durbal Yarragan (the Swan), Badimia (Murchison), Gascoyne, Ashburton, Fortescue, and De Grey. In the north of the Western Plateau, the rivers are less reliable and not always running. However in the far north, bays and gulfs indent the Kimberley region with major rivers being the Fitzroy, Lennard, Prince Regent, and the Ord. The Western plateau seaboard has two mountain ranges, the Darling Range and the Leopold Range (*Australia's Heritage*, vol. 1, 1989:31–35). The interior is dry and flat (Carnegie, 1982:162–63).

The northern part of Australia is in the tropics with warm to hot weather most of the year. Mangrove-lined estuaries typify this area and it is populated with Melaleuca and Eucalypt dry Sclerophyll forests, and gallery rainforests along rivers. The Cape York Peninsula is renowned for its seasonal variation, with a monsoon cycle from December to April. The monsoon season inundates large areas and flooding occurs in all river systems. Strong vegetation growth is a consequence of this high rainfall. The floods progressively subside when the season changes from wet to dry and these river systems become dry creek beds with isolated water holes. The south-eastern corner of Australia has warm summers, cool winters and snow in the mountains with frost occurring in the inland areas (*Australia's Heritage,* vol. 1, 1989:31–35).

The size of Australia means that there are great climatic contrasts. Australia is the world's hottest continent in regard to the duration of high temperatures. For example, the longest heat wave on record was at Marble Bar in Western Australia from 31 October 1923 to 7 April 1924, when for 160 days temperatures averaged 37.8°C. In contrast, temperatures can fall below zero Celsius: at Charlottes Pass in the Snowy Mountains in New South Wales. The lowest recorded temperature since colonisation was minus 22°C., on 14 July 1945. Alice Springs, in the Northern Territory, is recognised as being a hot region. However, at night in winter frost can bring the temperatures down to below zero. Australia's shape, size and topography determine the climate (*Australia's Heritage* vol. 1, 1989:31–35).

Australia is a chronically dry continent, one-third of which has a median annual rainfall of less than 400 mm. This means large areas of the Australian landscape are arid. They have an association of plant life that covers about 90 per cent of the arid zone. These ecological regions have habitats with diverse communities of associations of plants. Brigalow woodlands, saltbush plains, mallees and grasslands each carry different edible plant life (*Australia's Heritage,* vol. 1, 1989:31–35). The arid zone has a variety of vegetation type including shrubs (Acacia or Eucalyptus), small shrubs (salt bush and blue bush) and grasses (hummock and tussock). Clay pans, gibber plains and salt flats with some sand dunes typify the Australian desert landscape. Armed with the right knowledge and equipment this type of desert landscape is easily navigated.

Aboriginal traders traversed this continent to trade materials, which were not readily accessible in their own countries. Access to new materials and food substances encouraged intellectual creativity, the arts, technological advancement, and religious and political associations. Like all societies, Aboriginal people traded and bartered to improve lifestyles and health for the well-being of communities.

Travel was however dependent upon knowing how to read cultural maps, where to find water, and how to find food substances. To communicate with others across the landscape required considerable knowledge and skill. Aboriginal societies of Australia developed the ability to navigate, conquer, and mould the natural environment (for example by fire stick farming) so that they could travel and communicate with others.

The European imagination: the land and people of Australia

To traverse the Australian continent without European modes of travel and navigation seemed impossible to the newcomers. Without their usual means of travel and navigational tools, some Europeans discovered that travelling in Australia's inland with beasts of burden carrying their supplies could be fatal. And yet many perished in the belief that it could be done. For such explorers, travelling involved life-and-death situations. Thirst and sickness haunted them on long arduous journeys through the alien and unknown environment.

A basic assumption dominated the European imagination with respect to the Australian landscape: it was an impassable wilderness. The idea of wilderness presupposes a pristine state unmodified by human intervention. Commentaries from the eighteenth and nineteenth centuries did indeed regard Australia as a pristine landscape devoid of signs of culture. The etchings Europeans saw, but could not read, were thought to be crude and primitive art produced by uncivilised humans. That Aboriginal people were so-called primitive seemed evident from their perceived lack of material possessions. The Aboriginal landscape was viewed as utterly empty, and the black fellow country had no great architectural religious structures that could be recognised as sacred by eighteenth-century Europeans.

When the Nungas/Nyungars told their story of the invasion of South Australia by aliens on 28 December 1836 in *Survival in Our Own Land 1988*, they stated:

> The designated land, half a world away, unseen by those who passed the legislation, was described in the Act as 'waste and unoccupied'. The earth was untilled. The land was not disfigured by permanent man-made constructions. But it was indeed not 'waste'. In fact its resources were known and carefully husbanded. It was totally occupied by many and various ancestral groupings of our people. (Mattingley 1988:3)

In fact the endless featureless plains had been transformed by Aboriginal land management practices to present a landscape that Europeans thought of as 'a gentlemen's park' (Cowan 1989:23–27; Flannery 1994:348). Finally from the European perspective, Australia had relic forms of nature and a primitive people: 'It was a land of living fossils, a continental museum where the past was made in nature, a 'palaeontological' penal colony' (Griffiths 1996:9).

In modern Western thought, the recognition of the harmonious balance between Aboriginal social systems and ecological conditions has been theorised as societies influenced by nature – unlike their European counterparts. Again, this view is more ideological than descriptive. Tom Griffiths refers to Aboriginal travellers as *ecological beings* – whereby the Australian natural environment provided an abundance of native flora and fauna across all geological regions (Griffiths 1996:263). Terms such as Griffiths' (1996:263) 'ecological beings' or Tim Flannery's (1994:271–91) 'ecological agriculturist' are meant to suggest that the ways in which Aboriginal people gained food did not degrade the environment. This implies that their practices and innovations were driven by nature, rather than culture.

Environmentalists are less attached to the idea of a pristine wilderness and now consider that Australian Aboriginal people overgrazed the food resources available to them (Low 1987; Latz 1995). They hypothesise that bands always hunted large animals and that they had to follow these herds across large distances. This position is misleading because it negates the whole concept of Australian Aboriginal land management. The continent of Australia has its own distinct landscape, flora, and fauna not found on other continents. However, it is recognised that certain practices such as firestick farming depleted certain species of flora and fauna. Aboriginal people exerted other pressures on the environment through stone houses, hydraulic engineering, mining activities, and dam construction. All of these activities impacted on ecosystems and so challenge the view of Aboriginal people as ecological beings.

An affluent society or just hunter-gatherers?

Aboriginal people mastered the environment and because of this had ample spare time to pursue other activities, such as the arts and political gatherings. Not all people were engaged in food gathering activities, some were engaged in ceremonial activities and trade. Sahlins' (1972) term 'original affluent society' puts forward a distinction between work and non-work activities in 'literate industrialised societies' and 'technologically primitive societies' respectively. Sahlins' terminology exemplifies the process that contributed to the social fabric of Aboriginal people.

The notion that Aboriginal people did not produce crops or surplus food supplies for redistribution or storage means that they were not in a position to support those non-hunters who were otherwise specialists such as craft persons, armies, bureaucrats, religious leaders, and leaders. It has also been argued that Aboriginal people did not produce larger goods, or carry material property, because it limited freedom of movement. The argument here is that non-subsistence goods become obsolete because

Aboriginal people were slaves to the food quest, so that no time or energy remained to produce other material goods (Diamond 1998).

Ethnographers have continued to insist that Aboriginal people needed to move so that they could pursue sources of food (Braidwood 1975; Diamond 1998). In fact, some Aboriginal people chose to travel long distances to trade nuts, stories and material goods. An example of this is the gathering of Aboriginal nations for the bunya nuts that grow in the Black Butt Mountain Range in Queensland. Burnum Burnum (1988) discusses the great bora ground routes of the Bundjalung people in his *Traveller's Guide*, which took him into Queensland from the northern regions of the New South Wales coastal belt. These paths went from Lismore to distant lands to the north. The purpose of these paths was to connect people both ways, so that they could trade for new material culture, including the prized bunya nuts. He suggested that these trips became annual events based on the growing cycle and that there would be reciprocal visits, with bunya seed being traded for goods such as baskets and fishhooks. He points out that the bunya pines that grow in the Lismore, Woodburn, and Wyrallah districts were products of this trade. In those locations too, significant sites are connected by stories (Burnum Burnum 1988:82–83).

There is much evidence that Aboriginal society was, and is, dynamic with the sharing of ceremonies and songs with each other, and the adoption of various creator spirits like the Rainbow Serpent. Roth (1897) recorded that the Molonga ceremony, which had its roots in the Selwyn Ranges of north-western Queensland, has a story string that links people across vast distances from Alice Springs in the Northern Territory to Adelaide in South Australia (Roth [1897] 1984: 132–34).

> Macassans have visited north-eastern Arnhem Land over the last 400 years. In Arnhem Land much has been adopted from the Macassans, and the Berndts have pointed out that the Yolngu think that the two moieties, Yinrtija and Dhuwa, arose from contact. 'The Yolngu have adopted many Macassan words, ideas and skills. Macassan influence is also apparent in Yolngu ceremonies and art. Today, some Yolngu have both Aboriginal and Macassan ancestry'. (National Museum Australian (2004). *Aboriginal Gallery: Cultural exchange*).

The dynamic nature of Aboriginal society can also be seen in the development of technologies that master the environment. The spearthrower is a multi-purpose tool, which when used as a launcher would extend the throwing distance of a spear. It would also be used for carrying tools, so that it became a toolbox. The spearthrower was also used as a digging tool and a bowl for food, and the stone adze attached to one end would be used as a knife.

> Spearthrowers were also used as message sticks and were specially marked for this purpose. Designs were intended to remind the messenger of specific details about the time and place of gatherings. They also guaranteed safe passage for the messenger through the country of strangers. It is known from similar markings on the objects that circles may represent camps, notches may represent numbers and identity of

people attending, and other marks may indicate a meeting and the sender of the message. (Melbourne Museum (2004) *Bunjilaka Gallery: Journey of the Great Snake*)

In the Bunjilaka Gallery of the Melbourne Museum the spearthrower, shown in Figure 4, is on display. The lines on the spearthrower interpret the Journey of the Great Snake *Liru*, a Dreamtime ancestor. All the waterholes along that path are represented by circles (Melbourne Museum (2004) *Bunjilaka Gallery: Journey of the Great Snake*).

Several problems arise when trying to position Aboriginal societies as either affluent or hunter-gatherers. Sahlins' (1972) sympathetic view of the 'affluent society' rests in his definitions of work and non-work activities, which do not take into account ritual labour. The major flaw in prehistorians Braidwood (1975) and Diamond's (1998) work is that they have a static view of Aboriginal society. Much empirical evidence regarding Aboriginal societies has fallen victim to discussions about the various models of Aboriginal society. It is now apposite to slice through the long-held misconceptions that are held in the popular imagination, and reinforced by caricature.

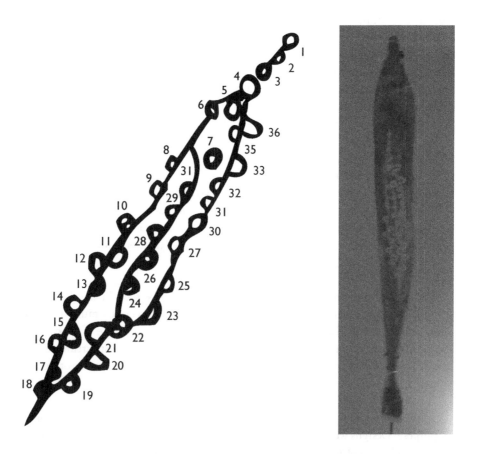

Figure 4 Pintupi spearthrower doubling as a map with the journey of the Great Snake Liru marked on it. Reproduced by kind permission of the Bunjilaka Gallery, Museum Victoria, Melbourne.

Aboriginal people as beings

Aboriginal movement over the landscape was the result of cultural practices and knowledge systems used to manage the land and harvest resources. At the end of the nineteenth century, Daisy Bates witnessed one such event which involved the flowering gum, as well as mullet and salmon moving up a river to their spawning grounds. In the south-western district of Perth, Western Australia, these fish would be caught with nets and spears. Bates commented that the sea was alive with the colour of their phosphorescence (Bates 1985:324–27). The Aboriginal people were taking advantage of the relationship between the appearance of the flowering gum, and the seasonal appearance of the mullet and salmon heading for their spawning grounds.

There is an increasing recognition that because the Australian natural ecology and Aboriginal experience are intertwined, they are better able to protect and provide, through local knowledge, the conservation of endangered species; the knowledge is dependent on Aboriginal knowledge systems (Griffiths 1996:268). For example, in 1991 the Anangu people from central Australia took part in a survey with Australia's Commonwealth Scientific and Industrial Research Organisation (CSIRO) to identify vertebrate animals in Uluru National Park; their knowledge was given equivalent value to the scientific investigation (Griffiths 1996:268). Danny McKellar, an Aboriginal Ranger at Currawinya National Park in south-western Queensland, stated that 'our knowledge about tracking, knowledge about the animals habits and what it eats is used to preserve and protect. Our knowledge is combined with that of the white fellow' (personal communication 2004). Aboriginal knowledge is to create habitats for endangered species, such as the bilby and wombats. Aboriginal people are successful, proven resource managers and this is recognised by employing Aboriginal people as community rangers in flora and fauna protected areas.

As a cultural phenomenon, the Aboriginal landscape had places known as story places which were used for the management of flora and fauna species. These places were closed to public access so that certain animal species were protected from over-exploitation. These story places would be well known and sung about; they became part of ritual learning and were ingrained management systems. An example of a story place can be found at Cooktown in north Queensland. The Gugu-Yalandji people considered the tree kangaroo to be an important resource. At the top of Mount Finnigan and Mount Misery are two story places where the rare Lumholtz tree-kangaroo is found. Outside these two story places the tree kangaroo had been over-hunted. While on an expedition in search of the 'boonary' [tree-kangaroo] in 1882–83, Carl Lumholtz reported that:

> We searched the scrub in the vicinity thoroughly and found many traces of boonary [tree-kangaroo] in the trees but they were all old. It could be hunted more easily here, for the reason that the lawyer palm is rare, and consequently the woods are less dense. The natives told me that their 'old men' in former times had killed many boonary in these woods. (cited in Flannery 1994:289)

Aboriginal people scheduled their travel to exploit the seasonality of resources, according to the optimal time to visit other nations for religious ceremonies and political gatherings, or to pay respects on the death of an important community leader.

The death of an important leader was an important reason for travel. Aboriginal beliefs entail intricate systems of ordering the universe, and magical devices designed to harness cosmic powers. The Elders and leaders are respected for their wisdom and knowledge. Mourning rituals draw upon specific religious and spiritual values and require that correct protocols must be followed. If these protocols are not adhered to, the lives of relatives and the clan may be affected by some disaster. These rituals have important social functions. In some Aboriginal societies, ceremonies are performed to assist the passage to the ancestral world. They help relatives to accept death and to express grief within socially-accepted traditions. The rituals also provide a means for patrimonial rites and succession to positions of importance (Warner 1969:402–22; Roth [1897] 1984: 381).

Ceremonies other than mourning rituals have an economic function in Aboriginal societies; they are courts or trade fairs, or even international courts. The courts are sought for counsel, and to settle disputes of a political nature, such as land boundaries. The courts are also used to settle criminal matters. William Gardner (1854) described one such meeting of clan groups: 'At certain seasons of the year various tribes of the interior meet at appointed places . . . their disputes were adjusted and settled' (in Carter 1987:163–64). Sometimes these ceremonies are held for feasts and hunting expeditions and all the surrounding nations would be invited to attend. During such gatherings, Aboriginal nations shared song, dance, and technologies, and they also forged alliances by marriage. All of these meetings, regardless of the reason they were held, were important as they enabled new knowledge to enter a community by trade and storytelling. The tradition of storytelling provided a means of finding out what was happening in other people's country. In addition, the trading of designs and symbols provided new means of communication.

The development of Aboriginal culture in Australia was dependent on two factors: internal innovation and the diffusion of ideas from external cultures. The diffusion of ideas helped Aboriginal nations to improve technologies for land management and to continue and maintain cultural traditions. The visual arts continue to be an important means of communication for spiritual purposes, and in establishing relationships across geographical areas. Aboriginal people stress that even in its contemporary form Aboriginal visual art is a mode of written expression, as it communicates to those who are learned in Aboriginal thought and tradition. M.J.E. King-Boyes offers the following interpretation of the importance of Aboriginal visual art:

those societies whose methods of imparting education patterns, ideas and general information through the medium of language, though not using the accepted forms of reading and writing which we use in our society, have developed a high-level transmitting system of conceptual and perceptual thought and expression. The Aboriginal people did have a literature; they did have an educational system. (King-Boyes 1977:13–14)

He also suggests that 'its [Aboriginal societies'] writing was a form of hieroglyphic geometric abstraction' (King-Boyes 1977:13). Paul Carter considers that Aboriginal forms of expression are 'oral' and 'vocal' (Carter 1987:346–47). Aboriginal writing is holistic, because corroborees, paintings drawn in the dirt, etchings on bark, wood, or rock, and body paintings, are all systems of writing. They carry a message and are tangible and independent of vocals. The messages conveyed are structured and follow set rules, which are dictated and taught by the Elders of a community.

> A dance on the earth, a pattern on a wall, a design on the body are systems of writing, spatial writing [*un geo-graphisme*], a geography. These forms of expression are oral because they possess a system of writing which is independent of the voice, which neither aligns itself with the voice nor is subordinate to it, but which is linked with it, coordinated within a radiating, multi-dimensional structure. (Carter 1987:346–47)

In north-east Arnhem Land (see Map 6), for example, the term 'darabu' refers to writing in general, as well as to a particular zig-zag pattern clan design (Berndt, Berndt 1954:36, 56). Ron Hurley, a renowned Aboriginal artist from the Gareng Gareng nation (Bundaberg, Queensland) said that this subject of art was a written communication tool, that 'each word spoken in my language can be painted or drawn by use of symbols. Through traditional law I have been given the right to paint by my mob' (Ron Hurley, personal communication 1998).

Aboriginal people had many reasons to travel: to renew relationships to families and to forge alliances through marriage. Aboriginal people also travelled for social events, to participate and attend small and large gatherings, because of weather patterns such as monsoons, and for the seasonal harvest of flora and fauna. Other reasons for people to travel were to maintain knowledge of the Dreaming tracks and ritually instruct others of their locations. People would travel to maintain these paths with fire management and to ritually dig into important water holes. This would keep the integrity of the places even along some of the most desolate tracks. Travel was also important for the purpose of obtaining goods from distant countries. Pituri (Aboriginal tobacco) from the Simpson Desert region was held in high esteem, and people would walk hundreds of kilometres to secure it.

An Aboriginal perspective

Clearly Aboriginal cultures are well-tuned into natural events. The flowering of gums and the abundance of certain species of fauna like mullet and salmon attracted and supported large gatherings of Aboriginal people. Through the use of visual and performance arts (ritual ceremony) Aboriginal people would relate the life-cycle of these fish to seasonal events within the environment. Aboriginal people know the environment and any change in the natural would indicate certain predictable events. Mick Leon (2004 Worimi country, Forster New South Wales), and Shane Coghill (2000 Koenpal,

Stradbroke Island) have commented on natural events and the harvesting of food resources.

From an Aboriginal point of view, work was divided amongst people of a group and these people developed skills accordingly. As with most societies around the world people contributed to the well-being of the community in various ways. Members of a community did not share food gathering equally, because they were needed to support children and Elders. Aboriginal societies had some members who toiled and collected sufficient food to sustain people in specialist positions, such as religious practitioners, specialised craft practitioners, and non-food-producing personnel, or merchants. Ritual work, such as food increase ceremonies, were part and parcel of the labour involved in the production of food (Rose 1992). Daisy Bates witnessed the close connection between ritual and work near Perth in Western Australia:

> Sometimes, when the visitors have all arrived for the fishing, an old totem man will sing the following: nagaija been yaan, naara beenyaan, woordoomanoo yaan, I come, dancing come, brothers come, naara been yaan. Dancing come. Yandaara gwabeen marra yanga goolong, beerart gwabeen. White ashes or pipeclay good, food going to give, fur ornaments good. This song is a reminder that the food must be paid for in native product, white fur for example, by visitors. (Bates 1985: 325–26)

The 'old totem man' was inviting people to partake in the produce, and in exchange the cost was ochre or fur products. The ritual life of Aboriginal people was in essence work. The 'old totem man' bartered for other goods with the fish.

> When the message was received, the two old men who were to become the eeko (guardians) of the women and younger men, collected all those who intended to journey to the jalgoo ground, and arranged what ornaments, weapons and other objects were to be taken for barter, the paints, fat, birds' down and other decorations being also collected. (Bates 1985:328)

Understanding the relationship of ritual and trade will help explain Aboriginal economics. For example, over a period of time the local mob that dwelt on the land would have noticed a correlation between the habits of the mullet and salmon when they swam in rivers and estuaries to spawn, and the flowering of the Red Gum. These resources would become the property of the local mob, theirs to be exploited. The mullet or salmon would become the totem of the peoples whose right it was to catch and trade the resource. The moiety with the mullet or salmon totem would prepare a weir out of wire-grass; the grass would also be used to make nets to catch the fish. Net making was the domain of certain people in the group, who would teach people the art of manufacturing this resource through ceremonial instruction (Bates 1985:328).

Shane Coghill, a Koenpal man from Stradbroke Island and an anthropologist, spoke about the trading and economics of his people on a trip to his country in 1999.

> We were a sedentary mob, we had a varied diet. Not only did we have the vegetation on the island, but the rainbow lorikeet, when gathering on the Brisbane River would

mean the mullet have come. We would travel across the bay and meet with the mob over on the mainland and catch the mullet and partake in festivals. In our calendar we have the movement of crabs, shellfish, tailor, and bunya nut to add to our diets. The stone we used in our grinding dishes was traded for from the Simpson Desert area. (Shane Coghill, personal communication, 1999)

Australian Aboriginal societies fit neither model of the industrialised society or technologically primitive society. The following section will address three commonly held myths in relation to Aboriginal people. First, that they were nomadic and non-sedentary; secondly that Aboriginal societies did not have people who performed specialist services, and thirdly that Aboriginal people were simply hunter-gatherers and did not produce food. Before proceeding to the chapters to follow it is important to examine these cornerstones of common myths, and enter into a discourse about the relevance of them in promoting concepts of the need to travel and the ability to travel for resources and goods for cultural use.

Myth 1, Aboriginal societies are nomadic and non-sedentary

Many Aboriginal people lived in established villages. Accounts of this lifestyle come from explorers and settlers who witnessed Aboriginal societies before the devastating effects of invasion and occupation sent whole communities to the brink of extinction. The following discussion refers to just a few of these observations.

> On the morning of the 20th January 1788 the first fleet arrived in Botany Bay in New South Wales preparing to establish a colony before moving to Sydney Cove. Botany Bay was an Aboriginal meeting place – in addition 'on the north-west arm of the bay, [stood] a village which [contained] more than a dozen houses and perhaps five times that number of'. (Tench 1789:58; Carter 1987:320)

In 1799 whilst on an exploration cruise to Hervey Bay in Queensland, Matthew Flinders observed some Aboriginal dwellings at a place now known as Stradbroke Island that:

> were beehive-shaped . . . in parts . . . framed with vines, with grass woven for the walls, roofed over with sheets of bark. The entrances projected out so the rain could not beat inside. The huts were about 1.5 meters high and one was double the size of the others – large enough to accommodate 15 people. (cited in Keith Willey 1979:98–99)

Thomas Mitchell's fourth expedition to tropical Australia in 1845, records that at the Barcoo River there were large huts with rafters and square pieces of bark laid like tiles.

> By 21 September the party was among the headwaters of what Mitchell called the Victoria, now known as the Barcoo. Here Mitchell remarked on some large huts,

which were better planned and of a more substantial construction than those he had seen further south. A frame like a lean-to roof had first been erected; rafters had next been laid on that and thin, square pieces of bark like tiles had been fixed on these. (cited in Baker 1997: 179)

Frederick Strange, a European naturalist, observed the Jindoobarrie people of the Moreton Bay area in early 1839:

Unlike most of the natives of Australia as yet discovered, they have fixed habitations, dwelling in little villages of six or seven huts in a cluster. Some of them are of great length, extending upwards of eighty feet, and covering a considerable space of ground . . . One of them was in the form of a passage, with two apartments at the end. The arches were beautifully turned, and executed with a degree of skill which would have not disgraced an [sic] European architect. (Fisher, 1992:11)

Sedentary lifestyles were not restricted to Queensland and New South Wales. Josephine Flood provides evidence of permanent villages with stone houses at Lake Condah in Victoria:

Stone houses with semi-circular bases and doorways all facing the same way are vis-ible at Lake Condah, and the finding of stone tools in some of these indicates their uses goes back to prehistoric times. Their walls stood about a metre high and the roofs were of bark rushes supported on a wooden frame. The remains of more than 175 houses have been identified, and 146 have been found in a paddock, clear evi-dence that Aborigines here were living in large, reasonable permanent village. (Flood 1990: 219)

In *The Aborigines of Victoria and other parts of Australia and Tasmania*, R. Brough Smyth includes a single sentence of note: 'The natives of the lacustrine district to the north of the Glenelg River in Victoria, and some tribes in the Northern Australia, used to construct substantial huts, and plaster them from the outside' (Smyth 1972:252). Sturt, who explored the Murrumbidgee River in 1828–1830, saw 'huts and foot paths in low-lying country with lagoons, seldom encountering fewer than 200 Aboriginal people daily' (cited in Campbell 1985:350).

In the western district of Victoria, archaeological work has uncovered several areas that were sites of villages. Dawson commented that these 'were the sites of large, perma-nent habitation, which formed homes for many generations' (cited in Critchett 1990:58). Elizabeth Williams, who participated in archaeological field work in 1989 on the remains of these villages which contained mud hearths, stated that they were located on high ground with good views and easy access to water and were numerous around this area. They were found in a cluster of around six or more homes, 1.5 metres and 3.5 metres long. It is believed that these mud hearths were the bases or platforms for houses. Williams has dated these platforms to be around 2000 years old (in Critchett 1990:58).

There are considerable accounts of well-constructed houses, as well as drawings of them by George French Angas, Mitchell, George Augustus Robinson, and writer William Thomas. Henry Fyshe Gisborne reported on his journey of 1839 across the southern area of Victoria, and maintained that the huts were 'substantial' (in Critchett 1990:59). Figure 5 was sketched by Robinson on his survey of Mt. Napier and Mt. Sturgeon in 1841. He recorded 13 large huts, and one in particular was 3.5 metres in diameter and 1.5 meters high, with two entrances. He maintained that these huts accommodated at least seven to eight adults (in Critchett 1990:60).

At a place below Mt. Eeles, now known as the Lake Gorrie archaeological site (unearthed through an archaeological survey in 1989), Robinson observed 'a sort of village, and some of their habitations made out of stone' (in Critchett 1990:60). James Dawson, who arrived in this area in 1869, concluded from a discussion he had with an Aboriginal male that each family had a permanent dwelling and that these dwellings were large enough to be partitioned (in Critchett 1990:60). Mitchell's expedition west across the Victorian Grampians came across several large 'Guneaks' of large dimensions; Granville Stapylton who accompanied Mitchell observed that 'one of these was capable of containing at least 40 people and of very superior construction' (in Critchett 1990:60).

Tindale's (1987) study of the Kaurna people of Adelaide plains in South Australia combines Aboriginal oral history with archaeological evidence to demonstrate that the

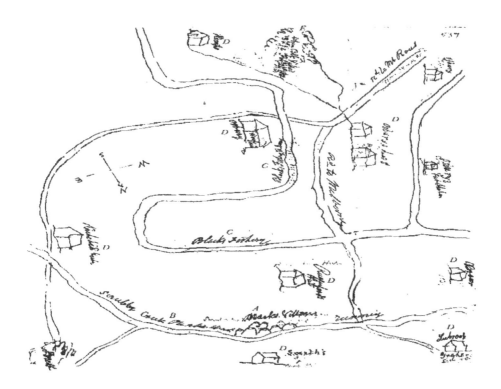

Figure 5 An Aboriginal village.

Kaurna people were definitely permanently sedentary (Tindale 1987:12). Furthermore, evidence of the long occupation of the desert country by Aboriginal people was recorded by David Lindsey in 1886. On his expedition he found that Boolaburtinna was inhabited on a permanent basis and that there were a large number of huts and well-beaten paths that led from them in all directions (Lindsey 1890:1–16).

In Western Australia, George Grey and Francois Perion also observed such dwellings. In central Australia, Earnest Giles sighted dwellings, and Charles Sturt reported sighting seventy huts along the Macquarie River (in Critchett 1990:60). Sedentarism was an important aspect of Aboriginal traditional life.

Myth 2, Aboriginal society does not produce specialists

A specialist is defined as a person or group who devotes themselves to specialising in one particular branch of human endeavour, such as study, research, or business. Roger Keesing suggests that 'specialisation in the division of labour, and the rise of full-time craftsmen created a greater economic interdependence of populations' (1981:59).

R. and C. Berndt and J. Stanton provide some details of specialisation in Aboriginal societies; they show that people were engaged as negotiators for the purpose of undertaking trade missions to barter and acquire goods at trade fairs. These people would travel along trading ways in south-eastern Australia.

> There appears to have existed a sort of traffic between the tribes of the Murray and those near the sea and curious sort of provision is made for it, the object of which may be the securing of perfectly trustworthy agents to transact the business of the tribes-agents who will not by collusion cheat their employers and enrich themselves. (R. Berndt, C. Berndt & J. Stanton 1993:118)

The Kukabrak nation in South Australia calls these people *ngengampi*. These *ngengampi* are trade agents who specialise in trading certain foods, fur rugs, fur and fibrous cloaks, nets, and lines. Berndt *et al.* indicate that value was added to these goods and concluded that 'values fluctuated according to supply and demand' (1993:129). Butlin has noticed 'special resource supply conditions' that define the value of objects traded over long distances (1993:85). Thus, baler shell (*melo diameda*) was traded from Cape York in Queensland as rainmaking devices, but if they were traded further afield from the point of origin, they became valued for a different function.

In most regions of Australia, Aboriginal people developed netting and basketry techniques. Not much has been recorded about skill development, although D.S. Davidson, an anthropologist, mapped the distribution and spread of certain techniques. In the South Australian Museum 'there is an emu net made of vegetable fibres 178 feet long by 2 feet 9 inches wide. The meshes are 9 inches by 9 inches' (Davidson 1933:257). We also know that Aboriginal people made nets for the capture of ducks; they would be spread across a river and the ducks chased into them. These nets would be constructed in considerable lengths; therefore they would require the skills and time of specialised craft persons. It is also reasonable to assume that at some point these nets would need to be continually maintained and mended because of damage inflicted by animals fleeing, debris, and weather (Butlin 1993:78). Just as significant as the construction and repair of nets is the manufacture of kangaroo waterbags for travel.

From 1883 to 1885 Ridley Williams was a Queensland drover who drove cattle across the northern fringes of the Simpson Desert to Alice Springs. He stated:

> We came to where they used to get water this was a well dug out of almost all stones and was evidently permanent water in this well there was a great lot of old discarded waterbags all made out of kangaroo skins . . . they prepare them by tanning them on the flesh side with bark so that they can carry water in them for days without it going bad. (in Kimber 1980:14)

He noted the manufacture and use of kangaroo-skin waterbags, mentioning that he saw Aboriginal men carrying kangaroo waterbags (see Figure 6). He also commented that these men travelled about 350 kilometres as the crow flies, drinking water from these kangaroo-skin bags (in Kimber 1980:14–15).

In 1979 there were Aboriginal people still alive who had knowledge of cultural practices before European goods changed manufacturing and production styles of certain items. As Rose points out most of the conquest of Aboriginal Australia took place within living memory and is still recounted by Aboriginal storytellers (1992:1).

Aboriginal artists are also storytellers and experts in their field. One such person was Yirawala, a painter of the Dreamtime. He was a ceremonial leader, law carrier, and

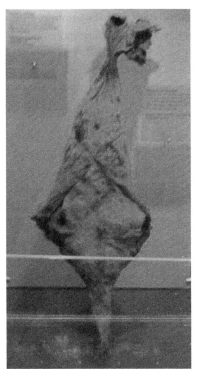

knowledgeable man who was born around 1894 and died in 1976. He left six paintings in his will in which he encoded symbolic instructions for his sons and his community. Yirawala described his art works as being 'not like white man's, but like pages of a sacred book' (Holmes 1992:3). He inherited his father's skills and intellectual property such as sacred designs, symbols, stories, and songs taught through ritual learning. As chosen heir he was instructed in tribal law and in turn, in the customary manner of his people, began instructing his son David Gumaraitj. This ensured that the tribal law and sacred designs, symbols, stories, and songs were preserved and taught to the next heir (Holmes 1992: epilogue).

Howitt describes a communication route where he was constantly informed about the

Figure 6 A kangaroo skin waterbag of the type used by Aboriginal travellers. Reproduced by kind permission of the Australian National Museum.

travels of John McKinlay 1862. 'Intertribal communication and barter was carried on by professionals in communication down from the Stone Desert of Sturt to Yanruwunta country' (Howitt 1882 papers 5).

A study undertaken by McCarthy and McArthur (in Sahlins 1972:19) in 1960 examined post-colonial labour and distribution in two Northern Territory Aboriginal communities. These communities had 'extraordinary relief from economic cares' and were able to maintain a full time craft person. 'Wilira was an expert craftsman who repaired the spears and spear-throwers, made smoking pipes and drone-tubes, and hafted stone axes (on request) in a skilful manner; apart from these occupations he spent most of his time talking, eating and sleeping' (in Sahlins 1972:19). Commentators on Aboriginal prehistory, Mulvaney (1975) and Micha (1970), have observed that a 'degree of specialisation did contribute to the development of trade' in Aboriginal Australia (Barlow 1979:2). Artists, tradesmen, and craftsmen are all specialist positions that require economic independence from food gathering.

The distinction between 'food collectors' and food producers' is drawn to argue that the latter were more civilised. It is common wisdom that civilisation began with the development of permanent villages and crop cultivation, and that food production led to a profound change in human societies. Kessing saw this as 'greatly expanding human population and revolutionising ways of life' (Keesing 1981:42–43). Jarred Diamond suggests that 'food production' occurred on every continent except Australia (Diamond 1998). Typically he argues, 'food producers' built reasonably permanent houses, cultivated crops, and entered into animal husbandry. He also suggests that Aboriginal people were food collectors and did not build permanent shelters, did not herd or domesticate animals, and devoted all their time to collecting foods (Diamond 1998). Stanner maintains that these assumptions are 'speculative' and have been challenged by detailed studies of Australian Aboriginal societies by archaeologists, anthropologists, and historians (1968:14). The studies examined 'function systems', which included the holistic view of processes that contribute to the social fabric of a society (Stanner 1968:14).

Myth 3, Aboriginal society were food collectors not food producers

A classic distinction between civilised and primitive societies is whether they produce and cultivate food, or simply hunt and gather food. Some Aboriginal nations built permanent settlements of wood and stone dwellings. This enabled those societies to harvest their environment and farm so that they could feed everyone in their village if the hunters came home empty handed. In his recent work, Diamond devoted considerable time analysing the differences between food collectors and food producers, and the evolution of farming and husbandry practices around the world. He comes to the conclusion that 'hunter-gatherers in some productive areas . . . possibly south-eastern Australia became sedentary, but never became food producers' (Diamond 1998:106). There is much evidence to contest this view of Aboriginal people as hunter-gatherers who lack farming and husbandry skills.

Explorer records of contact challenge the notion that crops were not produced in

Aboriginal Australia. Matthew Flinders explored the Australian coast between the years 1801–1803 and wrote in the *Investigator* that he went ashore in Port Jackson and communicated with some Koories. They informed him that 'on the west side of the mountains existed a people, who planted potatoes and maize . . . ' (Carter 1987:181). A.C. Gregory noted that at Coopers Creek, 'fields of 1000 acres were used to grow cereal crops'. Australian millet (*Panicum decompositum*) provided the means for a sophisticated seed grinding culture:

The natives cut it down by means of stone knives, cutting down the stalk halfway, beat out the seed, leaving the straw which is often met with in large heaps; they winnow by tossing seed and husk into the air, the wind carrying away the husks. The grinding into meal is done by means of two stones, a large irregular slab and a small cannon-ball-like one. (cited in Low 1988:29)

Thomas Mitchell recorded and named several such cereal crops in the central districts of Australia such as the Barley Mitchell grass (*Astrebla pectinata*) and *Panicum loevinode* (see Figure 7).

Travel was made more difficult, too, because much of the flat land was a vast sea of tall reeds extending to the horizon. On open plains near the marshes the grass was very rich, the best being *Panicum loevinode* which Mitchell had earlier found (Baker 1997:156) on the Darling pulled up and stacked in heaps, for some purpose he could not then discover. Kinghorne told Mitchell that its Aboriginal name was 'coolly' and that women gathered it in great quantities and pounded the seeds between stones with water to form a kind of paste or bread. (Mitchell 1848:60–61)

On the second leg of his expedition to 'Tropical Australia', which took him from Narran in New South Wales to St George in Queensland, Mitchell again noted that along the banks of the Narran River:

There were excellent grasses. The predominant species was *Panicum loevinode*. Dry heaps of this grass lay along Mitchell's path for many miles. He counted nine miles along the river-bank where only this grass grew. It rose as high as the saddle

Figure 7 Mitchell grass.

girths and seemed to grow back from the river as far as the eye could reach through an open forest. (Mitchell 1848:55–66, cited in Baker 1997:160)

During his exploration of the Belyando, Mitchell also recorded an area of land roughly about two acres, which he concluded had been 'broken by hoe' (Mitchell 1848).

Tony Swain suggests that rice was introduced into Australia several centuries ago through a long association with the Chinese and Macassans (Swain 1993:183–84). Once the Macassans had introduced rice it was planted and cultivated, so a new food crop was introduced to Aboriginal diet in the northern parts of Australia. Australian wild rice (*Oruyza meridionalis*) is called *Oruyza* (Low 1988:28–29). Bellwood, a researcher into Austronesian speaking peoples stated that, 'the first Austroneasian speaking peoples were a Neolithic, pottery-using society with rice and millet agriculture' (1989:1–59). These areas can be identified in Arnhem Land and are part of the song cycles of this area; the song cycles are performed to inform about how to find the location, as well as how to maintain and harvest the crop. Song cycles are also about moving through life, 'coming and going out of being, visiting the same camping places, sitting around a story place which has been used by ancestral beings long gone, reproducing and re-performing events that were taught from the ancestors' (Reser *et al.* 2000:49).

Similar evidence can be found further down south in Victoria at Lake Condah and 'Hopkins River these areas were rich sources of eels' (Critchett 1990:57). People who lived in stone house settlements also built these complex eel traps (see Figure 8). In traps set in Lake Condah 'many eels could be caught in a short time, providing food for large gatherings' (*The Bunjilaka Gallery*). This hydraulic engineering enabled local people to harvest large catches of eels all year round, and to live in permanent dwellings

Figure 8 Sketch of eel traps by Robinson, 1841, at Lake Condah, Victora. Reproduced by kind permission of the Bunjilaka Gallery, Museum Victoria, Melbourne.

(Lake Condah eel traps in *The Bunjilaka Gallery*, Melbourne Museum 2004, Critchett 1990:57).

A plant called *Duboisia hopwoodii* (pituri) grows in the south-western corner of Queensland; it is a shrub that grows up to three metres tall with narrow, willow-like leaves, small white bell-shaped flowers with dark stripes on the inside and small blackish berries. Pituri was also grown in plantations, as Groom observed:

> We travelled through about 100 acres [40 ha] of the pituri growing about 3 ft [1 m] high, very much like tobacco. Tamulju and Njunowa darted through it, selected and pulled leaves and piled them in bundles on camels until we resembled a travelling market garden . . . We take plenty back to Areyonga people. We get 3 shillings a sugar bag. Sometimes get more. (cited in Latz 1995:63)

Traditionally the leaves of pituri would be plucked from the branches and every twig would be removed, because only the leaf matter would be used for trade. The harvester owned the plant and monopolised the market; the picker's family owned the plantation (Terry 1974:64). The evidence indicates agricultural practices were developed by some Aboriginal nations, and also that the surplus was traded along Aboriginal paths. Aboriginal people also developed storage technology for critical foods and vegetable matter such as pituri.

In summary, the popular assumptions about Aboriginal traditional lifestyles obscure much detailed knowledge about Aboriginal society. Aboriginal social organisation demanded that specialists develop skills to invest in labour, to erect and maintain dwellings, fashion tools, and construct earth works for dams and weirs for the maintenance of fish and eel farms. With reliable year round food production, water conservation and solid construction of huts, people dwelt on their lands for long periods. The static view of Aboriginal culture underpinned the social Darwinist observations that it had not evolved to the highest level. Such ideologies have had enormous implications for investigations of Australian Aboriginal people and societies. Popular science, through natural history museum exhibitions, ethnographic and anthropological studies, consistently presented false conclusions based on shaky assumptions. Evidence to contradict the models of what Aboriginal societies were assumed to be from a Euro-centric perspective can be easily unearthed. In actual fact, for Aboriginal societies the cosmology and the 'social structure' formed systems of social relationships between persons and groups with which to manage the whole of 'human society' (Stanner 1968). Aboriginal people traversed and managed this 'sun-burnt land' of wide open spaces; they bartered, traded, travelled, governed, and built dwellings to support their communities and achieve a better standard of living.

Evidence indicates that there is now a need to reposition Aboriginal culture, and to rethink common assumptions about the lifestyles of Aboriginal people. Evidence has also shown that Aboriginal people are sedentary, and that some groups developed harvesting techniques and resource management, with a degree of regional variance in terms of the manufacture of certain types of equipment. Aboriginal nations across Australia had specialists who were not expected to procure food.

CHAPTER TWO

The Coming of the Aliens

For Aboriginal people land is a dynamic notion; it is something that is creative . . .
Land is the generation point of existence; it's the spirit from which Aboriginal existence comes. It's a place, a living thing made up of sky, of clouds, of rivers, of trees,
of wind, of sand, and of spirit that has created all those things; the spirit that has
planted my own spirit there, my country . . . It belongs to me; I belong to the land;
I rest in it; I come from there. (Father Pat Dodson MSC, in *Report of the Third Annual
Queensland Conference of the Aboriginal and Islander Catholic Council of Australia*, Jan.
1976:16)

This chapter examines some of the waves of contact between Aboriginal people and the
invaders since 1788, and the effects these had on travel and trade. The discussion focuses
on the introduction of smallpox in order to illustrate a later argument about trade
routes. During discussion about the effects of smallpox, the other means European
invaders utilised to create a wilderness are investigated. It is reasonable to suggest that
the effects of smallpox, along with wilderness creation, resulted in a depopulation of
the Aboriginal people's landscape. The investigation then focuses on the landscape and
clarifies how the European invaders constructed a wilderness that suited their needs
and which they could call their own. This discussion is important in terms of the argument that Australia was already a cultivated landscape with paths along which
information and goods moved.

The history of white colonisation and the settlement of Australia are well known
and do not need reiterating here. Some people, more than others, understand the devastating effects the colonisers had on the Aboriginal population, and are familiar with
the history of dispossession of lands.

The Wik nation was the first Aboriginal people to come into contact with
Europeans with the Dutch ship *Duyfken* that landed on the western coast of Cape York
in 1606. The place where the Dutch landed is now known as Cape Keer-weer (a Dutch
word meaning 'turn around'). Dirk Hartog landed on the Western Australian coast at
Shark Bay in 1616, and Abel Tasman reached the Tasmanian coast in 1642. All of this
is well documented, but somehow or other it has escaped the historical imagination of
Australia. Much less attention is paid to the earlier contacts, which is recorded in less
accessible language to the Anglo-Celtic historiographer. These contacts were made by
Chinese, Macassan and Papuan traders in the northern parts of Australia, probably well
before the well-known ones.

The Macassans conducted trade with northern Aboriginal people from their perahus several decades before European exploration of the northern parts of Australia (Mulvaney 1989:22–28). The Macassans are trepang fishermen, and they visited the northern shores for the purpose of harvesting and curing trepang. On returning to Macassar they sold the dried flesh to merchants from China (Butlin 1993:102–103). The trepang is an edible sea slug or sea cucumber that would have been harvested in the millions, and it was an industry that flourished for a long time before it was terminated at the request of the South Australian government in 1906. The Macassans also bartered for turtle shells and cypress pine (Altman 1987:2). Chinese navigators often commanded long journeys; the first recorded journey from Timor to Australia was made by a Chinese merchant in 1751 (Macknight 1976). But it is the British who commenced the scheme of dispossession. This did not begin until Lieutenant James Cook took formal possession of the whole eastern coast for King George III, and renamed the eastern part of New Holland 'New South Wales'. He did this from 'Possession Island' on August 22, 1770.

Then followed a succession of waves of boat people to Australia, beginning with the First Fleet in January 1788 that established a 'bridgehead that flowered into an overwhelmingly destructive invading force' on Aboriginal land (Butlin 1993:143). The flotilla of eleven ships and approximately 1044 people founded a new British colony that ushered in the beginnings of 'white fella artefact' with profound effects on the land, its resources, and its people.

Eora people and the first convict settlers

When the First Fleet arrived at Kamay (Botany Bay) its human cargo became aliens in a world where the trees shed their bark instead of their leaves at certain times of the year. There were no recognisable root plants that could be dug up, no identifiable berries, nuts or fruits; it was an alien environment. Displaced from their natural habitat, the Europeans were unable to recognise the abundance of food all around them so they continued to rely on the old stocks carried from Europe, but they fared badly.

The supplies that were brought out with the First Fleet were meant to last two years but the flour soon became ridden with weevils, the supply of salted meat shrank, and the livestock either died or was speared by the Eora people. The seed stock for planting was attacked by rats, mice, and insects and the soil around Tuhbowgule (Sydney) was found to be unsuitable for the planting of imported seeds. Stores were depleted as they cleared land for agriculture, set up encampments, established permanent dwellings and took part in probing expeditions into outlying areas. In addition, during the early months those who barely survived the passage from England began suffering due to the lack of fresh meat, green vegetables and fruit, so sickness from scurvy was a constant threat. In the first two years, they experienced serious problems with food stocks dwindling. Governor Arthur Phillip sought the help of the Eora people in supplying kangaroo meat and other edible foodstuff to alleviate the onset of starvation and scurvy. The settlers learned little from the Eora peoples about the variety of edible foodstuff or how to identify it; even the meat they were given was resented. In Surgeon-General White's view, 'Here, where no animal nourishment is to be procured the Kangaroo is considered as a dainty, but [in] any other country I am sure it would be thrown to the dogs' (in Willey 1979: 98–99).

A lively trade developed between the Eora people and the convict settlement. In the early days, crews on the transport ships were 'procuring spears, shields, fishing-lines, and other articles from the natives to carry to Europe' (Willey 1979:58). In exchange for these goods the Eora people received rum and metal tools.

From the early years of the British bridgehead in Sydney Cove, Aboriginal people were relied upon for expert advice on surveying the country. A famous and controversial figure in Aboriginal and Australian history is Bungaree, an Aboriginal man regarded as a diplomat. In 1799, Bungaree sailed on the *Norfolk* with Matthew Flinders to explore the coast from Port Jackson (New South Wales) to Hervey Bay (Queensland). He also sailed with Flinders on the *Investigator* to circumnavigate Australia in 1802–1803 (*Australian Heritage*, vol. 3. 1989:385–89; Flannery 2000).

Eric Willmot, an Aboriginal historian, brings to life this early period of settlement in *Pemulwuy: The Rainbow Warrior*, where he outlines the first Australian's resistance to invasions by alien people. The British knew *Pemulwuy* as a criminal, who burnt crops, killed stock, and attacked settlements and the British Marines. Willmot portrays *Pemulwuy* as a general who provided leadership for the guerrilla war fought over Eora lands. Willmot provides accounts of the early trade between the British settlers and the first Australians and argues that trade actually saved the fledgling colony. The Eora people provided scouting and interpretation services to the early British colonisers by guiding them over established paths and communicating to other language groups around the district of the early settlement of Sydney.

> Pemulwuy seemed to reach a compromise in dealing with the British and traded with them extensively in meat. He and his group hunted in Bushlands, mainly along what the British called the Georges River. The British did not like the meat of the country's marsupials, but they were desperate for fresh meat. The Bidjigals gained some metal tools from this trade. (Willmot 1987:31)

The role of Aboriginal collaborators in the European exploration and settlement of Australia is explored by Henry Reynolds in *With the White People* (1990). These people were generally scorned by Europeans as well as by their own people. The word 'collaborators' is used, because the majority of Aboriginal people see these historic characters as traitors who helped the British. A war waged between the British and Aboriginal nations for the control of Australia (Reynolds 1990).

Galgalla or smallpox

One result of this trade relationship was the spread of introduced diseases to which Aboriginal people had no resistance. Introduced diseases, such as smallpox, played a vital role in the depopulation of lands for colonisation and conquest in the south-eastern corner of Australia. It is important to consider the spread of galgalla (the Eora word for smallpox) across the continent and its relationship to European conquest (Willmot (1987:302). In Victoria it was known as 'Meen warann', and is remembered in a song 'Mallae mallaeae' that originated from New South Wales (Critchett 1990:77). The spread of the disease followed the established trade and communication routes which criss-crossed the continent.

Smallpox depends on a chain of humans; it is a virus that spreads from person to person via the air people breath; it is spread by sneezing, coughing, and saliva. It can also be spread by having direct contact with the sores of people who are affected by the virus and breathing micro dust particles from fabrics. Garments that have been used to cover the sick can carry the virus. Woollen blankets too would have spittle, vomit, or matter from the pustules left on them, which could infect a person by breathing in the micro dust. The virus can remain active on garments and blankets for up to two years given the right conditions, but the disease can quite easily be killed by sunlight. Wool provides the ideal conditions for the virus to remain alive and it releases fine particles that can carry the disease. The disease has a 21-day cycle that results in either death, or recovery; it is contagious/infectious at about 8–12 days after initial infestation (Butlin 1993). Smallpox was the most feared human disease; it wiped out millions of people in sixteenth-century Europe and was the third leading cause of death (Knapp 1989:83).

In Europe, smallpox was spread by trading missions and communication routes. Knapp argues that merchants brought smallpox into Europe when they traded with Byzantium and the peoples of the Middle East during the Middle Ages (Knapp 1989:79). In AD 164 and AD 189, when Rome was a hub of world trade, smallpox spread along established trading routes to Rome. 'By her contacts with distant lands and people, Rome opened her gates to pestilence' (Cartwright 1973:12). The smallpox plague wiped out millions of Roman citizens. 'It rapidly extended into all parts of the known world, causing so many deaths that loads of corpses were carried away from Rome and other cities in carts and wagons' (Cartwright 1973:13). Cartwright suggests that some 2,000 people died in a day; it was then called the 'Plague of Antoninus' or the 'Plague of Galen' after the physician who described the disease (Cartwright 1973:13; Diamond, 1998:205). The smallpox plague has been attributed with causing the first crack in Roman defence lines.

Because Australia was spared the ravages of diseases that swept through Europe and Asia, Aboriginal people had no immunity to these diseases. Any virus spread very quickly once Aboriginal people were exposed to it, as Aboriginal people were unaccustomed to infectious diseases so the whole community was at risk. Butlin calls this a 'potential for a true pandemic, wiping out large proportions of the total population' (Butlin 1993:104).

Opinions are divided about whether it was the Europeans (French or English) or the Macassans who introduced the disease into Australia. Campbell (1985) and Mulvaney (1989) believe the disease spread from north to south, so it must have been introduced by the Macassans. Butlin (1993) considers that the opposite occurred, because there were several outbreaks of the virus in Aboriginal nations: in 1789 (Sydney), 1828 (Melbourne), 1829 (Raffles Bay Northern Territory) and 1869 in the Kimberleys and these outbreaks follow a south to north pattern. The first outbreak occurred around the Sydney region in 1789, the year after the first fleet arrived. Butlin believes that the second outbreak of 1828 first occurred in Melbourne and spread to Bathurst, New South Wales by 1831 and west to South Australia in 1831 and east to Moreton Bay Queensland in 1837 (see Map 1). A third outbreak in Raffles Bay in 1829 is considered to have been an isolated localised infection. Butlin overlooks the fact that Raffles Bay was a British outpost between the years 1827–1829 (G. Taplin 1879:44–45; Ronald M. Berndt *et al.* 1993:292; Critchett 1990:76–77).

Taplin suggests that there were two waves of smallpox spread down the Murray from New South Wales to Adelaide in 1814–1820 and then in 1829–1831 (Taplin 1879:44–45; R. Berndt *et al.* 1993:292; Critchett 1990:76–77). This is interesting because witnessed accounts by Watkin Tench put the first outbreak of the disease in Sydney in April 1789, which had spread to Adelaide by 1814 (Flannery: 1996:102). This means it took 23 years for the disease to spread 1,665 kilometres. When the second outbreak occurred in 1829 it only took three years to spread the same distance.

Aboriginal people have long argued that smallpox was introduced by Europeans in 1788, and was a contributing factor that shattered Aboriginal resistance and decimated Aboriginal populations.The decimation of Aboriginal people by introduced diseases made it easier for Europeans to colonise and populate Australia, and at the same time to introduce animal and plant species within the environment. This is the case for New South Wales, Victoria and parts of South Australia. Willey suggests that smallpox was deliberately inflicted on the Aboriginal population by the 'First Fleeters', and the suggestion should not be dismissed lightly (Willey 1979:77). Willey asserts:

> There are certain circumstances connected with the medical history of the 'First Fleet' which arouse suspicion that the responsibility of the introduction attached to it. It was said that, before leaving Plymouth, the ship's company of the *Alexandria* [*Alexander*] transport had 'got a malignant disease amongst them of a most dangerous kind'. (in 1979:77)

It appears that some concerns about malicious intent were raised at the time. Watkin Tench, a marine with the First Fleet maintained that:

> No person among us had been afflicted with the disorder since we had quitted the Cape of Good Hope, seventeen months before. It is true that our surgeons had brought out variolous matter in bottles; but to infer that it was produced from this cause were a supposition. (in Willey 1979:77)

'Variolous' means having to do with smallpox, or pitted by smallpox. The disease spread and Phillip estimated that by 1792 over half the Eora nation in the Sydney district had died and a further quarter were dying. Occasionally the French are credited with the dubious record of bringing the disease into the country, because the outbreak happened not long after the ships of La Perouse departed from the harbour on 11 March 1788. However a sailor from the *Supply*, Joseph Jeffries, died from smallpox on 10 May 1789, not long after the disease had become an epidemic among the Eora people. If the disease did indeed surface in 1789 then the French seem an unlikely source due to the short incubation period (*Australia's Heritage,* vol.1, 1989:86–87).

In early May 1789 four Aboriginal people – two adults, a boy of six and a girl of about thirteen – were brought into the settlement from the Parramatta district suffering from the virus. This was the start of the dreadful calamity that was about to be wrought on the Aboriginal people of Australia. The two adults died of the virus but the two children survived. This means that the first infection of the Aboriginal poopulation around Sydney occurred in April 1789 (Willey 1979:106–107; *Australia's Heritage*, vol. 1, 1989:86). The first recorded Aboriginal person to die of smallpox was Arabanoo. Arabanoo was part of an experiment by Governor Phillip who had been trying to establish a friendly relationship with the Aboriginal population. Governor Phillip realised that without the help of the Eora nation, the colony would not make any progress. So in December 1788, Phillip set about coercing the local Eora people and Arabanoo was seized. He was given clothing, and manacles were slapped on him. He was then locked up in a hut close to a guardhouse to commence his training in civilisation. The experiment came to an abrupt end when Arabanoo died of smallpox on 18 May 1789. Governor Phillip ordered that Arabanoo be buried in the gardens of the first Government House (Mulvaney 1989:46).

It became a common sight for settlers and explorers to see corpses of Aboriginal people who had died from introduced diseases across the country. Bruce Elder writes: 'wherever whites explored they came across Aborigines covered with pustules and slowly wasting away' (1988:15). In the Sydney basin explorers would find small groups of corpses decaying, unburied, and forgotten. The Eora people were numerous; they managed their lands, hunted along the shorelines, fished in the harbour, and when they camped on the fringes of the new settlement, the smoke of their campfires could be seen. When David Collins took a trip with an Aboriginal male around Sydney Cove in 1790 to find the man's family, they witnessed the following effects of smallpox:

> The number that it swept off, by their own accounts, was incredible [in] . . . different coves we visited; not a vestige on the sand was to be found of human foot; the excavations in the rocks were filled with the putrid bones of those who had fallen victims to the disorder; not a living person was anywhere to be met. It seemed as if, flying from contagion, they had left the dead to bury the dead. (Elder 1988:15–16)

There was a dramatic drop in the Aboriginal population around the Sydney area in 1789. The disease then spread overland along trading routes and into the interior where it wreaked havoc as Aboriginal travellers passed from one small community and to the next. Edward Powell testified at a hearing over his conviction of murdering two Aboriginal men in 1799 that 'it was the intention of the Natives to come down in numbers from the Blue Mountains to the Hawkesbury and to murder some of the white people and particularly some soldiers' (in Robinson & York 1977:8). If Aboriginal people did cross the Blue Mountains, then smallpox could have crossed from Sydney along the same paths.

In 1828 the *Bussorah Merchant* berthed at Port Jackson in Victoria. It brought convicts to Australia and it was noted that this ship had an outbreak of smallpox on board. Its convicts were assigned to the upper Hunter River in New South Wales and all the material contents of the ship were supposedly destroyed. An epidemic broke out amongst the Victorian Aboriginal population six months after the ship berthed. If the contents had been just dumped rather than destroyed, the blankets and clothing would have been used by the local Aboriginal people. The infected convicts were moved to the Hunter region and the outbreak then spread north into Queensland and the Northern Territory (Butlin 1993:113 & 118).

Butlin's map (Map 1) below elucidates the observed spread of smallpox across Australia. In the eastern states, Aboriginal people used the river systems to travel; the river systems of the Murray and the Darling provided a highway for movement of Aboriginal people, so it would have been easy for Aboriginal people to spread smallpox along these waterways.

The Hunter region of New South Wales is located in the Murray Darling Basin river catchment area. The Murray–Darling is the fourth longest river system in the world and covers about one-seventh of the total area of Australia. The head of the Darling River is fed by the monsoonal downpours in northeastern New South Wales and southern Queensland. A tributary of the Darling, the Warrego, is also fed by rains in Queensland and joins the Darling at the country city of Bourke in New South Wales.

> The course of the River Darling itself over the imperceptibly gentle sloping plain of western New South Wales . . . is dissipated in a maze of outflowing channels, anabranches and temporary lakes, often spilling back into the river at some point. In effect they become giant billabongs when the water level drops and they are left isolated from the main stream. Beyond the largest of these groups of lakes, at Menindee, the river turns south and winds its way shadowed on the western side by its Great Anabranch until both streams join the Murray by separate mouths, one on each side of the town Wentworth. (Hardy 1969:xiii–xiv)

Critchett observed that 'The malady spread with rapidity from tribe to tribe . . . the infection being carried by the messengers who were sent forward to communicate the sad news of its ravages' (Critchett 1990:77). The news was spread by messengers who would recount a song to inform people of the sickness. One song originated in New South Wales and was relayed through Victoria and onto South Australia. This song cycle was called the *Meen warann*. It is thought that the news was spread along the river system and fanned out to other locations as messengers tried in vain to warn others (Critchett 1990:77).

Hardy makes specific reference to bearers of bad news in the Murray Darling Basin region of NSW:

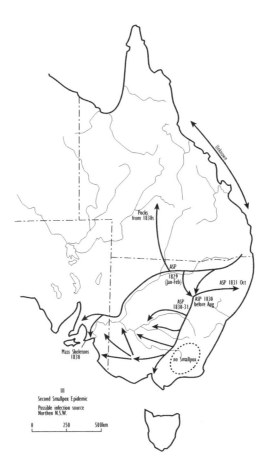

Map I Second smallpox epidemic spread by the movement of infected people along the river systems in New South Wales and Queensland. Adapted from Noel Butlin's *Our Original Aggression: Aboriginal Populations of Southeast Australia 1788–1850* (Sydney: George Allen & Unwin, 1983).

Less far-ranging journeys were made by couriers entrusted with messages for distant kinsmen – an invitation to join in a communal initiation ceremony perhaps. They carried a notched wooden message stick whose symbols outlined the venue and agenda. A messenger bearing tidings of death presented himself with a lugubrious, white-washed visage which left the recipients in no doubt as to the nature of his news even before its disclosure at the end of the prolonged preliminary rituals. (Hardy 1969:15)

Butlin argues strongly against the view that Macassans were responsible for the outbreaks further south. The Macassan trepangers who traded along the northern coast from the Kimberleys to Cape York used the prevailing winds of the monsoon season to travel to these locations from ports in Sulawesi. Butlin argues that the trip from

Sulawesi to the northern part of Australia would have taken too long for an outbreak of the disease to last, and that it would have decimated the crews of the ocean-going boats. Butlin explains that the crews on these boats were small and that smallpox needs large groups of people to remain active. He also points out that the northern Aboriginal communities would have been completely cut off from other communities by the wet season, so they would have become blocks or barriers that prevented the disease from spreading further south. Since trepang fishermen had visited the top end communities of Northern Territory and the Gulf area on a regular basis over a long period of time, these communities would have developed an immunity to the virus (Willey 1979; Altman 1987; Mulvaney 1989; Butlin 1993:120).

Macassan fleets also visited the Kimberley shores, but had much less contact with Aboriginal people there. Macassans could have introduced the disease to the Kimberley in 1869; however it is also possible that the disease was carried overland by Aboriginal traders. If the disease took 23 years to be carried from Sydney in 1789 to Adelaide in 1814, then it could have taken 40 years to reach the Kimberley.

Walter Roth (1897) notes that 'trade routes invariably run along water courses and water holes and that the length of time occupied by the journey varies with the travelling distance, from a few weeks, or months, up to a full year' (Roth [1897] 1983:8). It appears that the spread of diseases in fact followed Aboriginal trading routes and routes of communication. Explorers such as Watkin Tench, Matthew Flinders, Thomas Mitchell, Ludwig Leichhardt, and E.J. Eyre used Aboriginal guides as 'black ambassadors', to lead their parties to negotiate safe passage through other Aboriginal nations' country (Reynolds 1990). The spread of galgalla can be traced thanks to the accounts of the explorers in the journals of their expeditions.

I argue, as Hardy (1969) does, that smallpox was carried along Aboriginal trade routes. Hardy (1969) cites surveyor Mitchell's exploration of the Bathurst region and his sighting of smallpox. 'In 1835, Mitchell found some of the Aborigines of the northern Darling pitted with smallpox: it is possible that this early affliction with the diseases of civilization came from trading contact with tribes south of the Murray who contracted the complaint about 1830, probably as the result of an epidemic from the Sydney side' (1969:15).

There is mounting evidence to suggest that galgalla travelled along established Aboriginal trading ways. Mitchell's journals support this hypothesis about the spread of the disease. In 1831, Mitchell set off on his first expedition through New South Wales to the Queensland border; he was looking for the Kindur River, which he believed flowed through central New South Wales to the eastern seaboard. Mitchell took with him 19 European men, carts, drays, packhorses, and cattle. He crossed the Great Dividing Range along paths already established near Muswellbrook in the Hunter Valley. This was the first organised penetration of the hinterland by Europeans other than by runaway convicts (Baker 1997:40).

Here the expedition met with what Mitchell termed the 'remnants of the Geawegal people' who were suffering from the effects of smallpox (Baker 1997: 51). He described these people as 'a truly pathetic group', refugees escaping from the invading forces of the white man (Baker 1997: 51).

Once over the range, the expedition came across a remnant of a Hunter Valley tribe, probably Geawegal people, encountered a few days earlier ten miles or so south of Scone. They were truly a pathetic group. Not only were they suffering from smallpox, for which Mitchell provided medicines where he could, but they were also 'strangers in the land'. (in Baker 1997: 51)

During this expedition Mitchell had sought the assistance of Aboriginal people as guides, believing that they would give him an advantage in finding the best paths to move his equipment. Aboriginal scouts had local knowledge of the terrain, and edible food when supplies ran short; they were familiar with the best paths that demanded the least effort to move this contingent of men and equipment. Mitchell paid them with tomahawks, knives, and blankets. An Aboriginal guide named Mr Brown, for example, agreed 'to accompany the party in return for two blankets, one for his wife, the other for his use, and a tomahawk' (Baker 1997:52).

On Mitchell's next expedition of the Darling in 1835, he took 23 men, two light-weight whaleboats, a boat carriage, seven carts, packhorses and enough bullocks to pull the carts. He again used Aboriginal guides and one particular Aboriginal scout by the name of *Tackijally*. During the long journey, lack of water was a constant problem and its scarcity caused Mitchell some concern. Mitchell asked *Tackijally* to lead his group to water and he marvelled at how skilled he was in helping them to avoid obstacles and locate direct routes to waterholes (Baker 1997:68–73).

During this expedition, Mitchell came across several groups of Aboriginal nations who bore the marks of smallpox, which he described as 'confluent smallpox'.

A couple of days after the expedition reached Bourke, some Aborigines, perhaps Gunu people, appeared on the opposite bank of the river, shouting and calling but keeping a respectful distance from the Bullocks, some of which had crossed over. Presently they ventured across the river and sat down when Mitchell met them about two hundred yards from the tents. The party consisted of four men and a boy, followed by seven women and some children. The men were small and carried no spears. Most of them had had smallpox although the marks were no larger than pin-heads. It seemed to Mitchell that the disease had almost depopulated the district and that these people were the remains of a once numerous tribe. (in Baker 1997: 76–85)

Somewhere between present-day Wilcannia and Menindee in New South Wales, Mitchell came across what he believed to be mass graves of those who died from smallpox. A dead tree on top of a hill with bleached white branches pointed to the graves, thereby marking the gravesite. Mitchell describes the graves as 'oval shaped tombs about twelve feet in length and each had a tombstone made of a hollow tree' (in Baker 1997:85–86). Mitchell's notes show us that the destructive influence of whites long preceded their arrival at any given place. The only possible explanation for the spread of the smallpox virus is that it spread along trading ways. In other words, Aboriginal trading missions and communication routes spread galgalla from one nation to the next along their established trading routes. It seems likely that the colonisers continued to find peoples affected by galaglla, because they too were being guided along these established routes.

By the late nineteenth century, the disease had wreaked havoc on Aboriginal resistance. Campbell points out that the tribes around the Bathurst area in New South Wales who had been described in 1832 as 'the most ferocious of their class' had by 1845 become 'the most docile and peaceable in the territory' because of the devastating effect of smallpox (in Campbell 1985:344). Sturt's account gives a good indication as to the swiftness of depopulation. The first time he sailed down the Murray and Murrumbidgee in 1828–30, he saw 'hundreds to thousands of Aboriginal people' and commented that there was no evidence of smallpox in that area. But when he crossed the Murray at Edward Junction on 8 June 1838, droving cattle to Adelaide, he encountered a group of Aboriginal people many of whom had scarring from smallpox, and concluded that it must have 'committed dreadful havoc' (cited in Campbell 1985:347–53).

A Wilderness

A wilderness is an area 'where one or several ecosystems are not materially altered by human exploitation and occupation' (in Nash 1982:186). Therefore wilderness is essentially an uninhabited space where evolution can occur without human intervention. Generally, Europeans considered wilderness areas to be wastelands ripe for development. Aboriginal perspectives with regard to wildernesses have not been considered or included, and Aboriginal people view this perspective in terms of an extension of the concept of *terra nullius,* another colonising construct.

The notion that Australia was a wilderness is essentially a cultural myopia and is not borne out by the past. Lieutenant James Cook explored the East Coast of Australia at Botany Bay and described a well-managed landscape that could be transformed into English farmlands. When he led a party onto shore on 1 May 1770, he observed:

> We found deversified [sic] with woods, Lawns and Marshes; the woods are free from underwood of every kind and the trees are such a distance from one another that the whole country or at least great part of it might be cultivated without being oblig'd to cut down a single tree. (in Willey 1979:34)

Again on 3 May 1770,

> I foun[d] in many places a deep black soil which we thought was capable of producing any kind of grain, at present it produceth besides timber as fine meadow as ever was seen. (in Willey 1979:34)

The 'fine meadows' had not evolved without intervention. Aboriginal societies managed the landscape by various means including firestick farming, fish traps, and the clearance of pathways.

Several recent public campaigns by the Wilderness Society, such as Lake Pedder in the 1970s and the Franklin Dam in the 1980s, have lead to a growing public aware-ness of the need to protect large areas from deforestation. Nonetheless, the public still deems the wilderness to be 'vacant land' (in Thompson (ed.) 1989:198). Aboriginal people reject such conceptions of wilderness, and have seen government agencies and environmental groups trying to coin terminology such as 'Indigenous wilderness' that acknowledges Aboriginal ownership in and management rights in environmental areas. The term 'wilderness' as Australians use it, dehumanises Aboriginal people. 'Wilderness' has a Eurocentric definition, and in the Australian context was used to promote the concept of *terra nullius* – a land that belongs to no one or any state. British colonists used the term *terra nullius* to deny the existence of Australian Aboriginal people, Aboriginal laws and government (*Butterworths Australian Legal Dictionary* 1997:1160). Accordingly, wilderness is land that contains plant and animal life that have not been substantially modified by the influences of European settlement, which it remains remote from. Furthermore it provides opportunities for solitude and self-reliant recreational activities (*Butterworths Australian Legal Dictionary* 1997:1268).

In some ways wilderness is seen as almost sacred, something that should be revered; it is landscape complete with its own civilisation, but devoid of human beings (Griffiths 1996:262). European colonisers thought of the wilderness as a wasteland waiting for intervention from the civilised. Western colonised countries such as Australia, Canada, and the United States of America all adopted this perspective. Wilderness is also defined as one or several ecosystems that are not materially altered by human exploita-tion and occupation, and in which the competent authority of the country has taken steps to prevent (or eliminate) exploitation or occupation of the whole area. Accordingly, the competent authority is the state, and the state seeks to preserve and restore the landscape to how it was before colonisation (Griffiths 1996:262). Again, this definition is framed around European spatial awareness, and relates to boundaries and lines of sight. In 1921, Aldo Leopold described a wilderness area as, 'a continuous stretch of country preserved in its natural state, open to lawful hunting and fishing, big enough to absorb a two weeks' pack trip, and kept devoid of roads, artificial trails, cottages, or other works of man' (in Nash 1982:186).

Myles Dunphy, the father of wilderness protection in Australia, maintains that in the wilderness 'one may travel on foot in any direction for at least a full day without meeting a road or a highway' (in Thompson (ed.) 1989:198). These are Eurocentric notions, and are primarily concerned with remoteness, absence, and isolation.

A resolution was passed at an Ecopolitics conference in 1994 which read, 'The term has connotations of *terra nullius* and as such all concerned people and organisations should look for alternative terminology, which does not exclude indigenous history and meaning'. The common definition of wilderness has been thoroughly rejected by Australian Aboriginal people because it has connotations of 'vacant land' (Ecopolicitics IX Conference, Darwin, 1994).

Today, thanks in part to Eurocentric views of the wilderness, only about 33 per cent of flora are remnant native species, whereas the other 77 per cent have been introduced. In terms of authoring the landscape there is even less of the country inscribed with a traditional Australian name. In Queensland, only about one per cent of place-names

Figure 9 A road sign 'Aboriginal Land Permit', Sturt Highway. Approximately 50 percent of the Northern Territory is controlled by Aboriginal Traditional Owners (TO) groups. TOs have erected signage for the purpose of re-authoring and reasserting control/Aboriginal presence, thus creating a cultural landscape. Photo: Dale Kerwin, 2004.

and natural features have an Aboriginal name. Furthermore, there is no recognition of Aboriginal people in the Australian history that is taught. Aboriginal culture is cast as custodians temporised to a fixed point in time. By way of contrast, in Northern Territory (NT) approximately 50 percent of land is controlled by Aboriginal people (see Figure 9).

CHAPTER THREE

Only the Learned Can Read

At the heart of the identity of indigenous peoples is our distinct culture, deeply rooted in our traditions, our knowledge and the lands of which we are a part. Our being is steeped in the wisdom we have inherited from our ancestors. (Michael Dobson 1994)

The voices that come from the deserts and forests are not simply the spirits of the trees, but those of Aboriginal ancestors. These beings still continue to travel along the road and are located in the environment. For the road is a primal thing that is silent and scarcely obvious, except to Australian Aboriginal people for whom the roads are known as Dreaming tracks. The Dreaming tracks are the most humble and enduring of the original spirits of Australia; Aboriginal people inherited them from the ancestors who pioneered the paths. The Dreaming paths are as old as the continent of Australia, and were created before Australian Aboriginal people took their human form. The Dreamtime spirits used them to seek out food, and create paths to waterholes and soaks – which became their drinking places – and to assemblies by known tracks.

The Dreamtime spirits are wise; they know on which side an obstacle can be passed, where there is firm land which leads through a bog, and where the best going is: sand, rock, or dry soil. The spirits know the easiest approach. And through their work and through infinite time, the Dreamtime spirits sculptured the landscape and taught how the country should be read. Aboriginal people see the country in the landscape and the Dreamtime paths everywhere. As the rivers and long chains of escarpments were moulded, Aboriginal Dreaming tracks provided law to groups of men. Spirits, which are the forerunners of Aboriginal religion, flowed along the Dreaming tracks and leaped from Aboriginal village to village by way of stories. These became known as story strings and changed from one location to the next; in life too they have their own regional variants. 'As the ancestorial spirit travelled from place to place he sang many songs and performed corroborees which belong to [the] big one' (Minyanderri – Pitjantjatjara cited in Robinson 1966:91).

I have been told the last link of this story string, in which the blood of the Emu became the sacred red ochre of the Two Dog Dreaming story. The Emu paved the road for goods to flow from north and south. The Emu was killed and the two Dingoes (hunters) became hills, which were neglected in time. And with the spirits, everything such as communication ways, communities of language and ideas, flowed along these tracks.

Aboriginal humanity, which is a matter of spirituality, spread out over the landscape along these tracks and in turn these tracks became roads where material goods went with Aboriginal travellers. Once these tracks became established roads, commerce slowly got a foothold and these roads became established communication ways along which information flowed. These ways/tracks/roads became the means for Aboriginal philosophies based on the Dreamtime stories which were passed through other people's countries and around the continent of Australia.

Sacredness, which everywhere attaches itself to these Dreaming tracks, has its sanction in all these uses, but principally in that of the Dreamtime from which all things are drawn from, and with the word Dreaming. Dreaming tracks are the oldest monument of the life lead by the ancestral spirits. It is the oldest of stories with a continuous record and remains in the cultural patterning of Aboriginal people. The very horizon had been moulded by the Dreamtime ancestor's journeys. The Australian environment echoes the Dreaming; it is not an illusion but an ultimate reality that stands out when details are obscured (as can be seen in Figure 10). The sacredness of the landscape appeals to one's spirit, which increases as we pass further from the memories of colonisation and into the ancient memories of the mountains, where one is drawn closer and nearer to them. The presence of self is dwarfed by the Dreamtime ancestors.

The Dreaming is conveyed by these messengers after the present is manifold by the voice of the spirits who talk of lore and answering the perpetual questions of Aboriginal people. The Australian Aboriginal environment whispers away the vileness of the European Australian environment and articulates the accumulated wisdom of the

Figure 10 Scenic lookout, Macartney Range Kennedy Development Road near Middleton, Queensland. "The Dreamtime spirits talk to those who will listen." Photo: Dale Kerwin, 2002.

Dreaming, imbuing the presence with the spirit of country. The Aboriginal environment furnishes a symbolic text where Aboriginal people read their own intentions, identity, culture, and wisdoms. Both the landscape and the country is the text. The environment provides the very essence of Aboriginal ontology – relationships between individuals, society, nature, and time is based in the environment. Through ritual, alliances are forged with nature, and provide ownership to country and language. The environment through the country is sacred and spiritual, it is the very essence of Aboriginality (Reser *et al.* 2000:50).

Aboriginal culture's worldview is manifested through the interaction of people and the spiritual environment. This interaction is facilitated by ritual activities based on cultural affirmation and the practices of those people in connection with the use of natural resources. The natural environment of the land provides the foundations for religion, morality, and legal systems. The land provides a place for spiritual gratification and marital relationships, as well as being an economic base. The activities involved with culture reaffirm peoples' obligation to law, country, and hereditary rights. The interaction with country through ritual activities provides the means for the manufacture of, and production of, material property for trade, and the means to manage the resources that are of value to the community.

An important aspect of a distinct Aboriginal culture derives from the tradition of travel, and the tangible and intangible goods that were traded along communication routes that criss-crossed Australia. The external and internal trade of cultural products generated knowledge of other societies, and impacted on societies that traded. The movement of these tangible objects, and the movement of material culture, resulted in expert mapping and familiarity with the dispersion paths taken by Aboriginal travellers. In this movement, coastal estuaries, river systems, and catchment areas played a major role in assisting Aboriginal travellers to move deep into the very heart of Australia. These paths were also later followed by European surveyors and stockmen.

Re-authoring

This section provides visual pointers and lines of sight that penetrate the wilderness of Aboriginal history that has been stripped from the landscape. An understanding of the timeline and human occupation is fundamental to the act of plotting an Aboriginal spatial history above and beyond the Australian European chronology. The systematic clearing of Aboriginal history from the spatial landscape of Australia and the re-inscription of the landscape with a European history belies the fact that Australia has an Aboriginal history. Carter (1987) considers that the Aboriginal landscape is a geography of cultivated space:

> In 1788, Australia was already a highly cultivated space. Aboriginal occupation had created tracks and clearings . . . Instead of confronting chaotic nature, map-like in its uniformity, explorers and overlanders entered a country replete with directions. The very horizons had been channelled and grooved by Aboriginal journeys. (1987:337)

Aboriginal Dreaming Paths and Trading Routes

In detailing the major trade routes, and building a picture of these paths, we can also come to an understanding of the types of economic behaviour and social organisation that are generally deemed to be absent from traditional Aboriginal societies. Questions of how Aboriginal societies regulate goods and create value variations for tangible goods, undermine assumptions that Aboriginal society did not have a culture for travel or trade. Paul Carter describes this as a silence on the part of Aboriginal people, which is easily manipulated by European narrative (Carter 1987:343–44; Murphy 2000). The tradition of travel and trade in Aboriginal societies cannot be understood without referring to Aboriginal oral histories of the tradition of trade. Aboriginal peoples' history pushes back the geography and spatial history of Australia by many thousands of years. Aboriginal chronology can be gleaned from some of the major trade routes that were recorded by ethnologists, anthropologists and historians, and which also live in Aboriginal mythology and social memory. I now turn to extracts of Aboriginal oral histories taken from interviews with Aboriginal Elders and lore people between March–July 2004.

Kado Muir, a second-generation contact person from Wangkatha language group area Leonora, Western Australia whose Dreaming is *Dingo Dreaming*, is an initiated man who is also an anthropologist and represented the Greens in the Federal election of 2004. He talked to me about Aboriginal trading ways (see Map 2).

> 'Trading ways are roads '*urda*' with songlines and Dreaming Tracks and these are the ceremonies. My mob traded in songs, intellectual property, we traded in information technologies. If you know the songs, water and food resources are easily found.
>
> Map making cartography – our 'Yudurra' – is the information super highway. Along these Dreaming Tracks there were songs, dancers, designs, stories – these all come together as one construct: if you know the stories you can learn. You can learn these in one location and find all the resources needed to travel. Often they are associated with the waterholes. You know the dot paintings with circles here and there and paths in between. Trading was bundled up with a series of ritual, of songs, ceremonies; relationships, stories were the fundamental basis of Aboriginal trade. It is a universe where people know their relationship to the rocks, trees, earth, sky, people and animals. It is based on responsibility to everything. (Kado Muir, personal communication 2004)

Researchers such as McCarthy (1939), Micha (1970), Rose (1985), and Hercus (1987) have all noted trade in the arts. The Aboriginal Elders I interviewed on the subject of trade in intellectual property all recount stories of travelling performers who take their corroboree on the road. Rose points out that the best documents in a modern medium are those of the Kunapipi, the Molonglo ceremony, and the new religious ceremonies in the Kimberley (1985:28).

> Travelling songs are about the Dreaming and lore songs are related to place and are places along the track. They can be six to eight hundred kilometres long. However the song relating to a place along the track are two lines repeated and these can go a

further 50 kilometres down the track and a song will be a song about that place. We have a contemporary song about the train; people used the train to travel to ceremonies. This cut off a lot of walking time. This song was sung by a woman in the 1930s – she was a song maker. The old people still sing her songs and talk about her as special person and she is now in our folk history.

Trade and product depending on resources however the main was red ochre for ceremonies, there are two big mines, one was at Monkey Mia. It has been used for 20,000 years. Pearl shells from the Kimberleys and in my country they are secret and only men can use and people on the west coast every-body has one – women, children. Kal-bungale spears made out of the wood from a hard tree in my country and was very popular. Pituri was traded into our country and was scarce, the tobacco of my country was poor quality.

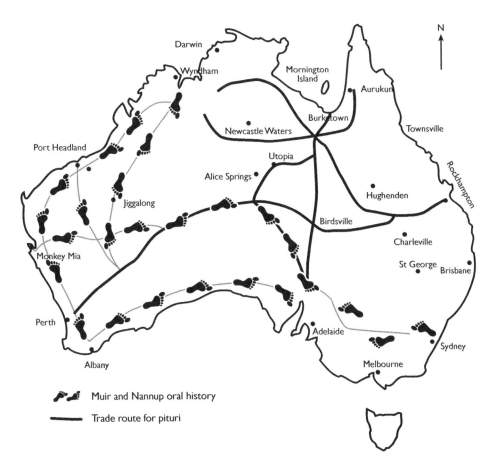

Map 2 An interpretation of the Dreaming tracks as told by Kado Muir and Noel Nannup. Kado Muir is an anthropologist and traditional owner from Leonora in Western Australia who represented the Greens at the Federal Election in 2004. His totem is the Dingo. Noel Nunnup, a Wajuk man from the Bibbulmun nation, he was awarded an Honorary Doctorate from Western Australian University.

Today people have put a frame around our 'traditions' and keep it in a time period, 'Dingo Dreaming, two men from Warlpiri kill a Mongali (dingo), they chased it along Gunbarrel Highway and joined up with a dingo from Leonora and headed to Port Hedland (see Map 2).

These two dingoes are then chased along the coast to Albany right across the country to Port Augusta then heads up to Chambers Pillar near Alice Springs Northern Territory and then back across to Jigalong Western Australia. This story also branches off the main songway into Sydney New South Wales. (Kado Muir, personal communication 2004)

We can compare the trading routes mentioned in Kado's story above (see Map 2) with the roads of today in Western Australia: the Gibb River Road travels south from Wyndham to Derby (see Map 3). Also the Northern West Coast Highway then links Derby to Geraldton and from here the Brand Highway links Geraldton to Perth. The

Map 3 An interpretation of Kado Muir and Noel Nannup's account of the trade routes, with the major highways and roads detailed.

Bibbulmun Track is a 650 km track that runs through the Jarrah and Karri forests of south-western Australia to Albany. The Coast Highway from Albany to Esperance, then links the Eyre Highway from Norseman to Port Augusta. The Stuart Highway links Port Augusta to Alice Springs. Part of the story string that branches from the main line to Sydney follows the Sturt Highway from Wentworth to Wagga Wagga and on to Canberra.

Noel Nunnup was awarded an Honorary PhD. in Conservation from the Western Australia University; he also was a senior heritage officer for the Council of Aboriginal Land Management Western Australia. He is of the Bibbulmun Nation forest people and told me that, The Milky Way and the Megilion Clouds are *The Seven Sisters Dreaming*; it runs a long way down from Pilbara region. The Great Spirit women *Chanark* collected spirit children *bwaiy kulongga* and put them into her hair, she had beautiful long hair (see Figure13). At that time there were no hills, valleys and at that time there was a Serpent and a heavy sky which was being pushed down. It made hills and valleys and all the other spirits sang and danced because it created this system of who would care for things. This Great Spirit Woman *Chanark* was picking up these children all over the place and putting them in her hair. Our belief is that the children were in groves of trees and rocky outcrops; they were everywhere and are still there now. She is the Milky Way. She sprang up from the ground and went up into the sky. We still see her long streaks of hair in the sky and we call *Yondle* and all the bright stars are the children.

Trading, it happened a lot. One of the things traded was ochre. Stories tell about why it is red, why it is white. They connect people to country, there are also songs attached. I have heard them called trading routes, songlines and spiritual paths. I have travelled over them, one of these is the Bibbulmun track, which was a trading route, but it has since been realigned because of mining. It goes from here Perth, Alice Springs and also Lake Gregory in the Kimberleys, it also goes from Perth to Waggle Mia in the Murray.

Seven Dingoes are a real part of the trading stories. They have their origins in Wargi country. South of the Black Stone range near a rocky outcrop and that's where they breed. There is a place that has Two Dog Dreaming, these two dogs run the trails they live in certain places. The story comes right through where there are hills near Swan River, it represents Seven Dogs (seven dog hills;) these represent life. The two dogs go from here onto Albany to Dog Rock. We know this is – as parts of the dogs along the track. The Two Dogs fought with a huge lizard and it got chewed up and became a large Island *Wingaleena*'. (Noel Nunnup, personal communication 2004)

Alf Nathan, aged 73, is a Pitta Pitta man born 60 miles (100 km) outside of Georgina Yarrie (meaning all small hills), Pituri Creek Glenormiston. He shared knowledge of cultural traditions of trade from his past.

Perra pitchrie to Glenormiston is on the intersection of the Georgina River, a large river and Pituri Creek people would trade. Pituri was mixed with coolibah ash or

Map 4 An interpretation of Noel Nunnup's story of traditional trading routes in Western Australia. These routes later became the Canning Traditional trade routes.

gidgee ash and mix it with spit, and chew it and swallow the spit and get high. We traded with the *Meiawali*, *Karuwali* mob for hair belt *juringa* made out of women hair. They would also bring shells and other goods. Towabmurrow, Lake Wynda, Lake Idomoda and across Georgina Creek, Walkaby and Roxboura, people would trade spears. Muncundia Creek, Diamantina and Windorah people followed their movement of water. There is a divide between everyone's country and it flows into the Burke or Wills and others come back into Cloncurry or the Leichhardt and Mt Guy, Wavell or Moonah all these flow into the Georgina. (Alf Nathan, personal communication 2004)

In the above extract, Alf explained the tradition of trade for the Pitta Pitta people; he provides an account of what goods were traded, who the trading partners were, and where the goods where traded from. Alf details the movement of Aboriginal traders along the water courses around the Channel Country of Western Queensland.

Jim Crombie is aged 64, and was born on the riverbank of the Diamantina Simpson Desert. He shared a Dreamtime story about Wunakaree that travelled down from Alice Springs to Lake Eyre on to Port Augusta.

It goes a long distance, Humawarria Mission means Milky Way; it travels to the ranges outside of Boulia-Rain Story. The Two Boys started walking from Dalhousie Springs and it was also a Snake story and King Fisher the story changes the Two Boys travel. The story travels along the rivers went across to Oodnadatta. The road (QAA Line into the Simpson Desert National Park from Birdsville passes Nappanerica Sand Dune Big Red) travels like the snake in the story it is the track and now the road is over it, it is like to me the snake in the story-same way. (Jim Crombie, personal communication 2004)

Jim provides an example of how a Dreaming story travels over the landscape and can change from one location to the next. At one location it is told as a Snake Dreaming story, but as the story follows the waterholes and rivers, a segment of this story is told as the King Fisher Dreaming story. The Two Boy Dreaming is a combination of several story strings that takes a traveller from Dalhousie Springs to Birdsville. The QAA[*] line is built on the original road that Aboriginal traders and snakes around the desert country between sand dunes. The Snake in the story is the road that Aboriginal people travelled over.

My mob travelled and traded with other people. See those grinding stones they don't come from here, not from the Simpson Desert, so they must have come somehow to get here. The stone is not found in this country. Water was the easy part of living in this country, knowledge of where to find it was recorded in song. (Jim Crombie, personal communication 2004)

When people went trading they had their way and used water bags and other skin bags to carry pituri – we had our ways. (Jim Crombie personal communication 2004)

Dick Smith is 72 years of age, an Aboriginal stockmen born at Beagle Bay, Broome Western Australia. His people are from Tennant Creek and Halls Creek Western Australia. He told me:

The traditional people had knowledge of the tracks. My mob were stockmen and we drove along the Canning Stock route and the Murinji track. The mob at Kununurra made hair belts and these would be traded across the country across Borroloola to Mt

---

[*] The QAA line is a dirt road that is accessed 18km north of Poeppels Corner. It is heavily trafficked and badly scalloped. The line travels through classic Eastern Simpson Desert country, and crosses Eyre Creek, which drains the Mulligan & Georgina Rivers. The line when flooded detours north to Dickerie crossing. The QAA line is a seismic line used by mining companies when blasting in the area in 1974.

Isa, Dajarra and Boulia. People took these on the Dreaming. We had our composers they would sing songs with clap sticks and boomerangs. The songman would put you on the right track. (Dick Smith, personal communication 2004)

Jim Wharton is aged 64; he is an Elder from the Kooma nation at Cunnamulla and a stockman. He too shared stories with me about trading that he knew of from his country.

The old people use to trade things but that was long time back. The big green axe was traded down from Mount Isa, again another one was from the Flinders Ranges and came with the story of the pigeon. Where it stopped it left blood and came in from Broken Hill. This story changes and came in from Port Augusta and up through this way (Cunnamulla) and up to the Cape. The story followed a footprint and travelled hundreds of miles.

Pituri was traded into my country from Cooper Creek. This real old women would pick the acacia bush and mix it with pituri, my mob would trade to survive. Travellers who did not know where to find water would have had a hard day. Knowledge on where to find the water hole like the one on the road near Moonie was taught through song. (Jim Wharton, personal communication 2004)

Mick Leon is a Worimi man who holds an archaeology degree from UNE. He shared knowledge with me about the culture of trade and travel from his country in Forster New South Wales.

'The old pathways that go down from the mountains onto the sea, if you fly over our country you can see them taper straight down into the lake system. There is a path down at Bulabdelah that the old fellows used time and time again, they brought live fish in kangaroo skin bags and put them into this pool. Every time the mob went through this location they had a feed. This was a way station, stop and have a feed and also this helps in knowing where you are and which way to go. At the end of the ridgeline there are camping places, shell middens, ceremonial areas and bora grounds. These are physical'.

We always traded in the resources we had such as stone ochre and fishhooks. These pathways are still there even though there are fences. This is where the trade in fishhooks began, we use the conch shell it is real hard. We also traded the sap and resin to the mob inland. They did not have this in their country, it went over the range. There are a lot of Bunya pines down here, we went to the Bunya feast. We would send representatives to Port Macquarie to be picked among a mob to go to the festival. We would receive an invitation on a message stick and travel through other country to the festival.

When whales would beach themselves we would send messages out over the country that a resource was available. People would bring things to trade so to partake, we also had tailor, salmon and mullet feasts. (Mick Leon, personal communication 2004)

Murrandoo Yanner is an Aboriginal leader from the Ganggalida nation, Mungubie (Burketown) North Queensland, he too talks about the tradition and history of trading.

We traded for steel axes, steel pots, metal knives, rice and outrigger technology for design of sails. This originated from Mornington Island, Mungubie (Burketown) and spread all over the place internationally to Java and Sulawesi and domestically to Broome and Port Augusta.

'Travel was made possible by songlines and the rivers are connected to the song-lines and naturally trade routes followed the rivers. River courses were often pathways as they made travelling easier and more comfortable. Most of the rivers are in song and these are the lines created by the Creator and trade routes are the physical evidence of the songlines. Through a song you can change direction twenty times, in one hour a chant can also change twenty different times aiding the direction'.

'We had our domestic trade routes that went north, south, east and west, my people the Ganggalida traded for oysters, sea turtle and dugong from the north and in return we had goanna and turkey. We went to Normanton for gidgee lancewood and heavy wood for spears and clap sticks, we went west to Garawa for spear flints and stuff. We went south to the Waanyi and we also traded for a stone axe from the Kalkadoons'.

'I made a personal journey from my beach at Goodamullawar looking to under-stand the journey of my people for this stone. I travelled to Mount Isa and onto Black Mountain at Dajarra where the spirit of this rock lives, I went to the site where it originated; it was a journey of renewing obligation to keep tradition alive. We also traded for pituri from central Australia and in return we traded shells and song to the southern groups. Shells are important for the lawmen, religious practices for initia-tion and making magic, these shells are needed in the magic for rain making ceremony. So we would bring in pituri and stone axes from our trading partners from the south'.

'We never just traded for goods, trading was a time for sharing of ideas and tech-nology such as the woomera and outrigger canoes with sails. The didgeridoo started in a small place in Arnhem Land and by the time whites arrived it had spread over half the distance of Australia. There was also a lot of ceremony sharing, of food, of stories, of culture and time together. Trade was a time of catching up both pleasure and business. My mob when travelling would grind up the Mitchell grass and make Johnny cakes out of it'. (Yanner, personal communication 2004)

Cheebalum (Mr Robert Vincent Anderson), aged 75, is a Ngugi man, Mulgumpin (Moreton Island). He was awarded an Honorary Doctorate from the Queensland University of Technology. Cheebalum shared his cultural memories with me on the subject of trade and travel:

Some time ago I was up at Tin Can Bay and I heard about this place called Mudlo and in my estate there is this island called Coochie Mudlo meaning red stone. Anyway we went along this track from the inlet side to the ocean side, and there were these two huge boulders of stone Mudlo. This is a distance of over 200 miles as the crow flies from Mulgumpin to Harvey Bay. I also share a common spiritual being Biamyi and identification as a Gorrie with people along the mid northern coast of New South Wales to Mulgumpin.

We ate the bungwall fern, the women would harvest the plant and grind the stem up and place it on a stone to pound it to make flour and a paste they would roast it on the fire and make biscuits out of it. The stones are made of granite and there is no granite on Mulgumpin and Minjerribah (Stradbroke Island). The nearest granite is around Toowoomba and Stanthorpe where the granite deposits are. That was traded to Musgrave Park, it was a bora ground and marketplace we would bring our dugong bone and fat, ugarie shell for scrapers and decorations like wise oyster shell for granite dishes from that region. We had expert bag makers, weavers, the dilly bag and these were traded we used them like shopping bags.

The people of Mulgumpin and Minjerribah were known as the people of the sand and water in song. One of our paths went through the bora ground at Musgrave Park (it should have an Aboriginal name) and further out along Vulture street along the high ridge at the dock area continuing out to Capalaba and out to Cleveland. Our spirits are still there along that path. (Robert Vincent Anderson, personal communication 2004)

Isabel Tarrago, a senior Aboriginal women from Arrente nation, is also a senior manager in the Queensland Department of Natural Resources Mines and Energy. She shared stories with me from her country, the Simpson Desert region:

My granny her Dreaming is the Dog that carries pituri, my granny was the holder of that story. The dog carries the pituri from the sandhills way up through to Lawn Hill; that's where its babies are and then vanishes. My granny sings this story in her traditional tongue.

Pituri was traded along the stock routes, it was traded down to South Australia and it was traded right up to the top end. People were coming through to trade for pituri and would disperse it. Pituri was grown in plantations on the sandhills. You know there are different pituri in different parts of this country but ours was the best. It is grown on our property. Through my granny and my grandfather, this is special very strong Dreaming.

The Dreaming for my country came with the dog and pituri to be harvested, it was also harvested for big ceremony. When harvested we had to splice it with the coolabah bark. My granny told my mum and mum told me that's our tradition. It was tied into a bundle and soaked in a stone bowl overnight until it was very soft. It would then be dried a little bit and put it into an earth oven. The earth oven would have the coolabah tree bark spliced into it so to help with the curing processes.

Mum told me about trading times and how we sing songs to prepare country to receive traders to trade for pituri. People moved pituri in bags and the women would weave the bags, I think from bulrushes. The bag would be strung across the head and hung down the back; pituri would be carried in this way. We also had kangaroo water bags for people who travelled. People knew the way by song and where the soaks are.

'The artworks on the ridges are messages for the traders. The ridgeline was a trade route. Mum would travel and sing songs. I remember my mum going to these places and at some of them she would sing. We are linked by song to people at Borroloola by the Dog Dreaming, the mob there are connected to granny and mum through this song and so am I. We are related across huge distances by extension of this Dreaming and song. The country is the text to be read and song is the means to unravel the text. My mother's birthplace is where the dog travels right along the Simpson Desert and that dog and pituri travels into the hills'.

'As a child I spent a lot of time at the water soaks and at times the Afghans would come in with their camels to drink at the soaks. These animals are pests because they foul the waterholes, these soaks are a part of our Dreaming strings and there is a chain of them to Alice Springs on to yellow water. My father was head stockman for Glenormiston Station he knew these routes and where the water was'.

'Red ochre was traded, we had no red ochre this came from South Australia. My mum and dad would paint themselves with it for ceremony. Mum was the song woman. The white cap came into my country and it was white ochre from the Pitta Pitta country the women would bring it with them, it was for mourning the dead. The nardoo grinding stone was also traded into my country because they were so heavy they would be left in certain places along the song cycle. We also had the stone axe head from Mount Isa. Through scientific testing of the materials we are finding out where they came from'. (Isabel Tarrago, personal communication 2004)

Alice James, is 72 years old; she is a Pitta Pitta woman from Boulia who shared cultural knowledge on the traditions of travelling and trading with me:

'People traded from the territory and came along special tracks for pituri. I used to be given a penny to go and get it. I collected it for the old people. They would burn the leaves into a coolaman and add old plug tobacco, they would cut it up into real small bits and add string to it and roll it into it, they chewed it. People would come in looking for pituri and offer sugar and tea, people were always trying to trade for it. One old bloke traded his wife for pituri. People would just walk in to trade for pituri, some rode horses in from the stations. People even came from Rockhampton and Winton for pituri'.

'Nobody smokes it now or chews it now, I never see anybody now. When white people come looking for pituri my granddad told me tell them nothing, tell them nothing about black fellow business. Granddad would sing about the sun and the stars and he would sing their names and point to where they would go'.

'You know the white copwi, it was used for mourning ritual. You would mourn for the old people in the olden days. When you mix it up you would burn it and it goes into ash you would mix it with water and it would go like cement. I had it on twice for two old people who died. The white clay there is plenty of it between Mount Isa and Boulia you can see it on the ridges'. (Alice James, personal communication 2004)

As we can discern from the stories shared with me, the tradition of travel and trading is still alive in the cultural memory of contemporary Aboriginal people. The stories all relate to real features in the landscape, and move along the songlines taking with them religion, identity, tradition, and goods. Some of the stories relate to Queensland and have their veins spread across the nation, carrying stories of faraway places and goods from distant lands.

The social game

The focus of this section is the social organisation of Aboriginal nations at the time of the collision of two worlds, in order to provide an understanding of the structural systems and symbols of office that operated in Aboriginal society. Commentators such as Norman Tindale, W. Stanner, R.M. Berndt, James Cowan and Tim Flannery have determined that Aboriginal society was far from egalitarian. The following examples indicate that there was a need for development of material culture in terms of class distinction, as well as the need to trade goods with others outside each societies' sphere of influence.

Nicholas Pateshall was third lieutenant on HMS *Calcutta* which was on an expedition to establish a settlement in Port Phillip Bay in October 1803. He mentions seeing 'a distinctively robed individual . . . being carried on the shoulders of other men'. He noticed:

> chiefs . . . who wear cloaks on their backs of small skins sewn very neatly together with grass . . . The chief's head-dress is composed of feathers of cockatoo and parrot, kangaroo teeth . . . In less than a half an hour a large party was seen carrying their chiefs as before described . . . Their King, who was with the centre party, wore a beautiful turban of feathers and a very large cloak. (Flannery (ed.) 1998:94–98)

This excerpt provides a small window into the stratified social systems that operated in Aboriginal societies of the southern regions of Australia, before they were destroyed by the annexation of Victoria from Aboriginal ownership. The irony of this is that in contemporary cosmopolitan society of Melbourne, Mayor John So was given a robe of possum and kangaroo skin on the 28 May 2003. The robe was presented to the mayor by Gary Murray of the North West Regional Aboriginal Cultural Heritage Board, Victoria. The mayor decreed that the mayoral robe was to be worn at all public ceremonies. The kangaroo skin robe is a symbol of authority and high position, that dates back to the time of Aboriginal spiritual leaders and lawmen.

Sociologists argue that all human societies have strata systems, that most operate efficiently and survive, and have certain characteristics and functional prerequisites. These are that 'all roles must be filled, that they are filled with people best able to perform them, that the necessary training for them be undertaken and that the roles be performed conscientiously' (Haralambos and Heald 1980:32–33). Sociologists consider that all societies have a mechanism for effective role allocation and performance, which has a reward system based on unequally distributed rewards, privileges and positions of influence (Haralambos 1980).

Reward systems are important, because they influence the internal dynamics of a society. What do Aboriginal societies identify as a reward? How does a society motivate its population to value such rewards? What were the factors in Aboriginal society that drove the need to travel and trade for goods? When seeking to clarify these points, it is important to keep in mind previous discussion in the Preface and Chapter 2, whereby the Australian landscape and the character of the Australian environment influences both Aboriginal culture and today's society.

> Elders are the custodians of the lore. They were, and are, honoured for their wisdom and experience. Councils of Elders made important decisions, helped settle disputes and guided the young. (Australian National Museum 2004)

In Aboriginal society this system of aristocracies, whereby the Elders owned 'country' or 'estates', and managed them by asserting authority over their localities through religious ceremony, is a sophisticated political form of land management (Kerwin 1998:97–98). In addition, once the produce is harvested from the 'country' or 'estate', it is divided according to obligations and social standing within the community. 'This topic of Aboriginal politics has had scholars seeking answers to whether or not Aboriginal societies are more accurately characterised as egalitarian or hierarchical in nature' (Tonkinson 1978:139).

Through ritual learning, men and women were able to gain positions of prestige and high ranking. As in all societies, once people gained these positions they had symbols or other paraphernalia that represented the position they obtained or the office they held. In some Aboriginal societies, these were ritually carved or incised on the body and/or objects that were worn. Fur would be incised using a stone flake; the point would be ground on sandstone to make its fine shape so that it would engave or incise (Berndt *et al.* 1993:112–16). Cuts made on the soft inside of the hide formed patterns, and ochre and animal oil would be rubbed into the underbelly of the skin (see ????). These symbols represent the office a person holds within their community, such as spiritual leaders and law people, and the patterns would tell people who could read them what that position is (Berndt *et al.* 1993:112–16).

Aboriginal metaphysical understanding of the self does not incorporate a European sense of time. The Aboriginal metaphysical world, manifested through mythical beings and natural occurrences and events, provided historical actors and important relationships with other Aboriginal nations across Australia. Aboriginal people have heroes from stories and the Dreamtime. (Australian Europeans have their historical heroes like the explorers already mentioned, and others such as Ned Kelly.) Early anthropology struggled to understand and describe Aboriginal ontology, and relied on ancient European and American Indian traditions to classify it in terms of totemism or animism.

Ideas of self can explain Aboriginal ontology and relationships with environmental elements such as totems or family. Stanner (1979) compares this with aspects of psychology that consider people's personalities to be defined in accordance to the environment. Psychologists such as Arnold Gesell, John Watson, Sigmund Freud. and Jean Piaget suggested that personalities are interactive with concepts of self and the social environment (Bernstein *et al.* 1992:31–36; Stanner 1979:25).

In Aboriginal ontology, totems form the basis of relationships between individuals, society, nature, and time (Stanner 1979:25). For example, when a Murri (Queensland Aboriginal person) is asked about laws governing relationships and family, the Murri might point to a tree and state that the tree is his brother-in-law. This tree is a totem that regulates his relationship to other individuals, his position in society, and his interactions with nature and the supernatural to a significant degree (Stanner 1979:25; Cowan 1992:79).

Bula (friend)

peoples are at pains to identify with their land as if it were a physiological or psychological 'echo' of themselves. (Cowan 1992:79)

Flinders records that Bungaree would spear fish to feed the crew, but whenever he speared a shark or stingray he would not eat them. 'The natives of Port Jackson have a prejudice against all fish of the ray kind, as well as against sharks and, whilst they devour with eager avidity the blubber of a whale or porpoise, a piece of skate would excite disgust' (Flannery 1998:80). Bungaree would reply 'they might be good for white man, but would kill him' (Flannery 1998:81).

Bungaree hailed from the Eora nation of the Port Jackson area of New South Wales. He was a salt-water person and it can be determined from the historical records that his totem was the shark. Lawlor (1991) argues that totems are central to all Aboriginal beliefs – they link humanity, nature and the gods, in the cycle of life. 'The natural world is guided by the same patterns that guide the formation of human culture and society' (Lawlor 1991:279). The aversion Bungaree had to the shark or stingray shows that there is a spiritual relationship between these marine animals and the clan members of Bungaree. According to Aboriginal beliefs there is mutual life giving between nature and humanity (Lawlor 1991:279).

These actors, such as the tree and the shark, still exist as metaphysical beings in the landscape, as do the stars in the night sky, the trees, certain flora and fauna, and the physical features in the landscape. For the Aboriginal worldview the land is sacred. All life is found in place and is worshipped from place through prescribed spiritual practices. In terms of the Aboriginal landscape, geological features represent human or animal forms, and they are at the centre of religious practices (Cowan 1992). These beliefs still persist today and can be found in family relationships and food avoidance rules (Lawlor 1991; Keesing 1981). This adds another dimension to the agricultural practices, religious and spiritual beliefs for Aboriginal people that developed over tens of thousands of years and manifest themselves in the everyday lives of Aboriginal people. Beliefs determine what a person can eat and when; to whom they can marry;

what tracts of land can be burned; and when a person can travel. Religious and spiritual practices contain the accumulated wisdom of past generations with regard to the best use of land resources. Rose (1985) argues that trade formed the foundation of Aboriginal morality. For individuals and groups, trading is based on an obligation to share resources that travelled along the Dreaming tracks, which were used to further the well-being of communities (Rose 1985:23).

Aboriginal culture developed totem systems and beliefs in the mythical world. Totems and the Dreaming were the results of the ritual observation of natural elements and natural occurrences, and which resulted in morality and laws (Lawlor 1991, Cowan 1992). Totems provide connections for families across vast distances, they provide knowledge of places that have not been visited, and knowledge of the country and law of other communities. Totems convey knowledge of the seasonal habits of creatures and nature; they inform when country needs to be burned, and when the mullet or tailor are running along the coast. They also specify the time for harvesting certain flora species, as well as the best way to communicate to others. The Dreamtime speaks of the antiquity of Australia; it tells us how the land was created and the people formed. Dreamtime also informs about Aboriginal relationships to land and law (Robinson and Munungguritj 2001:103; Gostin 2001:236).

Antiquity in Australia

This section outlines the human timeline of Australia, beginning with the European and then the Aboriginal, so as to bring to life the cultural landscape of Australia. My purpose is to demonstrate that during the long Aboriginal period of occupation, they developed the knowledge to map and traverse the continent of Australia.

Providing proof of how long Aboriginal people have occupied Australia is dependent on archaeological finds, and the validation of Aboriginal Dreamtime stories. Both of these depend on material evidence, so that finds of ancient human remains create excitement within the scientific community. One of the extraordinary problems these finds cause is that most of the human remains are found in the southern part of the continent. There also seems to be the suggestion that there were two forms of humanoids living on this continent.

The interest in the antiquity of Australia began with skeletal remains of megafauna, in New South Wales. 'In the 1830s the bones of a puzzling creature were discovered in a cave near Wellington' (Blainey 1975:51); it was part of a jaw that was sent on to London. The jawbone created excitement because it came from an animal previously unknown to the scientific community. Then in 1847, a full skeleton of a diprotodon was unearthed on the banks of the Condamine River in Queensland. Among the scientists who studied diprotodon was Ludwig Leichhardt, who believed that the giant marsupials might still be grazing on the grasses of regions of Australia as yet unexplored by Europeans. In a letter to Sir Richard Owen in 1844, he wrote, 'I should not be surprised if I found them in the tropical interior' (Blainey 1975:52).

In 1886, an ancient human skull was found near Talgai in southern Queensland; it was from a boy thought to be around fifteen. The find is known as the 'Talgai cranium' *Homo erectus* or 'robust', and is believed to be approximately 11,000 BP. However the integrity of the soil from the cranium is thought to have been corrupted and no firm date could be obtained (Griffiths 1996:64–66).

The next major find occurred in 1925. The 'Cohuna cranium' was unearthed at Kow Swamp near Cohuna in Victoria. The cranium is archaic, 'robust' in features, and of huge proportions. Professor Colin Mackenzie acclaimed it to be 'the oldest skull specimen in the world' (Griffiths 1996:64–66). However, dating of the cranium suffered the same fate as the 'Talgai cranium' because the soil samples were corrupted (Griffiths 1996:64–66).

Later, in 1940 on the banks of Maribyrnong River, Keilor, Victoria, the 'Keilor cranium' was unearthed. The fossil was radiocarbon dated in the 1950s, and confirmed the cranium to be 15,000 years old (Griffiths 1996:88–90).

Also at 'Kow Swamp' near the Murray River, a landowner unearthed humanoid skeletal (robust) bone material in 1962, while he was doing some excavation work on his property. The remains were sent to the National Museum of Victoria. Alan Thorne, a physical anthropologist, examined these remains: some bones, and a large skull of archaic (robust) features. He inspected the site and found it was a burial area for twelve people. Some of the skeletal remains were carbon dated to 9,000 and 15,000 years old. The burial site showed signs of ritual burials, and traces of resin on kangaroo teeth that had been made into headbands were found with the skeletal remains (Blainey 1975:47, Cowan 1992:10; Griffiths 1996:93).

In July 1968, the geomorphologist Jim Bowler was on location studying climatic change at Willandra Lakes in New South Wales, and also found evidence of ancient human occupation. While standing upon an eroding sand dune of the dry lake, he unearthed a bundle of burnt bones in a cemented material mass of sand and shellfish.

In 1974 Bowler marked the site with a steel peg and left it undisturbed so that when archaeologists returned the integrity of the site would not have been compromised. The bones were later dated by John Mulvaney, and he identified it as the oldest cremation in the world – at 26,000 years. The remains were identified as 'gracile', that is slender modern people. It was discovered that these remains were of a young woman, and she became known as the 'Mungo Woman'. 'Mungo Woman' was in her twenties; she was ritually cremated and her bones had been smashed using a stone axe. Near this site a body was unearthed in 1974; it was a male who had been buried in a grave that carbon dated at about 32,000 years old. He became known as 'Mungo Man'. However, new dating methods are now considering ages of 56,000 to 68,000 years (Dayton, 9 January 2001:8; Gostin 2001:234–35) (see Figure 11).

These examples challenge current theories of the human occupation of Australia as well as theories of 'modern man coming out of Africa' (Dayton, 9 January 2001:8). Allan Thorne's recent work on 'the origins of man' has changed how the evolutionary tree of humans is interpreted (in Dayton, 9 January 2001:8). In 1999 he undertook Deoxyribonucleic Acid (DNA) sampling of the male skeletal remains known as 'Mungo Man' and is challenging the dates of *Homo sapiens'* evolution (in Dayton, 9 January 2001:8). Thorne approximates the date of 'Lake Mungo man at about 62,000 years'.

Figure 11 In July 1968, the geomorphologist Jim Bowler discovered skeletal remains of what is now known as 'Mungo Lady'. Five years later he discovered new remains of 'Mungo Man'. The archaeological dig was excavated by Dr Thorne at Lake Mungo. In 1999 Allan Thorne undertook DNA sampling of the skeletal remains of 'Mungo Man' and approximated the date of 'Lake Mungo man at about 62,000 years'. Mungo Man was ritually buried between 56,000 to 68,000 years ago at Willandra Lakes in New South Wales. His hands were crossed over his pelvis and red ochre was ground into a powdery substance and sprinkled over his body. Published with kind permission of Willandra Elders. Photo: copyright and courtesy of J.M. Bowler.

The maelstrom of controversy that this date has raised within the scientific community questions past assumptions (Dayton, 9 January 2001:8).

So an Aboriginal man was perhaps ritually buried between 56,000 to 68,000 years ago at Willandra Lakes in New South Wales. His hands were crossed over his pelvis and red ochre was ground into a powdery substance and sprinkled over his body. The ceremonial burial is significant for two reasons: the first is that Aboriginal people have been proved to be engaged in religious practices, and the second is that the red ochre used in the ceremony is not found in the Willandra Lakes area. Red ochre is a highly valued substance in Aboriginal communities, and the fact that it was used in this ritual burial suggests that the substance was traded into the area (Dayton, 9 January 2001:8).

The findings also indicate that there were two humanoid species in Australia and that they performed religious rituals. In addition, evidence of ochre found on the human remains suggests that Aboriginal people were moving along known paths and a form of trade was taking place (Barlow 1994:6). Aboriginal Dreamtime stories in some instances fit neatly with the findings of archaeology records. Aboriginal culture also challenges European assumptions about modern man (*Homo sapiens sapiens*) thanks to these finds of human remains. The assumptions challenged concern the notion that man came out of Africa and the evolution of modern man. Aboriginal people can now lay claim to have been in Australia long before any part of the Americas was peopled or the mummies of ancient Egypt were first embalmed (Blainey 1975:5–6; Mulvaney 1979:42; Cowan 1992:7; Griffiths 1996:93).

The European chronology of events in Australia only represents 0.0016 per cent of the timeline of human history in Australia, but it also represents the fastest change in the geography of Australia. This change makes the Aboriginal cultural presence appear static. Regardless of any theory of origin, Aboriginal culture clearly has had a long association with Australia, and has developed land management skills that were compatible with the uniqueness of the country, and skills that enabled them to profit and multiply.

Allan Thorne (1977) hypothesises that Aboriginal occupation of Australia can be as old as 120,000 years: 'Existing skeletal evidence is quite consistent with occupation of the continent 60,000, 80,000 or even 120,000 years ago' (Thorne and Macumber 1972:196–97). The timeline that was held until the 1970s put the occupation at around 20,000 years. Most encyclopaedia and Australian history books continue with these dates, so they have become conventional wisdom since the early twentieth century. While scientific views of the extent of human antiquity in Australia have changed radically, Aboriginal views have remained the same.

The Aboriginal point of view is that 'we have always been here'. The country is the proof of ideas and creation myths, and indeed the country and its features have always been here: Australia has ancient land formations, such as Uluru (Ayers Rock) and Katatjula (the Olgas). The river systems are lethargic; they hardly change their course and can be crossed easily. Flannery states that 'the rivers of the east coast have maintained their position for tens of millions of years. Indeed, some have cut as little as a few tens of metres deeper into their beds in over 30 million years!' (Flannery 1994:78).

The landscape is splashed with massive lakes that periodically die, a low mountain range that is unaffected by volcanic disturbances; in short, the landscape possesses geological permanence. It is a timeless land with eroded hills with well-rounded and weather-beaten ridges, the plains seem perpetual, and the coastline orderly. This gives the landscape a worn character. Australia also has an extremely long geological history and a long history of humans exploiting the resources of the land (Flannery 1994:78; Griffiths 1996; M. Lawlor 1991).

Population density

Knowledge of Aboriginal population figures travelled along a similar trajectory. Traditional estimates have ranged from 350,000 to 750,000 but contemporary estimates are now putting the population at between 750,000 to 1,500,000. Research by historians and other social scientists over the two centuries of recording will be referred to in this section in an effort to reconstruct Aboriginal population density at the time of European invasion. The focus will be on the ability of Aboriginal people to store food through the harvesting and preserving of food, the availability of food stuffs in terms of per capita of natural resources. Discussion will also explore goods that are manufactured and foodstuff that is harvested as well as the techniques involved in these types of activities. The reason for this inquiry is to argue that a large population base generally requires outside stimuli.

The Australian population in 2005 numbered 20 million people, of whom 2.4 per cent are Aboriginal and Torres Strait Islander peoples (Saunders 2002). Roughly, 360,000 Aboriginal and Torres Strait Islander peoples live in Australia today (O'Dwyer 2002). Some estimates conclude that this number of Aboriginal people represents the pre-contact population. Some historical accounts suggest that the continent was sparsely populated. Joseph Banks observed in 1770 from the HMS *Endeavour*:

> This immense tract of land, the largest known which does not bear the name of a continent, as it is considerably larger than all Europe, is thinly inhabited. We never but once saw so many as thirty Indians together, and that was a family, men, women, and children, assembled upon a rock to see the ship pass by. (in Willey 1979: 32)

Between March and April 1793, the Spanish docked at Port Jackson Sydney Cove on their voyage of 'scientific and political' discovery. They too inferred that the land was thinly populated:

> The inhabitants of all these parts are without doubt very small in number, and more inclined to Fishing than the Chase, as being less painful and less uncertain means of subsistence than that draw from the latter. The unequivocal proofs of this are, the difficulty encountered by the colonists in trapping Kangaroos, and in hunting them, in spite of the excellent Dogs with which they pursue them, and the marks in the trees, referred to by Sir Joseph Banks, and seen by us almost daily, which show how much cost in time and fatigue it takes at other times to procure for themselves the miserable meat of a single bird, not seldom quicker than the Pursuers themselves, by

which they are mock of. This scarcity of Food should then have influence, and actually does influence, not only in the small proportions of their bodily structure, and particularly in their inferior size, but also in the absolute lack of strength which the English acknowledge after a thousand trials of every kind of labour including even the softest. (in King 1986:53)

This perceived sparsity of population has been the basis for political claims over uninhabited territories. Reynolds' research highlights estimates that were made in 1838 by a subcommittee of London's Aborigines Protection Society. It concluded after examining every reasonable account and estimate that the total population could not 'be stated as short of 1,400,000' (Reynolds 1996:20).

A.R. Radcliffe Brown was responsible for providing the early estimates on the Aboriginal population. In 1930 he wrote a letter to the Editor of *The Times* London calling for humane consideration and a better effort by the Australian Government to do more for the surviving 'black fellows', explaining that his estimate had been based on his assessment of the carrying capacity of the country in 1788:

> As I am the person responsible for the estimates of 300,000 as the total population at that date I may say that in the course of the studies on which the estimates were based I come to the conclusion that this was about as large a population as the country could support so long as the inhabitants had to depend on the natural food supply of wild animals and plants. (cited in Stanner and Barwick 1979:45)

Much current literature on Aboriginal populations repeats these grossly underestimated figures on Aboriginal populations. Mulvaney, for example, also quotes population figures of 300,000 Aboriginal people pre-contact. However he revisited these figures in 1989 stating that: 'archaeologists and historians argue that population numbers have been underestimated and that a drastic revision upwards is necessary. 'The conventional number of 300,000 for the continent may be doubled, at least' (Mulvaney 1989:97).

Butlin proposes that estimates performed by earlier theorists only took into consideration the two colonies that were populated by the colonists early in the invasion period. He also argues that there is strong evidence that adjustments need to be made because of the depopulating effects of smallpox right across the country. The areas that were not taken into consideration on the main land were Queensland, Northern Territory, South Australia and Western Australia. Butlin suggests that the figures for New South Wales and Victoria alone were close to the early figures proposed for the whole of Australia at 260,000 (Butlin 1993:133–39).

Some observers claim that we are able to estimate population according biomass of the landscape. But, as Anne Brown points out, 'the relationship between Aboriginal population and biomass of the landscape cannot be measured' (Brown 1990:4). She states that 'biomass is the measurement of the total quantity or weight of organisms in a given area'. This is arguably a very ineffective tool, because Aboriginal farming and pastoral practices have been completely overlooked.

Brown points out that there is plenty of evidence of plant curation in Australia, and that fire was used to remove plant species that compete for soil nutrients. Brown details the diversion of streams and the building of weirs to supply water for use in species, such as yams, taro, nardoo and grass species. Aboriginal people fine-tuned agricultural practices to suit the unique environmental conditions of Australia. Consider the unpredictability of the Australian weather, where droughts last for months and in some cases for years, but then overnight it might flood. On the other hand, in the northern regions of Australia the predictability of the monsoons had a different, but marked effect on population density (Brown 1990).

There is also a propensity to overlook the 250 language groups at the time of colonisation, as well as the estimated 250 dialects associated with these main language groups. This linguistic differentiation suggests that the number of Aboriginal people would have been more than the accepted view of 300,000 people, since an average of 1,200 people is insufficient to sustain a language, much less a further division into dialects (McConvell & Thieberger 2000; Schmidt 1990; Yallop 1982).

A report by Patrick McConvell and Nicholas Thieberger explores revisionist figures that are based on linguistic studies of the numbers of people needed to keep a language alive. The numbers average 3,000 to 4,000 people per language. This figure is based on the Warlpiri nation in present-day Australia (Patrick McConvell and Nicholas Thieberger 2000:18). Annette Schmidt's research estimates that pre-1788 language groups were larger than this. She maintains that before European settlement, each language group had 'roughly 4,000 to 5,000 speakers' (Schmidt 1990:8). These figures suggest a population base in Australia at contact time of around 1.2 million.

In conclusion, the pre-contact size was much larger than estimates have routinely suggested. It is possible to say that there were about one million Aboriginal people living in Australia at the time of contact with Europeans. The question that needs to be answered is: how does a population of this size sustain itself? This can be answered by considering the practices Aboriginal people used to manage resources.

To whom the land belongs

Ancestral Beings are incised on the land in features such as a river, a hill, the ridgelines of a mountain, and also flora and fauna. Wandjuk Marika (Foreword 1980) spoke about the relationship of Dreamtime stories and the role that they played in the creation of the landscape:

> Our people of the desert in the centre of the continent speak of the Tjukirita time when land was a flat disc, a vast featureless plain which stretched to the horizon without rivers or hills. But as the ages passed many different giant mythical beings emerged from beneath this crust and wandered about. (Wandjuk Marika, 1980)

The developmental models of social evolution from hunter-gatherer to agriculturist harbour the idea that sedentary societies were able to master and harness nature, whereas earlier ones were dependent on nature. But Aboriginal people were as firmly committed to the idea that they could forge strategic alliances with nature through ritual, whereas the early settlers subjugated nature by felling trees and damming rivers. The latter have subsequently been proven wrong.

Because assumptions about Aboriginal exploitation of the land inform the various models developed and keep Aboriginal society in a biological context, Aboriginal people are viewed as ecological beings, at the expense of recognising their political being. Aboriginal people were organised in political and social groupings and engaged in work that transformed the natural environment to meet their needs. Aboriginal people constituted a real socio-political value for the land. It is customary for the young to seek advice and guidance from the Elder and repay this advice by providing material property and foodstuffs. However, to Europeans the apparent imprecision of Aboriginal knowledge and notions of the Dreamtime and the physical extent of these notions were sources of confusion and mistrust. Justice Toohey, when commenting on enacting legislation based on Aboriginal Dreamtime knowledge for land rights and heritage protection, argued for an overturning of these earlier European conceptions, stating:

> In my opinion sites should be thought of as places usually possessing some particular feature such as a hill, creek or waterhole, but not delimited by the precise amount of space occupied by that feature. . . . In considering the existence of sites and their relationship to the land claimed I see no reason to take a narrow approach and every reason to take a broad one. (cited in Neate, 1989:235)

Mythological places aid in the creation of Aboriginal intangible knowledge and can be represented in the form or shape of 'naturally' occurring rock formations, trees, sandhills, caves, and plains. Aboriginal political structures, only recently entered into the study of Aboriginal culture and the Australian judicial systems, are coming to recognise Aboriginal relationship to the land through connection to sites within the landscape. The above quotation provides an insight into the recognition of Aboriginal Native Title in Australian judiciary systems. The court decisions of Mabo 1992 and Wik 1996 (see page xi) are important turning points in the Australian legal system for the recognition of Aboriginal values for land and ownership for land.

Reynolds cites Collins, the Deputy-Judge Advocate in 1791, who observed, 'they have also their real estates'. Collins explained further that Bennelong assured him that an island in the harbour was 'his own property' and was 'his father's before him', and moreover, that there were 'other people who possessed this kind of hereditary property, which they retained undisturbed' (Reynolds 1996:25).

Typically, in the Aboriginal system of politics a local power governed small areas thereby providing status for a ruling group of Elders. The Elders passed their authority to their children depending on whether the lineage was matrilineal or patrilineal. This is a gerontocratic system of power. However, there are exceptions to the rule, as young people can climb the hierarchical order by performing great feats.

The knowledge of ownership of land and cultural property is controlled by Elders of the community in conjunction with other Aboriginal nations. The knowledge of Aboriginal nations and the obligations of these societies are passed on by ceremonial instructional practices. In both men's and women's business, Elders were knowledge-able about survival, and they passed their knowledge on by way of dance, song, story telling and pictures. Tonkinson (1978) notes that:

> Elders spend much of their time in camp as guardians and entertainers of the small children. As story tellers and singers of songs, and grandparents. From these elders children acquire much of the lore of their people; a great deal is also learned from their observations and emulation of peers and older members of the band. (Tonkinson 1978:84)

Forde (1968) warns us that land and resource ownership cannot be viewed through ethnocentric lens of 'what is of value'. Each society has its own notions of 'value', partic-ularly in relation the different values applied to land and resources (Forde 1968:375).

These values may change over time, as they have in Europe, where population pres-sures occasioned a shift from valuing land in terms of the labour that works it, to valuing land as a material asset in itself. Tony Swain points out 'agriculturalist' or 'anti-feudalist' principles of land ownership manifest in John Locke's 1690 definition:

> Whatsoever then he removes out of the State that nature hath provided, and left in, he hath mixed his Labour with, and joyned to it something that is his own, and thereby makes it his Property. (cited in Swain 1993:78)

Swain points out how in Locke's view 'one has to dig one's spirit into the land by ritual labour' (Swain 1993:79). This ontology comes very close to Aboriginal ideas about their relationship to land. In Aboriginal societies land ownership was recorded in various ways. When people moved to manage their estates they would leave markers indicating which part of their estate they would be managing (Jones & Sutton 1986:8). Aboriginal people mapped the country they owned; every tree, cave, rockhole, saltpan, creek bed or land formation would be known and mapped. The knowledge of these places would be recorded as a series of symbols and lines which were drawn on the body, on objects or in the sand. Most Aboriginal art is a record of the land.

Summary

This chapter discussed Aboriginal trade through the use of cultural processes in devel-oping material, cultural and spatial orientation methods. The text drew upon Aboriginal oral history and published sources to consider map development, with the purpose of providing a context for Aboriginal movement through the landscape. It was argued that Aboriginal people established communication networks across Australia that linked across vast distances and territories. This network was important for estab-lishing a tradition of travel and trading systems. The focus on trade meant it was also important to establish population size and density by referring to languages. I have now established that Aboriginal society was larger than the suggested figure of 300,000 at the time of contact with Europeans. The population size of one million suggests that Aboriginal people would have communicated with other Aboriginal societies across the landscape. A further motivation to communicate with others and to seek goods unavailable within their domain is class distinction and stratification. The discussions of antiquity focused on scientific procedures, and the investigations and testing of human remains and buried material culture suggests that there was a culture of trade in ochre.

Aboriginal connectivity to the natural environment enabled Aboriginal society to acculturate the landscape and use the resources to provide a better standard of living. This was achieved by managing resources and mapping the country by cultural means. In comparison, some ignorant white explorers died without acknowledging Aboriginal utilisation of land to feed whole nations (see Figure 12).

Figure 12 A Dig Tree and Interpretative sign at Nappa Merrie Station. Burke and Wills were offered food by the local Aboriginal people, but refused it. As a consequence they died from hunger despite the availability of edible and sustaining food in their travel environment. Original photo by the Sydney Mail newspaper, 1911. Kind permission to use granted by the State Library of New South Wales.

CHAPTER FOUR

Maps, Travel and Trade as Cultural Processes

Australia's Aboriginal and Torres Strait Islander peoples have exchanged goods and ideas for many thousands of years. Pituri, pigments, stone and shell, as well as technological and cultural ideas, travelled along ancient trading routes. These exchange networks connected people throughout the continent and the Torres Strait. (Australian National Museum [2004] *Trading Goods and Culture: Crossing Boundaries*)

The Australian landscape was mapped with established paths and goods that were treasured, and which Aboriginal travellers traded at communities visited. Goods would be taken back along the path to their respective communities (Barlow 1979:5). Rose (1985) sees trade as establishing 'sets of relationships' between individuals, the collective, and communities, with the purpose of enhancing well-being (Rose 1985:23). People desired and needed new ideas and goods, which they did not have at home and the only way to obtain these goods was through the establishment of social relationships. Stone axes from the Mount Isa area, for example, found their way to areas along the eastern coast. In addition, 'the engraved pearlshells from the Dampier Peninsula, north-western Australia, actually reached the shores of the Great Australian Bight over 3200 kilometres, and the oval baler-shell ornaments from Cape York, north-eastern Australia. These are used by the Aboriginal people of the northern Flinders Ranges of South Australia, almost the same distance away' (Mountford 1976:50).

People with bales of pituri on their heads moved south, while others carried ochre from southern mines into the north. Stone artefacts travelled from east to west. Every exchange involved more than material goods. It also brought new ideas, songs and ceremonies. (Australian National Museum [2004] *Trading Goods and Culture: Crossing Boundaries*)

Charles P. Mountford (1976) noted that there were 'multitudinous' trade routes that spread in all directions across Australia. These paths were not only used for travel and trade, but also as lines of communication, or as Bob Munn labels them, the 'common ways'. 'Commodities, mundane or magic, were exchanged between far distant peoples and it is some indication of the wide range of these transactions'; trade items were not only material objects, such as ochres and shells (Hardy 1969:14). Materials that helped in the manufacture of tools and weapons, but also songs and dances, were traded with nations thousands of kilometres away. Trade routes linked Aboriginal nations via chains of ritual relationships and links of language. *The Glimmer of Fires in the Night* exhibition brochure on Aboriginal culture in the Australian National Museum, explained that:

> People from neighbouring clans gathered together regularly for the purpose of exchange. As well as materials like ochre and stone, they traded manufactured goods such as spears, shields and stone. Women traded possum skin cloaks and belts, baskets, bags and digging sticks. Cultural knowledge too was carried over great distances. (Australian National Museum 2004)

Having already demonstrated the importance of travel in Aboriginal culture, this chapter examines particular travel technologies and guiding devices that enabled this extensive movement over vast distances.

Kaiou kampa lari janda maleiri turuka turuka	Going along sleep calf, legs walking, walking
Kalka na mara janbi janbi	Sun-colour (red sky after sun sets) fades down
Kalka na mara lari janda	Red sky fades sleep
Karti tjak:ala ko manu ngeitja	Pitjuri tree cut (break) go back
Kop:iri koko wilataruka	Soon come back everybody cook it
Koro koro teit:ako	Come back (return from collecting) kill it (break it up)
Wantji wantjiri	And cutting into bag.

> (Ngameni travelling song for collection and harvesting of pituri, recorded by Tindale 1934a)

Trade, by definition, involves:

> Operations of a commercial character by which the trader provides to customers for reward some kind of goods or services: trade consists of traffic by way of sale or exchange or commercial dealings. The practice of some occupation, business or profession habitually carried on, especially when practised as a means of livelihood or gain, is a trade. (*Butterworths Australian Legal Dictionary* 1997:1175)

Trade and commerce refer to 'all those commercial transactions, dealings, and exchanges between people encompassing either tangible or intangible goods and services including their transport' (*Butterworths Australian Legal Dictionary* 1997:1175). This section focuses on the various systems of trade used by the Aboriginal people of Australia as well as some specific to Aboriginal nations in Queensland. This chapter also highlights Aboriginal songlines, roads, and the regional variance of goods. Stone axeheads and stone bowls were traded into grain-growing production areas, and became part of the trade network systems (Rose 1985:25). Where these networks existed, goods and ideas travelled along the network systems and marketplaces became established.

Aboriginal nations across Australia had access to various resources and the raw materials to manufacture goods, such as ochre that was used for ceremonies as well as painting. Some had stone materials used for spear points and stone axes; others had wood to make clubs, tools and weapons, or even the knowledge required to manufacture fishhooks, baskets, mats, and bags (Bourke *et al.* 1980:105). Regional variance is perhaps a prerequisite for stimulating trade. Aboriginal nations each specialised in niche areas such as nets, fishhooks, growing tobacco or song.

Maps

Maps tell us a lot about a people's culture, including where they travelled, what they traded, and how detailed their knowledge of the land was. It is often thought that people who developed maps were from societies that were literate, that is societies that

Figure 13 A compass rose used by medieval navigators.

had systems of reading and writing. However people believed to be preliterate also used maps to travel over the landscape and return to their place of origin. We also know that medieval European navigation was based on the compass (see Figure 13). This enabled medieval sailors 'to navigate successfully without literacy, writing, sophisticated instruments, the scientific methods or Western schooling . . . these sailors sailed the world without having either a map or foreknowledge' (Turnbull 1989:50). Inuit people of the Arctic Circle etched directional finders into wood and bone, and the Polynesians of the Pacific Islands made maps by weaving cane into a chart to indicate tides, currents, and wind direction. Other seafarers used astronomy to navigate by charting the stars and making cultural maps from them (Thrower 1996).

Numerous examples exist which indicate the antiquity of mapmaking. One such example is a small clay tablet that was engraved in Babylon ca. 2300 BC, which details an estate and a mountain-lined valley. Egyptians also made maps as early as 1300 BC. One of these outlines a route for the transportation of Nubian gold to the Nile Valley. In addition, Claudius Ptolemy, a scholar from Alexandria (Egypt), made maps around AD 150 (Thrower 1996:14–18). Mapmaking and cartography has a relatively long history in human development and is a reliable indicator of cultural activity. Maps represent perceptions of worlds that people understand, and they create spatial awareness from emptiness. The design of maps, as graphic depictions of geographical locations, are an aid to reading the Earth and spatial phenomena. They are also a storage and retrieval system for information. Maps effectively interpret three-dimensional data, which in turn provides knowledge of geographic relationships and spatial awareness. Norman Thrower describes this function as a method of viewing the changing world 'through time'; maps are 'excellent indicators of culture and time' (Thrower 1996:1).

Thrower suggests that, in recent time, collectors of maps of antiquity saw them as works of art or great ethnographic creations. One such example is the Bedolina petroglyph from northern Italy, ca. 2000–1500 BC. It was engraved over several developmental periods up to the Iron Age, and readers of this map are still debating the abstract symbols or pictorial representations. Turnbull states that 'spatiality is a central element in almost all our representations of the world and fundamental to our consciousness' (Turnbull 1989:1).

Thrower suggests that, in more recent times, collectors of old maps conceived of them as works of art or great ethnographic creations (Thrower 1996:1). But is mapping simply an art, whereby the knowledge required to understand the various abstract symbols or pictorial forms is not 'automatic' (Turnbull 1989:1)? A map-reader must be taught how to interpret the contents irrespective of the form in which the information is presented (see Figure 14). A map may be drawn in the dirt, on a rock wall or a bark panel, woven into a fabric or etched into bone or rock.

The form of the representation does not matter; it is the information conveyed that enables predictable movement. Maps can be pictorial, terrestrial, or celestial and the many forms are an indication of the importance of cartography in terms of cultural processes. 'Maps are graphic representations that facilitate a spatial understanding of things, concepts, conditions, processes, or events in the human world'. Map reading is a 'cognitive schema' (Turnbull 1989:3).

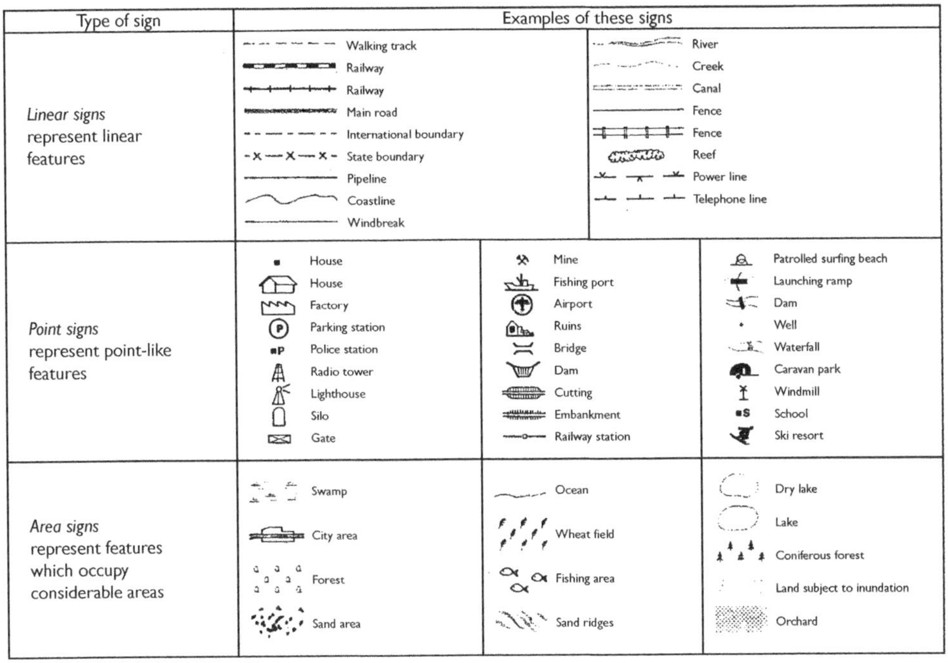

Type of sign	Examples of these signs		
Linear signs represent linear features	Walking track / Railway / Railway / Main road / International boundary / State boundary / Pipeline / Coastline / Windbreak	River / Creek / Canal / Fence / Fence / Reef / Power line / Telephone line	
Point signs represent point-like features	House / House / Factory / Parking station / Police station / Radio tower / Lighthouse / Silo / Gate	Mine / Fishing port / Airport / Ruins / Bridge / Dam / Cutting / Embankment / Railway station	Patrolled surfing beach / Launching ramp / Dam / Well / Waterfall / Caravan park / Windmill / School / Ski resort
Area signs represent features which occupy considerable areas	Swamp / City area / Forest / Sand area	Ocean / Wheat field / Fishing area / Sand ridges	Dry lake / Lake / Coniferous forest / Land subject to inundation / Orchard

Figure 14 A Queensland State High school year 8 activity sheet for map reading. Children are taught how to read a map, what function maps serve, and what the symbols on maps represent.

Astronomy and Astrology

Maps also chart the sky and navigational points can be drawn to link the stars and make abstract concepts readable. Stars can tell us what time of the year it is, provide us with directions, and teach morality. They are consulted when crops need to be harvested, they explain mythology, and inspire thought (Burra 2003:7). People throughout the ages have used the sky in their charts. They joined groups of dots (stars) to represent figurative forms and moulded cult figures out of them. Over time, these become reference points for their knowledge and beliefs. Shapes made from the stars became maps much the same way as the landscape was mapped.

The heavens and the night sky also inspire the Aboriginal imagination. When he finished creating the Murray River, the creator, Nurrunderi, shaped all the tributaries as he travelled, and then looked for a place to hide his magic canoe. He decided that having completed his task, he would travel overland to find his wife, so he decided the best place to put the canoe was in the sky so he could easily find it. The translation of Nurrunderi Juki is the canoe of Nurrunderi (the Milky Way) (Burra 2003:8). Nurrunderi's canoe still absorbs the attention of people when they sit around their campfires at night. Norman Tindale collected elements of this story when he was researching in South Australia over many years. From 1928 to 1964, he interviewed several people who shared the story and named it Tjirbruki. Tindale spelt the name of the great being 'Nugurunduri'. He attributes the story to Milerum (Karagari clan), Karlowan (Jarildekald tribe), Reuben Walker (Ramindjeri people) and Sustie Wilson (Kaurna). This particular story relates how Nugurunduri was fishing for a gigantic Murray codfish, which he pursued from the upper reaches of the Murray River in the Riverina district, west of the Great Dividing Range. The story involves travel through country that already has an established human presence (Tindale 1987:5).

Other Aboriginal mythology of the stars includes Yirran Yambo the hawk (Sirius), and Moolka and Kudda (Alpha and Beta in Centaur), the guardians of love. Then there is Balleroo the hunter (Orion) who tracks the devil women (Pleiades) across the night sky; Kara the spider (Rigel in Orion); Poolkamee the swan, who travels down the great lake with its neck outstretched, hissing at Jirradilli the thieving lizard. Jimbun is the old man who controls the love affairs of the tribe, and is marked by a cluster of stars to the north, indicating his camp. Old Gerda weaves the strands for Yammacoona's net, keeping it taut and strong for the Wizard Woman so she may cast it wide to draw the souls of the dead safely to their resting place. Mittakoodi the heron (Mercury) awaits his beloved Monkeemi, the dawn winds, and together they greet their son Macumbara, the cloud gatherer, who goes around collecting fire sparks from the fires to light the sunrise. These legends lead the traveller on a never-ending trail across space and time (Duncan-Kemp 1961:84–85).

Dick Smith told me a story about how he used to navigate by the stars when he was droving horses and cattle from Victoria River Downs to Dajarra.

> If I fixed the pointer stars of the Southern Cross on my shoulder and kept it to my right I would make it to all the water holes along the Murranji track and make it to Dajarra. (Dick Smith, personal communication 2004)

Mr Robert Anderson also told me that,

> When travelling on Mulgumpin if you face Bege, the sun and rise your left hand and hold Bege in your palm and look over your shoulder that's north. (Robert Vincent Anderson, personal communication 2004)

People all over the world and through the ages have used stars as directional markers. For example, to locate north in the Northern Hemisphere people used Polaris, the North Pole Star. In Australia we have a South Celestial Clock, which is the Southern Cross. The Spanish and the Portuguese also used this system to chart the southern hemisphere (Burra 2003:7). The Southern Cross was conceptualised by Aboriginal people and several stories describe the movement of this system across the sky. Salt-water people (an Aboriginal colloquial term meaning Aboriginal communities who live by the ocean) see the two pointers as shark fins chasing a stingray. In Central Australia, the mob (an Aboriginal colloquial term that means family, or community) sees the Southern Cross as talons of the wedge-tailed eagle. The Coal Sack is its nest and the pointers are its throwing sticks. As a travelling story from the northern region of Australia, the two pointers connect people across distance with the story of fire and how it spread over the landscape. The two pointers are the firesticks, and the smoke rising from the fire created the Milky Way (Burra 2003:14).

The Celts and the Druids told stories that featured the landscape and their entire natural world, so they could travel from one place to the next. We know this because their imagination has survived for generations and is remembered in stories recorded in modern media. In the past, Aboriginal knowledge of the stars was not considered: 'too often we look at other countries for these stories but we have a celestial bounty of lore right here in Australia' (Haran 2002). Aboriginal constellations include 'the celestial emu, a giant stingray and the pointer stars as sharks, pursuing a canoe' (Haran 2002). Scientists now acknowledge Aboriginal celestial knowledge partially because of the secrets once told by Elders that are now shared to enlighten Australian society about Aboriginal history (Burra 2003:67–71).

Bill Yidumduma Harney is an Elder from Wardaman country, a country surrounded by the Victoria, Daly, Fizmaurice, Flora, and Katherine Rivers, roughly 350 kilometres south-west of Darwin. Yidumduma told his story to Hugh Cairns in 1998:

> The Dreaming Track in the sky! The planets come straight across like you and I doing walk, pad up and down, walking backwards, forwards, make a little track there, a pad. A walking trail become a pad, then a wagon road, two wheel tracks, somewhere, I say, yes, follow me and I'll take you straight there. Pad is straight across country: Yondorrin shows, how! If I'm down the east and I've got to go to Hugh Cairns, I'll walk straight down to you. I'll make a road there. We call that Murrujarriyn, mean you're going on from generation to generation: that's what they do, and places you see. (Yidumduma Harney in Cairns 2003:9)

Myths

Ancestral myths explain events in the natural world. The beings of the Dreamtime were ancestral beings; they explain things that once happened and events that might occur. These myths contributed to the culture of Aboriginal people and transcend time and space. Ancestral beings provide the existence and dimension of time and add to the physical, spiritual, and social fabric of Aboriginal people. The events of the Dreamtime and the spiritual forces that helped to shape Australia still exist. They inhabit the landscape and reside in place. Nancy Munn describes this as ancestral transformation, meaning that ancestral beings metamorphosised into natural features of the landscape. She also states that they left some imprint of themselves, such as footprints, tools or rivers, and finally an object or thing, which the ancestors remove from their bodies and which become sacred (Munn 1970:142).

Some stories are localised and tell of ancestors that inhabit the local region; however, others are a part of a 'storyline'. These 'storylines' can move through one nation and travel great distances over other territories. These stories, as they move over the landscape, may tell of the same events and use the same characters but they differ in that they use localised knowledge and features of the landscape. These are important variations because they teach different aspects of law and depict the country as maps. For maps, the stories are important as they direct movement over country. In this respect they tell people where water and other resources can be found and provide knowledge of a country the traveller may not have had. Daisy Bates notes that people living in Ooldea in South Australia had detailed knowledge about the tribal relationship of individuals who lived up to 1,600 kilometres away (1985).

As travellers move over the landscape, these stories are shared along the travel routes when travellers encounter other peoples. Ancestral beings sang stories as they moved across the country, and they left a record of the stories in the form of natural features, such as rivers, mountain ranges, and waterways. One favourite song recorded by an early observer was performed from the Monaro highlands to Gippsland. It was composed by Mrgagula, a songmaker of the Wolgal people, and describes his attempt to cross the Snowy River in a leaky canoe during a flood (Australian National Museum 2004).

Figure 15 depicts an interpretation of the Wangkangurru Dreaming that hangs at Birdsville, in the Simpson Desert Rangers information centre.

Songs such as these are ostensibly records of the travels of ancestral spirits, and relate to the major routes of communication and trade. As travellers reach one of these song places they perform a ceremony and recount verses that have been passed on from generation to generation since the Dreamtime. As the traveller recounts the verse, they sing the song of that site or feature, which in turn leads to the next stanza, which represents the next site or feature in the songline or cycle (Edwards 1988:17–18).

Art

This section provides an explanation of Aboriginal art and what it means to Aboriginal people. All Aboriginal communities of Australia practised art. Art is the way

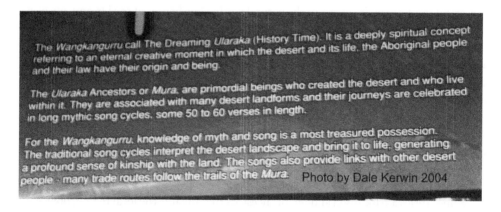

The Wangkangurru call The Dreaming *Ularaka* (History Time). It is a deeply spiritual concept referring to an eternal creative moment in which the desert and its life, the Aboriginal people and their law have their origin and being.

The *Ularaka* Ancestors or *Mura*, are primordial beings who created the desert and who live within it. They are associated with many desert landforms and their journeys are celebrated in long mythic song cycles, some 50 to 60 verses in length.

For the *Wangkangurru*, knowledge of myth and song is a most treasured possession. The traditional song cycles interpret the desert landscape and bring it to life, generating a profound sense of kinship with the land. The songs also provide links with other desert people – many trade routes follow the trails of the *Mura*.   Photo by Dale Kerwin 2004

Figure 15 The painting Wangkangurru Dreaming provides information of the dreaming tracks, lore and history of the Aborigines. In the Simpson Desert Rangers Office, Birdsville. Photo: Dale Kerwin, 2004.

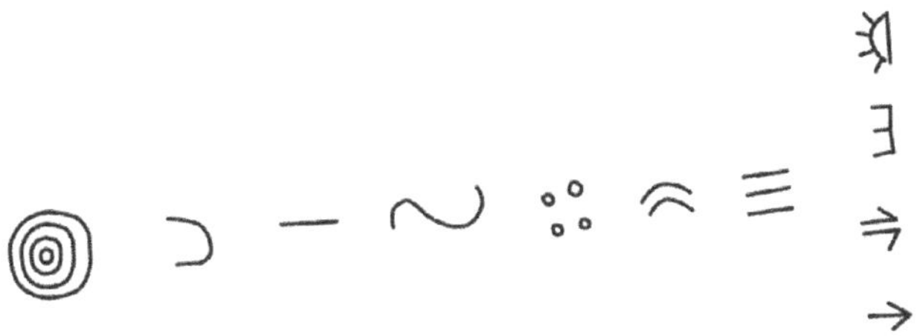

Figure 16 Generic Aboriginal symbols used in Aboriginal art, in Peterson 1981:46.

Aboriginal people articulate intangible property (such as thinking and stories) and real-world occurrences via symbolic abstract artforms (see Figure 16).

The various art forms – dots and lines in the sand, paint on a person's body, dance, a story sung or told, or an enactment of a story from the Dreamtime – represent intellectual knowledge. A comparison can be made between most Aboriginal paintings of the land and topographical maps (Kerwin 1998).

Body painting is also an important part of ceremonial life. This art form is symbolic; the representations of sacred concepts are painted on the body, and differ from region to region. Some are elaborate and associated with a whole ritual performance, while others are small and based on instruction. The symbolic representations of movement, events, and tracks link ancestral beings to the present day. Most designs include the

Figure 17 Sand drawing of Honey-ant Dreaming, in Charles Mountford 1976:60.

71

symbolic representation of the clan, and after various initiations become more elaborate and detailed.

Ground paintings have many purposes. They may be used for instruction so that the ground is used like a blackboard that is wiped clean after a lesson. Symbols are drawn in the dirt and stories are told to accompany the figures. The symbols represent a feature in the environment and children learn their meaning. The stories can also be about everyday life, family relationships, or morality.

Sand drawings were used by most Aboriginal nations, but the people of the central desert regions used them (as many still do) as ritual instruction for ceremonies (see above Figure 17). At times of large gatherings each clan would gather at a preselected location and members would prepare the material needed to add their story to the painting. These events could take up to two weeks depending on the reason for the ritual and occasion.

Material would be prepared through gathering wild cotton, natural dyes and ochre, crop harvesting, and head and armbands; clan groups would then participate in the piecing together of a sand painting. These paintings range from 7 metres by 7 metres to the size of a large football ground – over 100 metres in length. The paintings relate to movement and country, and each clan adds its country to the story. Every waterhole, mountain, or grove of trees where people camped, and the food they ate on the way, would be symbolically represented.

> The dancing and artwork is your whole life. You have your traditional artwork that ties in with the land and ties in with the creation, where your boundary is, how far your ancestor has travelled. It's all written in art. That is what the traditional art means – owner to the land. (Banduk Marika 1992, Melbourne Museum, *Bunjilaka Gallery: Knowing Country* 2004, Melbourne Museum)

Modern Aboriginal art maintains these features. In 1996, Galarrwuy Yunupingu addressed the Australian Arts Board with the following words:

> I would like you to remember this . . . that the paintings are not just beautiful pictures. They are about Aboriginal law, Aboriginal life. They are also about resistance over the past 200 years, and our refusal to forget the land of our Ancestors. They are about cultural, social, and political survival. (in Mercer 1997:vii)

Aboriginal art is not just a representation of land, but a representation of the politics of land. A thorough knowledge of culture is required to understand such representations, and viewing them as simply art can detract from their function and value (see Figure 18). Reading Aboriginal paintings requires a large body of esoteric knowledge (Turnbull 1989:49).

> Aboriginal people have a detailed knowledge of the land, which is necessary for physical and spiritual well-being. This knowledge is expressed through art. Designs mostly represent the journeys of ancestral beings. Specific symbols represent partic-

Figure 18 Map of camps and routes of honey-ant totemic beings, in Charles Mountford 1976:60.

ular landscape features they created. Some symbols even represent the ancestral beings themselves. In this way, designs are condensed versions of elaborate stories associated with both everyday and religious life. Knowledge is the key that allows the symbols to be read, like a map. (Melbourne Museum 2004 *Bunjilaka Gallery: Mapping country*)

C.G. Brandl interviewed an Aboriginal Elder and Ngarluma mekigar (medicine man of the Pilbara region of Western Australia) called Parrarura, and they discussed war shields (see Figure 19). Brandl initially assumed the incisions on the shield were purely decorative. Parrarura sang:

> The snake got up, got up from the north and made a deep trench in the land, digging it halfways, and come along the river from the north. He cut off two halves (of its halfway course) by making waterholes at the edge. (in Brandl 1972:3)

Brandl then realised the symbolic designs on the shield were a map, for it became evident that the country was diagrammatically represented. The shield represented the Fortescue River, with bends and waterholes marked on it.

James Cowan observed,

> Shield or sand drawings (also message sticks and clubs) formed a geographic map of regions from which trading parties or visitors could draw on knowledge when it came to travelling through unfamiliar territory. (Cowan 1992:12–13)

The landscape is represented abstractly or symbolically by circles, lines, figures, and colour. By such means Aboriginal people learned complex techniques of navigation and mapping, which were passed on through the generations. Turnbull calls this 'spatial

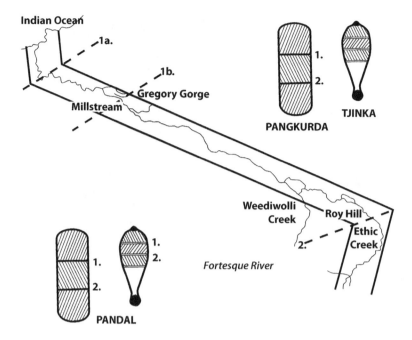

Figure 19 Cartography drawn on a shield, from Western Australia, in Cowan 1992:12.

connectivity' whereby the landscape and knowledge are one as a map (Turnbull 1989:30). The landscape is mapped with a series of narratives that are related to specific ancestral spirits. These beings acculturated the country; they named it, and engraved it with paths for their descendants to follow into the future.

To provide a better understanding of the many devices used by Aboriginal people to move over the country, knowledge is required of tangible objects like the shield. Some of these objects are sacred while others are commonplace, everyday objects. The landscape, knowledge, story, song, graphic representation, and social relations all mutually interact, forming one 'cohesive knowledge network' to create way-finding devices (Turnbull 1989:30).

Way-finding devices

The shapes and forms of material objects, and how they provide information about the trade routes and songlines, are crucial to discussion about Aboriginal people and movement. Songlines are the Dreaming, and the Dreamtime connects the paths by footprint. Songlines travel from place to place and are sung at many corroborees, but songs are only part of a much bigger story. Aboriginal trading paths should be understood in the context of Aboriginal material culture. Aboriginal art (intangible) and material (tangible) objects can be read. Many devices are used as directional finders. These include: the human body, stone, and wood tjuringas (churingas), stone cylcons (see

Figure 20), carved trees (see Figure 21), wooden boomerangs, wooden message sticks (see Figure 23), and wood and stone Toas (see Figure 22) Shell middens and art (such as bark, rock and ground paintings) all convey a message, and they often represent knowledge so as to assist navigation for the purpose of travel and trade.

A wooden tjuringa is a personal item that represents the heritage of a person's birthplace and is modelled on a stone tjuringa. The stone tjuringa is held in the heart of that person's birthplace or country (Cowan 1992:15). To Aboriginal people, tjuringas are deeds to land that were passed down from one generation to the next; they embody the essence and spirit of country.

Wood and stone tjuringas were highly treasured in the nineteenth century by museum collectors as curios of an ancient society. Australian museums began trafficking in these sacred objects with the aid of field researchers, including E.C. Stirling, Director of the South Australian Museum, and Baldwin Spencer, honorary Director of the National Australian Museum in Victoria (Mulvaney 1989:117). As a result of this ethnographic interest, tjuringas were pillaged from special Aboriginal keeping places. As a consequence, tangible evidence of Aboriginal ownership of the land was forgotten in the dungeons of Australian collecting institutions.

Another material expression of Aboriginal title deeds are Cylcons (see Figure 20). Cylcons are sacred objects, some of stone, others moulded from clay. Some were known to be fired and were cylindrical in shape. They were about 30 centimetres in length, and about 7 centimetres wide, and are incised with totemic emblems that represent movement across country. These are believed to have been in wide use in central New South Wales (Ellis, 1994:104; Hill 1981:95).

Carved trees were used by some Aboriginal nations as markers of their boundaries (see Figure 21). For example, the Wiraduri nation in New South Wales carved trees at

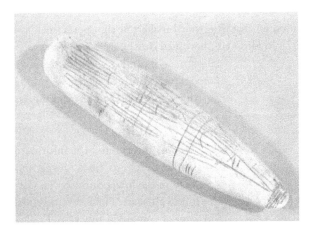

Figure 20 Illustration of a cyclon. Aboriginal material culture, in Marji Hill 1981:95. Cylcons are Aboriginal title deeds, considered as sacred objects, often carved from stone or moulded from clay. Some were known to be fired and were cylindrical in shape. They are about 30 cm. in length, and about 7 cm. wide, and are incised with totemic emblems that represent movement across country.

the edges of their country, so that people entering their country would know that the Wiraduri people owned the area. It is estimated that there were more than 300 of these carved trees *in situ* in Central Western New South Wales, between the Lachlan and Macquarie river systems. Relatively few have survived. In 1989 Mulvaney was able to locate 78 of these markers, including some as curios in private collections and as ornaments in a private poolroom (Mulvaney 1989:84–85).

Toa

Toas are colourful objects used by people on the move to indicate where they were heading and which route to follow, or to indicate when people left and when they would be back. Reuther, a missionary in the late nineteenth century, observed their use when he worked in the Killalpaninna area of the lower Cooper Creek. The purpose of the toa was to inform friends where they were (in Hercus 1987:59). Toas have attracted interest because of their iconographic imagery and the scientific world (H. Morphy 1972; P. Jones & Sutton 1986; L. Hercus 1987) considers them to be artefacts from the Lake Eyre basin. The Lake Eyre basin and the adjoining area of far south-west Queensland is 'an area of much cultural and linguistic diffusion' (Hercus 1987:59).

Typically, toas would represent some feature of the environment or a totem figure (see Figures 22 a, b). Toas were used as directional markers or signposts but were also statements about territory; they were 'expressions of myth and topography' (McConnell 1976:65). They were made from wood and some would have 'bird feathers, human artefacts (netting, stone tools), body parts and products of animals (lizard feet, kangaroo teeth), human hair, teeth, animal bones and bark or wood splinters then painted (Jones & Sutton 1986:8).

It is worth mentioning that directional makers or sign-posts (such as toas are) were not at all unusual in traditional Aboriginal Australia . . . Through their shape, colour, design, or appendages, toas represented conspicuous topographic features which in turn, are linked to mythic wanderings of the Dreaming. (Jones & Sutton 1986:8)

Hercus interpreted the information encoded on a Wutjukana toa to be a gorge in Wangkangurru country in the lower Simpson Desert where water can be found all year. 'These we find illustrated on the toa by way of row upon row of red dots. All the streams trickle together into a deep red waterhole at the bottom of the toa' (Hercus 1987:63) (see Figure 22b).

Figure 21 A carved tree of the Wiraduri nation, in Mulvaney 1989:85.

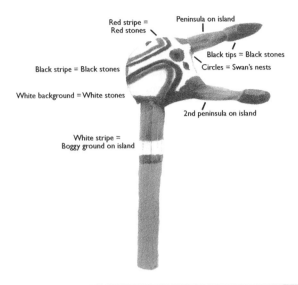

Description		Potential meanings
Dots*		Trees, bushes, stones, grass, feathers, knots, ants etc.
Circle	●	Waterhole, campsite
Oval	❶	Waterhole, Coopers Creek, low flat, watercourse
U-shape	∪	Waterhole
Vertical dividing line	ϒ ʃ	Waterhole, Coopers Creek, waterhole in Coopers Creek, watercourse
Meandering line	⧢	Watercourse, snake
Thin line			Watercourse, deposits, line of stones, cracks, path etc.
Band	☰	Watercourse, sandy bank, soil, elevation, plain, line of trees, sand, shallows, limestone/ironstone hills, shores etc.

Figure 22 A toa from Lake Gregory providing interpretative information through the use of symbols, in Jones and Sutton 1986:62.

Message sticks

Message sticks were widely used as notes of introduction when travelling or as invitations to an important ceremony (see Figure 23). They are marked by lines, circles and totemic figures which represent movement and indicate time. Walter Roth concluded that message sticks were a guarantee of 'good faith, and may at times act as a passport over hostile country' (Roth [1897] 1983:8).

He provides an figure of how they might be used: an Aboriginal trader from Boulia heads to the pituri markets in the Simpson Desert area to undertake a business transaction. The message stick was used as an introductory note, and if accepted, the order for pituri would be placed in a queue. Then 'a dilly bag of pituri is then handed over with the message stick' (Walter Roth [1897] 1983:9). If walking a traveller would need to know where to find water, where to obtain food, where the best locations are to rest and which was the best route to take.

Shell middens

The word 'midden' is an archaeological term that describes an accumulation of debris resulting from the discarded inedible parts of foodstuffs. In Australian archaeology this usually refers to the accumulation of shell deposited after the collection and consumption of shellfish. Mick Leon told me, 'that is whitefella terminology, those shell middens are signposts. They link resources across the landscape; they are thoroughfares' (Mick Leon, personal communication, November 2003). Archaeology is gradually piecing together Aboriginal trade routes. Everytime there is a find of an object that appears to be of some antiquity and is from Aboriginal material culture, questions are raised. At Cobham Lake in the Darling region of New South Wales 'pearl shell from the Torres Straits area was found', which is a distance of over 4,500 kilometres from its origins (Hardy 1969:14).

In another conversation I had with Mick, he went on to explain that 'the knowledge of where these are located are sung about, told in story, drawn on tools and other instruments, and all these things are cultural maps' (personal communication, November 2003). They are also used as landmarks. 'If you are walking along the beach and the ocean is on your right, because we are on the east coast of Australia you will be heading north. If the ocean is on your left you are heading south. Local fishermen are using these middens to navigate along the beach. They count the middens as they are four-wheel-driving along the beach and stop when they have reached their destination – the best gutter to fish' (Mick Leon, personal communication, June 2004). Mick Leon also pointed out that they are a record of Aboriginal occupation and ownership of country.

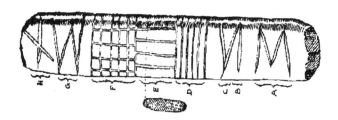

Figure 23 A message stick from Boulia, Queensland, in Roth 1897:137–38.

Bora grounds

Bora grounds are an Aboriginal institution that were used for many purposes and for many functions (see Figure 24). However, they were generally located close to resources such as water and food. They are represented by a large ring and a small ring with tracks connecting them. Most are circular with the centre of each ring scooped out and cleared of vegetable matter. In south-east Queensland there were 120 known bora rings. Bora, or kuppa, rings are important and significant areas to Aboriginal people as these sites are used for council and political deliberations, courts, judicial hearings, and for trade; they are important Aboriginal institutional and ceremonial areas and were used up until the late nineteenth century (Colliver 1970:3). They could be an arrangement of stone, a circle of earth rings (mud rings) and be as large as 60 metres in length; they could have several little kuppa rings connected to the largest ring. They would also have trees incised with lines and geometric shapes and have clay or wooden sculptured figures standing near them (Colliver 1970; Steele 1983; Kerkhove 1985). Steele (1983) has plotted these sites in the Brisbane landscape and found they had several things in common, such as well-defined paths connecting them across distances. One of these sites was located at Musgrave Park, in West End, Brisbane, but it has since been destroyed (Steele 1983). In 1824, when John Oxley was surveyor-general, he drew one such 'Aboriginal Ceremonial Ground' (Colliver 1970:3). F.S. Colliver (1970) also undertook a survey of these grounds, and noted that 'these earth works have been likened to our modern university' (Colliver 1970:3).

Clem Lack (1966) describes the 'Burung' ceremony which was practiced by numerous tribes from the Murray to the Barwon – a distance of over 400 miles – and the pathway that was called 'Dharambil' which was 55 chains long (1 mile) and lead to a bora ground. Another path called 'mooroo' leading to a bora ground was 15 chains long (1,500 feet) (Lack 1966:118–19). Lack reported that 'a messenger, or messengers, went to neighbouring tribes. A message stick, 'dharral', on which symbols were carved' would be relayed to other people of the area as an invitation to attend (1966:120). They were meeting places and ceremonial centres, and messengers with invitations would be sent out along tracks that linked people across the landscape.

At Bestman Road, Toorbul Point in Queensland, there is a well preserved bora ground (see Figure 24). The missionaries, Nique and Hartenstein, recorded that in

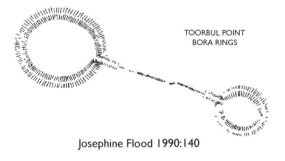

TOORBUL POINT
BORA RINGS

Josephine Flood 1990:140

Figure 24 A Bora ring at Bestman Road, Toorbal Point.

1841 over 2,000 Aboriginal people attended a ceremony there, and among them were people from the 'Noosa area and Bonya natives' (Steele 1983:170–71).

Aboriginal people across Australia developed technologies that were fine tuned and adapted to suit their environment. The technologies assisted in identifying particular country such as whose country the traveller has travelled to, or was planning to travel through. The objects were functional tools that were grounded in country and represented a medium for reading country. The spirit of place is marked or incised on the object, as are lines of movement that piece together songlines or story strings. The incisions cut into objects represent movement and geographical features combined with storylines, and made travel possible. As functional tools, these objects would act as a map, a connection to political affiliations, and a personal note of identity. Some of these travelling guides are simple, others are elaborate, but all have the major purpose of contributing and maintaining the social connection of people across the landscapes of Aboriginal Australia.

Travel technology

There are four important ingredients to travelling-story, song, dance and art. People here would carve their journey on special boards and as you are journeying you would record it on the board. We have it on the spearthrower and they would be lines, we also have pearl shells and these would be put on a belt and the zig zag would explain where to travel. Ochre, possum skins plucked and spun into belts, there were also special people who made them. We also traded stone axe to the French. (Noel Nannup, personal communication 2004)

This catalogue of ways for recording country suggests that Aboriginal societies developed techniques for cartography for the purposes of navigation around the landscape of Australia. Moreover, contact with neighbouring regions of Papua and the Indonesian archipelago increased their knowledge of navigation across land and sea estates. Throughout the long period that the trepang industry operated in Australian waters, the Macassan trepangers employed many Aboriginal people as deckhands, some of whom would travel to Macassar when the season finished. Some returned to their communities to tell their stories (Ganter 2006).

Djalajari, a Wonguri man from Elcho Island off the Arnhem Land coast, recounts a story of his travels while employed as a deckhand on a assan prau in 1895:

We spread our sails and went north-westwards, going outside and above Djowadjowa, Melville Island . . . On our way through the sea we come to Djadja Island, but didn't stop for water . . . At last we come to Leti Island, where we dropped anchor; and here we loaded more stores and fresh food that Wonabadi, our boss, had bought with trepang. It was on Leti that we saw balanda [whitefella] for the first time . . . We walked around the town with its houses, just the same as Darwin, and there were coconut trees too. After about two days we left the port, and sailed to Danangigu

Island. There were more houses there, and the people were the same as those at Leti; there were people from Java there too. We stopped there one day, and weighed anchor that night; we sailed on fast through a smooth sea, and saw no land until we came to Lant'djau Island, too without stopping. Then we came to the big island of Madada, and to another called Laga, and further on to Bandei. From there by climbing to the top of the mast we could see Danagigi [Danangigu] (Tanakeke Island, south of Macassar), called by same name as the one we had passed before. (R.M. Berndt and C.H. Berndt 1954:51–58)

Over the long period of contact between the Macassans and the Yolngu of Arnhem Land there was a cultural exchange of language (shared words), arts, food, and knowledge (Isaacs 1980:264). In a Macassan song, Wandjuk Marika sings about the practices of the crews of these boats and their preparations for departing the shores of Yirrkala country to sail north. 'The crews of these boats would pull their masts up and lay them on the deck of their boats and weigh anchor. They would sing this song as they were departing and sail out to sea and head for home' (Wandjuk Marika in Isaacs 1980).

To travel across water, Aboriginal people developed watercraft technologies ranging from rafts to cross small bodies of water, to bark canoes and dugout canoes to travel across large bodies of water. However, to date these have been viewed as ethnographic curios, so they were rarely examined in their social and historical context. The history of their introduction is obvious. For the static view of Aboriginal society, they appear as inauthentic add-ons. Researchers such as R.M. Baker, Berndt *et al.* and Ellis all have commented on the manufacture and varied use of these different types of canoes. Coastal seafaring was developed independently of external contact. Abel Tasman observed small fleets of bark canoes off the north-west coast in 1642, as did Lieutenant Cook and Joseph Banks off the New South Wales coast in 1770. Similarly members of the first fleet saw several canoes as they docked at Botany Bay in 1788, and at Flinders in 1802 (Baker 1988; Berndt *et al.* 1993; Ellis 1994).

In the main, when rafts and canoe styles used by salt-water people and river-dwelling Aboriginal nations are mentioned, the focus is on their functionality and their ability to mobilise Aboriginal people so they could communicate with others for trade. The varied descriptions of watercraft across Australia suggest that these are regional variances as well as intellectual creativity in terms of designs and ideas for watercraft. This adds to our appreciation of the extent of knowledge Aboriginal people had of travel techniques and their skills in the production of these vessels. The crafts were used for fishing, as well as for crossing rivers and open bodies of water. They were also used to move up and down waterways, as vehicles for the transportation of goods and to attend important meetings.

Rafts were made using strips of kangaroo hide, or twine made from the bark of trees; vines were used as lashing. Several logs were tightly bound together and paperbark piled on top to raise the platform above the waterline. Some observers have noted several of these rafts lashed together as a floating platform that were able to carry six to eight people. Others have also seen houses constructed on the rafts and fires lit on them at night. The fire would be constructed in the middle of the houseboat and mud used as

81

a base to protect the raft from burning. The fire had several purposes: to cook food, to act as a lantern to guide movement, to keep warm on cold nights, and for security. The rafts were steered and propelled by a person using a pole (Davidson 1935; Thomson 1957; Baker 1988:179; Ellis 1994:96–97).

Bark canoes were in use nationwide, but differed from region to region. Some used single sheets of bark, sewn together with sinew, strips of skin, fibre, resin and mud to seal the seams (Berndt *et al.* 1993:83–86). On his voyage in the northern regions of Australia around the Edward Pellew Group in 1802, Matthew Flinders described two canoes 'formed of slips of bark, like planks, sewed together, the edge of one slip over-laying another, as in our clincher-boats' (Baker 1988:180). These craft would be used to navigate long rivers, for bay hopping, and also as ocean-going vessels.

Dugout canoes were used in the northern parts of Australia. They were a relatively new technology introduced by Macassans (see Figure 25). Some scholars suggest that the logs to make the dugout canoes were floated down the Fly River in Papua New Guinea and traded into the Torres Straits (in Wilson 1988:118). The dugout canoes of the type used in the Torres Strait were ocean-going vessels, approximately 20 metres long. The type designed and made in the northern regions of Australia were between two and seven metres long (Hiddins 1998:95; Baker 1988). However, some communities along the northern coast of Australia made their canoes out of softwood (Leichhardt pine, *Nauclea orientalis*), but in the Arnhem Land area they were fashioned

Figure 25 Painting of a dugout canoe from Prince of Wales Island coming along side the Monarch, as described by Gregory 1857:7–8, in Birman 1979:99. The Aborigines bartered several articles with the crew of the schooner.

from hardwood (*Melaleuca*) (Davidson 1935; Thomson 1957; Baker 1988: 179; Ellis 1994:96–97).

Depending on their use, the crafts carried one or two people. There were also rafts designed for inter-island hopping that would carry up to 20 people. These larger crafts would be equipped with stone anchors, fixed seats, and sails woven from the leaves of pandanus palms. Stone axes, stone or wooden chisels, and adzes were traditionally used to construct these crafts, and paddles were used to propel them (Davidson 1935; Thomson 1957; Baker 1988:179; Ellis 1994:96–97).

The men who constructed canoes were specialists and it would take several months to construct the larger craft. Handling a canoe was also a skilled task.

> The expert canoe makers knew from experience exactly how far a tree could be spread without cracking it . . . Mac and George Rily made the best canoes: everything they cut was good because they knew how to line them up and straighten them, they cut them with the timber and they were really good boats they made. If the tree wasn't good enough they wouldn't start on it. (Baker 1988:177)

Complex skills to navigate and travel were passed down through the generations from Elders and craftpersons specialised in the art of iconographical mapping. This helped travellers to come to terms with unfamiliar lands. Rock art and engravings on cave walls and rock faces are locational markers comparable to the steles and temple walls of the Egyptians and Sumerians. Steles are upright slabs or pillars of stone, bearing an inscription or sculptural design. These markers speak to those who have been introduced to the art of their production and interpretation.

As indicated above, certain material objects representing features of the landscape were used as a form of cartography. A further aid for spatial orientation resides in mnemonics and rote learning associated with oral traditions and songlines. This orientation technique relies on the ability of the traveller to recall ideas and experiences that have been imprinted into social memory. Carter suggests that 'recollection is not passive imitation inspired by antiquarian zeal. It is active recreation . . . that living space in which places have histories and implements are put to use. For Aborigines, to travel country it is to "tell it", to represent it to oneself' (Carter 1987:346). Environmental elements were also used, such as 'brown hawks'. These birds are scavengers that circle campsites where food scraps are left and spiral up into the atmosphere; they are distinctive signs, which can be seen from long distances (Roth 1897:132–33).

Aboriginal people developed the means of undertaking long-distance travel; they developed technologies to conquer the tyranny of isolation, to trade, and to communicate with others. The material culture of Aboriginal people seems simple on the surface, but there clearly existed travel technology and a culture for travel. Hence the general term 'walkabout'.

Travel

'The travelling culture heroes are believed to have not only brought combined religious and social institutions, but also to have acted as inventors of technical advances' (Micha, 1970:292). Travel represents a crucial part of Aboriginal culture. It is a response to the need to renew relationships with the country of ancestral birth and the ritual journey to renew relationships with people across the landscape. On the mainland the most common form of travel was on foot. Before European invasion there were no suitable beasts of burden to carry people and goods, and the use of canoes was restricted to river and salt-water (ocean-dwelling) peoples. Queensland ethnographer Walter Roth recognised the 'walkabout phenomenon' as an economic institution. 'It is part and parcel of the great trading or bartering system which is more or less continually going on throughout the various districts' (Roth 1897:132).

Tindale (1987) documented the travels of Ngurunduri and his people throughout eastern Australia over a period of 36 years and remarked that 'it continued up to present day'. He recognised that over the long period from the Dreaming to the present, the Tjirbruki story spread along Ngurunduri Dreaming tracks, because messages sent about impending events along the storyline were constant in the story. What Tindale called 'kindred tribes' (but later 'clans' and 'families'), would come to the gathering place (Tindale 1987:10). Once on walkabout, various signs and signals were used to indicate the traveller's presence. For example, Roth noted the use of 'smoke signals' and 'boomerangs as track-signals'. Roth explained that Aboriginal people of the Hamilton River area would leave two boomerangs placed crossways on the ground, which would tell those who are following that the route was the correct one (Roth 1897:132). Roth lists these devices as 'smoke signals, finger posts, footprints, geographical names' (Roth 1897).

Roads and trading routes

In the Top End of Australia the languages are rich with words for 'which way', the track is rich with language, as the Dreaming moves with the path being overlaid on the rivers, the sandstone escarpment and plains being the road. In Arnhem Land the principal word for road is 'djukurr', which Reser et al. describes as having 'affinities with the word for kidney fat' (2000:48). This has implications in terms of 'conditioning, usability and consumability, and deadly powers' (Reser et al. 2000:48).

> Roads to new lands brought new ideas. How the blackman must have chanted his latest songs as he moved down the dreaming paths of trade. Everywhere over the land these trails brought different rituals to tribesmen. In memory and imagination, they still operate. (Harney 1950:43)

A road, according to a dictionary definition, is 'A way from one place to another which enables passage between the two. A road includes any bridge, tunnel, causeway, road-ferry, ford, or structure forming part of the road. It includes the airspace above the road and soil beneath the road' (*Butterworths Australian Legal Dictionary* 1997:1036). Stock routes are roads and have also been overlaid on Aboriginal Dreaming ways. It should also be noted here that roads are not claimable through the Native Title processes, but are claimable under state, federal, and international laws for cultural heritage.

Roads have become part of our popular culture and our cultural consciousness as artefact. The road is a symbol that has created its own image; novels have been written about them, movies have been made about the road, 'road songs, road culture, genre in books and a cultural icon and landscape' (Reser *et al.* 2000:42).

Humans have a long memory of roads that stretches back to antiquity; 'roads have always been human arteries, just as intersections have always spawned commerce cities, and the crash of cultures (Reser *et al.* 2000:43). Archaeologists have pieced together ancient trade routes, such as the trade in flint implements produced by the Danish Ertoboll culture about 4,000 BC. Mined and napped in large workshops these instruments were transported to Norway and into the interior of Germany. In central and eastern Europe about 1500 to 300 BC, there were four major trade routes known as the 'Amber Roads', along which the Etruscan traders would take statuary, jewellery, and medieval medicines made from amber, a major commodity of the time (Schreiber 1962:1–3).

Other roads that have been used over time are the Royal Roads of Persia and the communication routes used by the Persian monarchy of 500 BC. One such road, which is 2,400 kilometres in length, was used by the monarch Darius 1 (521–485 BC) (Schreiber 1962:10–12). The 'Silk Road', which has been described as the longest road in the world, brought great bales of silk, tea, and other treasures to the Western world and has been in existence for over 2,200 years (Schreiber 1962:28). Vadime Elisseeff suggests that the Silk Road was not only simply a functional link, it also provided the means for trading partners to exchange cultural wealth along its length. He also suggested that those who crossed the mountains and deserts propagated religious beliefs and travelled to increase knowledge and trade. The Silk Road encompassed parts of China, Eurasia, India, Serindia and Iran, just west of China, and has been known for centuries (Elisseeff 2000:2). Ray Gonzales notes the cultures of China and Mesopotamia, which otherwise would have been separated by a vast, hostile wasteland, came into contact by way of their use of the Silk Road for trade (Gonzales 2004:1).

There was also the 'Incense Road' on which merchants were able to bring aloes, balsam, myrrh, incense, and rare tress to Oman and the Hadramauth to Egypt and the Mediterranean ports of Syria. This road was in use for about 2,000 years and serviced the needs of such queens of Egypt as Hatshepset and Cleopatra (Schreiber 1962:79). Finally the 'Inca Roads' of the year 1500 travelled along the coast a distance of 3,600 kilometres and the 480-kilometre long Andes Road, which was also used by the Incas (Schreiber 1962:183).

Generally, as cultures 'advanced', increased specialisation and trade gave people more access to goods and services, and the increased number of trades gave rise to merchants. The Babylonians and the Arabs are historically recognised as great traders who took their wares or merchandise by foot or on camels and donkeys over great distances. Elisseeff notes, these roads are:

> The descendants of natural roads following the patterns of vegetation whose ecological qualities enabled man . . . to thrive in the days when palaeolithic hunters tracked their game. These historical routes are also terrestrial and maritime, running from east to west and corresponding to waterways that run from north to south. They introduced sedentary and nomadic populations, and opened up a form of dialogue between the cultures of East and West. (Elisseeff 2000:2)

Elisseeff also notes that archaeology has expanded our knowledge of the trade of goods between Mesopotamia, Indian and Chinese territories in the Neolithic period. Trading took place in all directions, but especially from oasis to oasis across the Pamirs (a region in central Asia). Artefacts that have been discovered made from 'lapis lazuli, jade, bronze, and iron' indicate fairly conclusively that such exchange occurred (Elisseeff 2000:2–3).

The Pituri Road

Aboriginal people also had roads.

> Aboriginal people had organised networks of exchange that extended from one side of the continent to the other. Red ochre, essential for ceremonial use, body decoration and cave painting, was carried along trade routes for thousands of kilometres. Pearl shell travelled even further. People in the Great Australian Bight wore shells collected in the north of Western Australia as pendants. Baler shells from Cape York found their way to Central Australia, Lake Eyre, the Flinders Ranges and eventually the coast of South Australia. (Australian National Museum [2004] *The Importance of Trade*)

Aboriginal people of the river areas 'travel through outback tribal lands for various reasons, mainly concerned with trade' (Hardy 1969:14). The river Darling has its catchment area in Queensland; it flows through New South Wales, Victoria and South Australia. The Aboriginal nations near the Darling River 'had their part in the complex of routes that criss-crossed the continent, and their couriers travelled far a field over the dry expanses of the inland bent on barter' (Hardy 1969:14).

Barlow (1994) argues that maps highlight the 'routes along which particular trade items travelled'. In the Aboriginal world, one of these particular trade routes or trading chains links the people of the Kimberley in north Western Australia to those on the Eyre Peninsula in South Australia; they trade mostly in pearl shell. Other goods that moved along this road, as Barlow points out, were 'beautifully carved with designs, bamboo necklaces and boomerangs, wooden dishes, dillybags, and red ochre' (1994:13–14). As cultural landscapes, roads in the Aboriginal world 'converge and separate' the human form from the Dreamtime, as the human foot signifies presence, use and ownership, management, identity, but also direction, orientation, script and passage. This 'sacralises and humanises the path'; footprints in paintings provide human presence, so the space can be visualised and the thoroughfare walked and maintained (Reser *et al.* 2000:44).

One of the most important Aboriginal Highways is the 'Pituri Road'. Observers spelled the word 'pituri' differently: pitjuri, pitcheri, piuri, bedgery, petchery and bedourie. In addition, it is not to be confused with other native tobaccos such as wolaria of the Katherine and Victoria River areas or Alice Springs, because most areas of Australia had wild tobaccos (Harney 1950:44).

The Pituri Road 'encompassed a river system where the headwaters of numerous streams [flowed] north into the Gulf of Carpentaria' (Watson 1983:29). These streams also lie close to the catchment area for the Channel Country, where the tributaries of the southward-flowing waters of the Diamantina and Georgina Rivers flow (Watson 1983:29). The Diamantina and Georgina Rivers form the floodplains of the Channel Country and the Lake Eyre basin. In this area the 'Finke and other river systems flow south into South Australia and Central Australia' (Watson 1983:29). The direction of the water formed the main trunk route for trade; it also flowed along other numerous river systems branching out from the main trunk (Watson 1983:29). Pamela Watson's (1983) monograph on the production, distribution and consumption of pituri, states that the Pituri Road brought together 'religious and social institutions and inventors of technique' (Micha 1970; Watson 1983:29).

Pituri is a narrow-leafed plant (see Figure 26) that was chewed in the days before European tobacco took its place. 'The proffering of a well-masticated quid was a friendly gesture not always immediately appreciated by the white man' (Hardy 1969:14). Pituri grows in large parts of the desert areas but the most sought-after pituri comes from the south-west corner of Queensland. 'Special bags were woven for its transport and it was carried over a system of recognised trade routes that covered a large part of the continent. Aborigines from the West Darling travelled as far as the Birdsville Track to obtain supplies from southbound traders. Others waited for it to be brought down to a main centre at Goyder's Lagoon where in autumn, as many as five hundred customers would be waiting for its arrival' (Hardy 1969:14).

Traders carried these hand-woven bags of pituri on foot along the Musgrave and Everard Ranges to Ooldea where the Transcontinental

Figure 26 A Pituri plant.

railway is situated. It was also carried to Lake Nash through Arltunga, along Harts Range from Alice Springs (Terry 1974:64–65). Some was brought from Alice Springs, with the southwards movement of water to Lake Eyre; the main Pituri Road ran the length of the interior of Queensland, across New South Wales beyond Lake Eyre (Terry 1974:65). McConnell (1976) also notes that it moved through the Lower Diamantina, Lake Eyre, Lake Torrens, Kopperamanna, to North Flinders Ranges, Cooper Creek, Thargominda, Charleville, William Creek, Boulia, Cloncurry and beyond (McConnell 1976:18).

Pituri, *Duboisia hopwoodii* (see Figure 26), is also known as emu poison and belongs to the Solanceae family (Latz 1995:163). Pituri is like a tobacco, which was either chewed in wads or smoked. It is not related to the American tobacco that is part of the nightshade family *solanaceae*, genus *nicotiana* species *N. tabacum*. Pituri produces a nicotine considered to be four times more potent than that found in commercial tobacco (Latz 1995:63). There are three types of pituri: *Duboisia myoporoides*, which grows along the coast of Queensland, *D. hopwoodii*, which grows in south-west Queensland, and *D. leichardtii*, which grows between these two areas (McConnell 1976:17). The three small trees named *Duboisia* also belong to the potato family, and are 'first cousin to the mandrake, jimsonweed and deadly nightshade. The alkaloids atropine and scopolamine extracted from pituri contain nor-nicotine, chemically akin to nicotine (Taylor 1966:145; Terry 1974:63).

Traditionally pituri was dried in sand ovens and crushed into small flakes, before packing it into specially designed woven bags for trading. As a final process, pituri was mixed with the dried plant, as well as flowers and ash from particular acacias, which enhanced the nicotine. This mixture was bound together in quids by various native flax (*Psoralea* spp.), which made it easier to transport and trade. The plant contains the alkaloid nicotine and nor-nicotine, and is poisonous if introduced to livestock (Low 1987:257–60). Aboriginal people also used pituri for catching game. Dried and crushed pituri put into a waterhole would stupefy game once they drank, so it would be easy to catch. Game such as emu, parrots, and wallabies were caught in this manner (Latz 1995:163; Barlow 1994:19). Aboriginal travellers also used pituri to control hunger and thirst, as it has a stimulating effect that staves off hunger and increases endurance and stamina. Low cites an example, 'One Aboriginal boy supposedly walked 260 kilometres in two days with no other sustenance' (Low 1987:258).

Pituri is traded over a large area, but the processing area is located in the south-western corner of Queensland, near Bedourie. It has been suggested that the name of this Queensland town derives from pituri (Low 1987:258; Barlow 1994:19). Bedourie is a small isolated desert town accessible only by four-wheel-drive vehicles. Pituri grows in even more isolated locations than Bedourie, at places such as 'Pelunga Springs, Idumea (Glenormiston) Station, Monterita and Bulkra Springs, west of the Mulligan, and across the ninety-mile dry stage from Merrica Spring to Nelica corner on the wire-netting fence of Western Queensland' (Harney 1950:43). Bancroft (1884) noted that one of the growing areas was near 'Bindiaca (Sylvester Creek) at the junction of Mulligan and Pitchery Creek and Idumea (Glenormiston) Station on its banks (Johnston and Cleland 1933:211). Roth (1897) subsequently added Cluny Station on the Herbert River, east of Lake Phillip, and Monkarra, on the Diamantina (Johnston and Cleland 1933:211).

Low (1987) and Watson (1983) suggest that the drug was traded over '550,000 square kilometres, and that the drug was traded south to Lake Eyre, north to Cloncurry, and west into the Northern Territory' (Low 1987:258; Barlow 1994:19). However, the best quality pituri was grown around Bedourie and it was here that the intellectual knowledge and secrets on curing the plant for consumption were held. George Aiston, Protector of Aborigines, wrote of the trade and use of pituri. He stated that a patrimonial right of succession existed in the ownership of plantations and production of the plant (Aiston 1937:372–77).

Aiston also noted that the tobacco traded at markets attracted 'up to 500 traders':

> After everybody had rested and fed, one of the party would throw down a bag in front of the assembled camp; anyone who wished to buy would throw down, perhaps a couple of boomerangs, perhaps a grinding mill, or whatever he could spare; the pitcheri seller would leave his bag until something that he wanted would accept by picking it up and buyer would then pick up the bag of pitcheri. Perhaps another of the member of the pitcheri party would see something in the goods offered and would throw down another bag; if the buyers were not satisfied they would pick up their offerings, and if the seller was not satisfied he would pick up his bag of pitcheri. The camps near the pitcheri grounds never became big markets because the pitcheri was more valuable farther away it was traded. The near camps were only used to get enough utensils and weapons for use when travelling to more profitable markets. (Aiston 1937:372–77)

Rose (1985) concludes that the harvesting of pituri demanded specialised skills and knowledge. She also describes where the best pituri is cured; 'through highly skilled management, including harvesting and artificial drying by a process designed to maintain the highest levels of nicotine' (Rose 1985:35).

Pituri is still used today by Aboriginal people throughout the Channel Country, particularly when resources are stretched and funds are scarce; it is a substitute for European tobacco. In addition, to make European tobacco go further, pituri is mixed at a ratio of one third to two-thirds of store tobacco. The Pituri Road is estimated to have been over 3,800 kilometres in length and possibly surpasses in extent and antiquity of the Silk Road, the Incense Road, the Inca Roads and other ancient trade routes (see Map 5).

Whitefella knowledge of pituri

Although colonisers had a strong interest in the acclimatisation of plants and the discovery of Aboriginal plant uses for commercial purposes, pituri did not come to the attention of the new Australians until 1861. This was when they first heard of a plant with 'rather remarkable properties that grew in the interior where both desert and scrub abound' (Taylor 1966:144). No mention was made of pituri by the explorers Sturt,

Stuart, Barclay, or Gregory in their journals (Johnston and Cleland 1933). However, in May 1861 Burke and Wills' party of men were given fish and nardoo cakes as well as pituri when they were in the Cooper Creek area. One of the party by the name of King describes his experience of pituri (Johnston and Cleland 1933:202):

> After chewing it for a few minutes I felt happy and perfectly indifferent about my position, in fact much the same effect as might be produced by two pretty stiff nobblers of brandy. (in Moorehead 1963:118)

Map 5 The Two Dog Dreaming story has several Aboriginal Dreaming ancestors associated with this story line; it also involves the movement of cultural property such as pituri. For example, the Rainbow Serpent Dreaming story chasing the Nightjar is associated with the Two Dog Dreaming story. Also associated with the Two Dog story is the dreaming story line of the Emu, Kuringii, being chased by the Two Dingoes. Further across the central desert the mythical Kangaroo, revenging the death of the blue-tongued lizard Nintaka, chased the Ninjuri lizard-man. Two Dogs also incorporates the Two Boys story of the Wangkangurru people as well as the Pigeon Dreaming of the Gurindji people of the Victoria River region. These stories represent the movement of pituri across Australia, starting at the place of harvest in the Channel Country and radiating outwards along the Dreaming tracks. These Dreaming stories are found within oral histories collected by McCarthy, Roth, Tindale and Rose.

Howitt (1861), the leader of the rescue party, found King near Innamincka, on Cooper Creek on the border of Queensland and South Australia, where the mob gave him a small ball of pituri in friendship (in Johnston and Cleland 1933:203).

Again, in 1862, when Howitt led a search party for Burke and Wills, he was met by an Aboriginal man in full ceremonial body painting, which Howitt describes as painted like a skeleton. The man offered him a plug of the tobacco (Morrehead 1963:137). Pamela Watson clarifies that this meeting occurred when Howitt was 'crossing Sturt's Stony Desert route used by Aborigines from Lake Hope, Cooper Creek on their journey to procure pituri' (Watson 1983:8).

Later a physician named Joseph Bancroft went in search of pituri in 1872. He took several samples back with him to Brisbane and sent these on to Europe for analysis. Results confirmed the identification of a new alkaloid, called 'nor-nicotine' (as described earlier). Bancroft also documented pituri's economic value to Aboriginal people and the trade in the tobacco along northern and southern Aboriginal trade routes. Bancroft spent five years searching for the main plantation area, but with little success (Bancroft 1877; Watson 1983:8–9).

In 1876 explorer and surveyor W.O. Hodgkinson led the last government-funded expedition into the Simpson Desert, ostensibly to find land suitable for pastoral expansion. But Hodgkinson's diary revealed his main purpose was to discover the source of a valuable native narcotic (ABC Radio National, Radio National, *Hindsight*, 09/01/2000). Pamela Watson's research details European searches to unlock the pituri secrets. She notes that Hodgkinson was frustrated in his efforts because Aboriginal people would not show him where it grew, so he found only one plant growing on a sand ridge. Hodgkinson recognised that the local mob were willing to give him some samples and show him how it was cured but not to disclose the plantations (Watson 1983:9–11).

> The Aborigines were willing to give him some of the prepared pituri, taking it from a trench in the sand where it was undergoing a drying process, but they were not prepared to show him where it grew. (Watson 1983:9)

By the turn of the twentieth century other researchers, such as Charles Winnecke (1887), Walter Roth (1897) and others, had all tried to locate the plantations but none were able to get the information from that area's mob. Aboriginal people guarded the secret. Nevertheless, Roth's research describes in detail the trade in pituri from Carlo on the Mulligan over a wide area of Queensland and the Northern Territory (in Watson 1983:9–11). However, there must have been prior knowledge of Aboriginal tobacco because Mitchell mentions that 'Yuranigh found more of the native tobacco, which the men eagerly asked for some of' (Mitchell 1848:352) while surveying Possession Creek on 16 October 1846,

There is wide debate about when the pituri trade ended. Some historians have recorded the historical processes that affected Aboriginal trading. When the first white settlers moved into the area and took up large pastoral runs in the 1860s, a significant disruption of Aboriginal community life occurred. Like many other places in Australia,

Aboriginal people in this area suffered significant losses to disease and the gun. Bruce Elder notes one such occurrence, when large numbers of Aboriginal people from the nations of Wardamba, Midaga, the Wanganguru, the Nyulubulu, the Wangamadla, and the Yaluyandi were killed (Elder 1988:158–59). The Wardamba massacre, as it is known, took place near Poeppel's Corner, Eastern Simpson Desert. Elder states that the incident is blurred by time, but it began with the kidnapping and rape of a Wardamba woman by a stationhand. The Wardamba warriors retaliated by spearing the station-hand and killing him.

> News of the murder of the white man took some days to filter back to the police forces stationed on the edge of the desert. During this time the tribes in the area . . . had joined the Wardamba people for a corroboree. They gathered near Poeppel's Corner to the west of the Diamantina River . . . The festivities were well underway when the police and their trackers arrived. Once again the opportunity for a large-scale slaughter was there. Driven by irrational hatred and revenge, the police shot randomly at the gathering. Large numbers of innocent people were shot. (Elder 1988:158–59)

Mrs Ditton, from the Tjilpat Aboriginal Land Claim Association, provided evidence (during a Native Title land claim hearing at Birdsville, Queensland, on 8 December 1993), of the disruption to traditional life by the massacre that occurred in 1878 at Kalidjawarra (Poeppel's Corner), Eastern Simpson Desert.

Evidence about the trade in pituri can be found in Australian museums where they document usage of the bag. Such information includes how a pituri bag is made, and the museums also collected several styles of the bag. They note how people carried the bags, what was carried in them, how much the bag would have weighed and the purpose of carrying a bag of goods across the country. Museums have pituri bags on display or in their repositories, and the relevant information regarding manufacture, use and biographical details is stored with these bags (see Figure 27). The information tells us several things, such as provenance, context of the trade and direction of trade (Taylor 1966:145; Terry 1974:63).

Associated Dreaming tracks related to trade in pituri

Contemporary Aboriginal people from the growing areas of the pituri still have traditional affiliation and connection to the country of the Simpson Desert. The Wangkangurru and Wangamadla people lived on the land and used all the resources for a long period of time. Their descendants are familiar with their ancestors and the stories of the Dreaming. These stories, knowledge, and practices have been handed down orally from one generation to the next generation, along with associated historical, social and cultural factors. The knowledge of the Elders from the Wangkangurru and Wangamadla nations will provide context with respect to some of the trade routes.

Figure 27 A Pituri bag on display. Reproduced by kind permission of the National Museum, Australia.

Figure 28 Painting of Two Boys Dreaming. On display in the Simpson Desert National Parks Office, Birdsville.

The Simpson Desert is criss-crossed by the travels of the Two Boys' Dreaming from Witjira (Dalhousie Springs) (see Figure 28). Their travels circle the desert and link with other Dreaming strings such as Emu Dreaming from Mulligan River. The story enters the Lower Simpson Desert via Arrernte country and travels to Parra-parra (a mikiri) in the central Simpson Desert on the South Australian side. They then travelled east, passing through Yarluyandi and Wangamadla country, returning through the desert to Dalhousie. Throughout their journey, the story changed and took on a regional variety, but when they entered the Witjira they would turn back to the original story (Jones 1993:50). The Two Boys' Dreaming took in such locations as Diamantina and Georgina Rivers, north to Glenormiston, on to Mulligan waterholes to Birdsville (Wirrari) (Jones 1993:50). The Two Boys' travels became a major route for people to collect pituri at Dickerie waterhole, north of Birdsville (Jones 1993:50).

Across the Aboriginal landscape, the flow of languages or linguistic affiliations, and the penetration of Dreaming tracks into different language associations and country, connected Aboriginal nations. The flow of stories is associated with activities of the Dreaming heroes and their impact on the landscape in a particular area. Dreaming strings traversed large areas, connecting people and country across the landscape of Australia, and people who move along these communication paths assist the transmission of knowledge. Micha (1970) saw corroborees as a trade in goods, as corroborees increased the knowledge of clan groups, and new corroborees are learned from distant Aboriginal countries (Micha 1970:301).

The Urumbula (Malbunga, or Native Cat) Dreaming is an example of a story string that travels through country from Port Augusta to Alice Springs, and then on to the Gulf of Carpentaria; it has its own regional variants. As the story moved, it travelled over the landscape by way of the Pituri Road. This storyline is part of the much larger Dingo Dreaming or Two Dog story string, which crosses the Simpson Desert where it takes on various regional variants. For example, the eastern Simpson Desert Fire Story connects the peoples of Wangkangurru and Wangkamadla with the Diamantina and Georgina through Pitta-Pitta country and links with the Arrernte people.

The Fire Story is about the journeying of an ancestral fire striker. The place of origin is near Horseshoe Bend on the Finke River, and the course of the fire striker travels south-west to Mulligan River, where it links up with the Two Boys' Story. The Fire Story is about two men from Wangkangurru nation camp on Mararu claypan (Kudnanara) in South Australia, which is a Wangkamadla camping site near Mulligan River. An argument ensues, and as the two Wangkangurru men call the fire toward the camp, they sing to it in Wangkamadla. As they lure the fire into Wangkamadla country, it destroys everything in the camp, except a barking gecko. The two men who caused the fire to come into the country escape by riding away on the backs of two ancestral snakes. The barking gecko is injured by the fire and limps off, heading southwest to Poeppel Corner. As the gecko travels he sings verses in Wangkamadla language. While singing in that language he is moving over the landscape. He loses his tail along the way and enters Poeppel Corner at a salt pan associated with the Rain Story. The gecko is a knob-tailed gecko. The story is told by Mrs Crombie, an Elder from Birdsville, as it relates the Two Boys' story:

Well we stopped at Muncoonie, but we are still travelling south with those Two Boys. They went to those two hills there, just the Two Boys. Totilla – when there at that – dancing there all the mystery, all the story dance. Everybody meeting there and they all dance there. Warrthampa there to dance. And they went down to Annandale then they went south. They danced at Muncoonie like they danced at Taranga, then they danced at Totilla. They took them rocks just outside Annandale, they had big corroboree there then – history there. (*Aboriginal Land Tribunal Report* 1993:314–15)

Mrs Crombie went on with the story:

Those two Boys are still travelling, they go back to Dalhousie, so they are coming down and the next place we have got on the map is Dickerrie. There two trees at Dickerrie one big one and one special tree – well, you can actually see where it's been burnt sometime, the rock has been burnt, and traces of burn mark, which is more or less now petrified and turned into sort of like white – kopi. Fire history also travels through here following down from Cudivera waterhole. At Dickerrie, there are rocks with the burnt and big corroboree place. The name of the place where they got burnt Mukatukapilli. The two Boys go to Dalhousie from Dickerrie where they got burnt at the rock. (*Aboriginal Land Tribunal Report* 1993:318)

Like the Native Cat Dreaming, the Two Boys' story moved pituri; this story travelled into Birdsville from the north for ceremony and then left the way they came, towards Birdsville. Ms Crombie explains the Dream Story of Two Boys as told by the Wangkangurru people from Andado:

The Two Boys come across, through the desert. They come across there to Jardine and Ngalparangurru. At Andado is important site of Wadi tree; it links with the lower Southern Arrernte and Wangkangurru, it symbolises that connection right over the other side of desert' (*Aboriginal Land Tribunal Report* 1993:255). At Ngalparangurru was an important Warrthampa (corroboree) people come from many places Bedourie and people come from Annandale, they come back here, and from Pandi Pandi come up here for big meeting and some from Filayuarratu. All-them come everywhere. People walked to this place, no buggy, no cart, nothing, walk across the desert, the meeting lasted about a couple of weeks, two weeks. People singing and dancing all the time, Ngalpura-Ngura (hand clapping).
    The Two Boys from Dalhousie, that they come across there and they stayed there, and there's no one allowed to swim in water. They'll kill you (*Aboriginal Land Tribunal Report* 1993:259). It big camp for mikiri people for Warrthampa ceremony, Two Boys place. (*Aboriginal Land Tribunal Report* 1993:259)

The Two Boys' story also has history at Jardine Crossing and passes through to Tunkalawarkathi. Kenny Crombie explains the story of place: 'In the river there's rocks

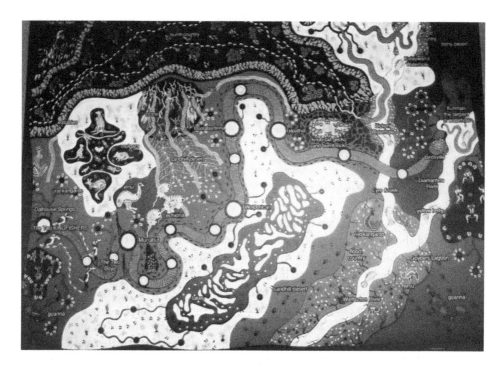

Figure 29 Wangkangurru storyline (trade routes) of the Mura. Painting on the wall of the Simpson Desert National Parks Office, Birdsville.

down there it's a men's place. They come from Jardine's Crossing to have their last drink. They then moved onto Ethabuka up further north' (*Aboriginal Land Tribunal Report* 1993:262–63).

The storyline (see Figure 29) moves through a place called Two Boys, Kadna or Two Boys Hills. Kenny Crombie states that it is an important men's place.

> They did ceremony, like men's business, and then moved on and went on their journey (page 269). They moved heading through to Ethabuka to the north; they turned around at Carlo on Tobermory Station, coming back in a south-westerly direction. They travelled through well-known country but that country is in other people's country, which is at the limits of this country. Arrewerte is a spring where the Two Boys came into Queensland and they headed south-west. That place is the northern point of our country and they turned to Dalhousie. These stories are of great spiritual connection with the land and connection with people; how we relate to them; same as mob in Boulia, that way big connection. (*Aboriginal Land Tribunal Report* 1993:269, 275, 128)

Pituri was also traded along these same story chains into Western Australia. The material was moved along the Two Dogs' Dreaming story, which formed a major trading route (Bourke *et al.* 1980:107).

Sandstone grinding dishes quarried at a site near Stuart Creek, south of Lake Eyre, were also taken north into Bedourie. Material culture of high economic significance was moved from one Aboriginal nation to another stage by stage. This may have taken years; and the value of the object increased the further it got from its point of origin. These items were moved along a major communication route from the west of the Flinders Ranges in South Australia and north to the Gulf of Carpentaria in Queensland. The latter route also linked with the route across Mount Isa to Cloncurry. Material culture that travelled up from the Flinders Ranges was red ochre, fine sandstone grinding dishes, and pituri. Material culture traded south from Cloncurry and the Gulf of Carpentaria was baler shell, stone axes, and pituri (the latter being the major commodity). The trading parties undertook major trading expeditions to the Flinders Ranges for red ochre and to Madlhu for pituri. These parties would travel several hundred kilometres, while others would possibly travel over 1,000 kilometres.

The Simpson Desert was the hub of a major trading route along which goods travelled in all directions. It was a meeting place and a major trading centre for pituri. Tangible cultural material property as well as intangible cultural knowledge passed through the region. One such road that ran from Pituri Creek, on the Northern Territory and Queensland border, to Rockhampton is over 1,600 kilometres long. Just outside of Rockhampton at the Carnarvon Ranges baler shell stencils can be found. At the source of one pituri plantation at Woodnunajilla waterhole (Apwertetywernkwerre) (known as Salt Lake and related to the Snake Dreaming in Arrernte country), Urtneye was harvested and taken to Lake Caroline, where many groups would travel to trade for the tobacco (*Aboriginal Land Tribunal Report* 1993:274). A.W. Howitt, W.E. Roth and pastoralist Lee Reese have all noted the great distances that pituri trading took place – such as the 1,600 kilometre Pituri Creek to Rockhampton route. McConnell (1976) noted that 'Boulia, Goyders Lagoon, and Kopperamanna' also served as pituri trade centres (McConnell 1976:18).

Trade goods

On Wigram Island, off north-east Arnhem Land, people of the Buralpala nation gather diremul (grinding mortars), light grinding stones that are traded all over Arnhem Land. From nearby Elcho Island, red ochre is traded into Arnhem Land and further afield; from Inverway cattle station, the Kurindji (Gurindji) would mine chert and manufacture bifacial spearpoints to trade farther afield. From Daly River, the Wonga traded dance and would travel with traders, offering them 'brinkins' (throwing sticks and bamboo spears). From Borroloola, the Charrada performance would travel with songmen who would also take special ochres and magic string youalya with them. The Irapindji song man would also lead his delegation of traders to the market grounds to trade their spearpoints with the mob from Newcastle Waters, who brought kurabuddies and waradillas (boomerangs) with them (Harney 1950:43–44).

Kevin Tibbett (2002) undertook an archaeological analysis of stone axe exchange in the Lake Eyre basin; he states 'the evidence supports the hypothesis for trade' and that 'stone axes were traditionally brought from Mt Isa to exchange for Pituri along the

Milligan River' (Tibbett 2002:25). The trade in stone axes and pituri flowed along the Mount Isa, Boulia, Glenormiston and Lake Eyre basin trade route and into markets further afield (Tibbett 2002). The Kalkadoons produced a large stone axe designed specifically to be traded at markets; this precipitated a flow of goods through the Channel Country (Tibbett 2002). C.G. Austin's article for the *Special Journal to Mark the Centenary of Queensland 1859–1959* (republished in 1959) acknowledges that the Kalkadoons had access to pituri and exchanged stone tools for the tobacco (Austin 1959:218–29).

Travellers traditionally (and in contemporary times) have commuted across the isolated 'Kalkadoon Road'; it has a long memory, journey men have moved along it from the Townsville area on the east coast to Wyndham area on the west coast. Tourists, law people, business people, profiteers, and people relocating moved along this road, it has long been recognised as a road to travel, complete with its major intersections. Along the Barkley Hwy between Mt Isa and Camooweal is a sign that simply states 'Kalkadoon Road'. The Kalkadoon nation near Mount Isa in Queensland mined for stone tools that were traded far and wide along this road.

Rose (1985) provides a description of what happens when goods are traded along a route. She details the contents of a load or packages that will be passed along a trade route, and points out that these vary after they have passed through one community to the next. All items considered of value locally will be taken, and fresh material will be added for the next community to pass along the route (Rose 1985:31). Hardy notes that 'the strong timber of the north Darling area made excellent boomerangs and spears, which were valuable commodities for trade with areas that lacked supplies of suitable wood' (Hardy 1969:14).

Down the Paroo from the Leichhardt Ranges of Queensland came hard 'greenstone axes and nardoo stones. The axes were delivered unhafted: the handle to be affixed by the new owner. This trade extended down to about Wilcannia' (Hardy 1969:14). Not only did material culture move along these trading ways, but practices such as mourning rituals did as well. In museums around Australia are collections of widow peaks or caps; they were made from gypsum, mixed with water, that was plastered on the hair of women related to the deceased, through marriage or blood. This practice has been recorded in the lower Murray River region, stretching from the New South Wales border to the mouth of the Murray in South Australia. The widow peak falls off after several months and is left on the ground. Mrs Alison James, a Pitta Pitta Elder, told me in an interview that when her husband died she wore one (personal communication, 30 March 2004).

Shells

Earlier it was noted that shells were broadly valued, and in this section I provide a more focused discussion on prototype routes and items. The trade in engraved pearl shells (*ringili*) is described by Mountford (Mountford 1976:50). Engraved pearl shells (see Figure 30) from Dampier Peninsula in north-western Australia were traded as far south as the Great Australian Bight, over 3,200 kilometres from their original point of manu-facture. The oval baler-shell from Cape York, northeastern Australia, was traded as far south as the Flinders

Ranges in South Australia – over 3,000 kilometres from origin (Mountford 1976:50). The shells were used in important ceremonies, which differed from region to region. The engraved pearl shell would be used in initiation ceremonies or circum-cision rituals. Others in the desert regions would use the shells in rain-making ceremonies. Once they had been used, the shells would be traded, and as they moved from their original trading source they would take on a different significance; they might be used as magical devices like love charms (Lonka-lonka) (Mountford 1976:275). The shells would be traded for goods that could not be procured locally and they commanded a high price. Mountford observed that a single shell was traded by the Pitjantjatjara, for 'a large bundle of spears and several spear-throwers and many head-bands' (Mountford 1976:275).

Material culture, like shell pendants, served a largely decorative function in their homelands, but became prized objects that took on a sacred meaning in locations hundreds of kilometres from their place of origin. The baler shell (*Melo diadema*), for

Figure 30 Engraved pearl shells. Reproduced by kind permission of the National Museum of Australia, Canberra.

example, was used in rituals some 1,600 kilometres away from its place of origin in the Gulf of Carpentaria. Shell pendants have been found on rock walls as far south as the Carnarvon Ranges near Rockhampton in Queensland along the Pituri Road (Rose 1985:14).

Baler shell is chipped and ground to form an oval ornament up to 12 centimetres long, which is then suspended on a string through a perforation. From the Gulf, shells became incorporated in the trading system and shell specimens have been collected in South Australia where they were worn as pendants by men to signify status. It has also been reported that baler shells have been traded into Western Australia. On the Kimberley coast in Western Australia pearl shell ornaments were produced in large numbers and they too were traded over areas of 1,700 kilometres. As ornaments they were either worn as plain shells or incised (Isaacs 1980:94).

Other material traded along these paths was gathered from distant coastal shores of the Gulf of Carpentaria, and these included pearl shells gathered from the north-west shores of Western Australia. These shells were used as scrapers, water carriers, chisel bits, and ornaments. However, as they were traded further from their place of origin their value increased. As the value of the shells increased they would acquire ritual significance through the long chain of contact with other groups across the country. Materials that were traded and valued for practical purposes were wood, fibre, and resins which were made into wooden shields and spears, string made from human hair, boomerangs, stone for grinding dishes, and axeheads.

Fur cloaks

There was a lively trade in cloaks made of possum, kangaroo rat, wallaby and kangaroo skins, and some were specially made and designed specifically for trade rather than local use (see Figure 31). Other fur cloaks were manufactured as a status symbol or symbol of office. 'Only five possum-skin cloaks made in south-eastern Australia before 1900 have survived. Two are in Museum Victoria's collection. There are others in museums in Britain, the United States of America and Germany' (*Bunjilaka Gallery*, Melbourne Museum, Victoria 2004).

There would be different preparation techniques for these cloaks according to consumer needs. For example, plain skins would be made for the general community's use, whereas others would be prepared as status symbols with bark fibre plaited in the hem; these were for people who held some rank in the community. For those who held high office in the community, such as lawmakers or spiritual leaders, feathers might also be attached and the skin be engraved/incised with the symbols of office on them. These would also be made of the finest furs and be destined for trade markets (Berndt *et al.* 1993:113).

A trader once exchanged a possum skin rug for three pieces of axe-stone. The axe-stone was considered valuable because of its quality and scarcity. On the other hand, a possum-skin rug required a lot of work to make. Seventy or so possums had to be caught to make one rug and their skins had to be cleaned, dried, worked and sewn into a cloak. (Barlow 1994:12)

Ochre

Many stories relate to trading ways and some of these have a strong connection to the trade in ochre. Red ochre is one of the most important trading items and is used as a pigment for a variety of 'artistic and decorative purposes' (Peterson and Lampert 1985:1). It is used in rock art on wooden and stone material culture, on fur products and to '[adorn] the human body' during corroborrees and spiritual ceremonies. Red ochre quarried from the mines at Parachilna in the Flinders Ranges of South Australia was traded widely in South Australia, the desert areas of Lake Eyre, and the Simpson Desert, New South Wales, Queensland and the Northern Territory. Finds of red ochre at major archaeological sites such as Kenniff Cave in Queensland have been dated at 19,000 years. Other archaeological digs including Miriwun in the Kimberley, Arnhem Land, Cloggs Cave in Victoria and Lake Mungo in New South Wales (Peterson and Lampert 1985:1). This indicates that ochre has been used since antiquity in Australia.

All Aboriginal nations had a form of ochre that was used in everyday life. The best ochre came from only a few sites and was treasured for ceremonial purposes. The ochre from Pukardu Hills was highly sought after and was used for important gatherings and as a tradeable commodity. There are several colours of ochre and each has a geographical and spiritual significance and story. For example, the white ochre from the Lachlan River was kept by the giant kangaroos of the creation period, Wirroowaa. Yellow ochre was traded from the Yirritja moiety group of northeastern Arnhem Land.

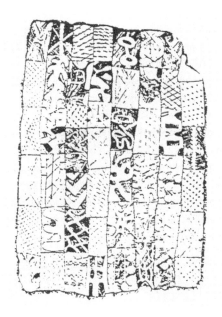

The sacred red ochre, karku, is found in the Flinders Ranges at Parachilna in South Australia and is collected by the Diyari (Dieri) peoples (Stevens 1994: 31–35). The other valued red ochre comes from Western Australia at Wilga mia 'and was quarried on a grand scale' (Peterson and Lampert 1985:1).

The red ochre is the blood of Emu, which was killed by Marindi (Mindari) the dog (Horne & Aiston 1924:128–30). Takaweejee said 'that traders would come from Cloncurry in Queensland to trade their wares of shields made from bean-wood and from New South Wales with

Figure 31 Drawing of a possum/kangaroo skin cloak. Reproduced by kind permission of the Museum Victoria, Melbourne.

their spear shafts and from Alice Springs for the red ochre' (Horne & Aiston 1924:128–30). In the 1930s, the anthropologist A.P. Elkin also traced the songlines of the Mindari, which travels over the landscape from south-west Queensland to Port Augusta (Elkin 1934:187–89). Furthermore, the Two Dogs' Story involves real geological features and provides practical significance to people travelling in the Channel Country. The Two Dogs' Story tells how the red ochre is traded and how it was formed. Non-Aboriginal knowledge systems find it hard to grasp this concept; it is abstract and seems repetitious. However, poetry and song are composed of these mixtures, and verse is about repetition and rhyme, as are Aboriginal stories and songs.

Berndt and others traced the trade routes of the Narrinyeri peoples of South Australia:

> Small parties would go travel through Coorong to Milipi or from the Lower Murray to Encounter Bay via Goolwa. From Goolwa . . . to Currency Creek to Mt. Compass and then on to Willunga and McLaren Vale, down to Tainbarang (Noarlunga) River (the Onkaparinga or Ongkeperinga) to Red Ochre Cove (Mulgali or Putatang, both names meaning red ochre). Another route ran from Encounter Bay up the Inman River, through Muwerang to Yankalilla, meeting other parties from Rapid Bay (Patapungga) and continuing to Myponga (Meipongga), to Aldinga and down the Onkaparinga River. Red Ochre Cove was an important meeting place: Lower Kaurna people would meet those from Encounter Bay, the Lakes and Coorong and exchange various commodities (e.g., gum, shields and spears) for indigenous tobacco, itself presumably traded down from further north, usually through the Dieri (Diyari) from what became the Queensland border. (Berndt *et al.* 1993:19–20)

The extract above provides an example of the movement of people for the purpose of trade in ochre. Berndt noted that this did not only occur in South Australia. Goods flowed through to New South Wales and Queensland along an artery of this route.

Hardy points out that South Australian red ochre found in the Flinders Ranges, and at Noarlunga, were sanctified by myth as the only 'acceptable pigment for the ceremonial painting of Aboriginal bodies. Messengers were dispatched from the Darling to offer spear shafts in exchange for a load, which must have been a cumbersome parcel to carry home' (Hardy 1969:14). Along the route where ochre was traded, the loads would become stories of travel, which are just as important as the cumbersome loads to cart back home. As the Dreaming story is the pathway for trade in ochre, ochre then became the vehicle with which other material property and intellectual property moved along the artery. Alongside ochre that travelled the major commerce routes of Central Australia, were also boomerangs and heavy spears that were to be distributed into Northern Territory, Western Australia, Queensland and along the Murray–Darling Rivers into Victoria, New South Wales, and South Australia.

Marketplaces / trade centres

It is known that on the east coast of Australia people met in large gatherings when resources were being harvested. Some Aboriginal nations had plentiful resources, such as ochre, which was used as a paint pigment, or quality stone for making tools; others would trade stories, song, and dance. Bob Munn, a Gungari person from south-western Queensland, commented in an interview that economics and trade were central to ritual relationships:

> In most cases, trade was conducted on mutual soil and tracks were used as common ways to get from one place to the next even through hostile territory. These routes connected nations. Culture is a series of paradigms linked by economics and surrounded by language, but not linked by language, linked by shared country, display of ability, and dance. Dance acts as a conduit for negotiations. (Bob Munn, personal communication, 16 July 2000)

Trade items read like a veritable shopping list that included various types of ochre, trapping devices such as bird nets and fish traps, various ornaments, hair-belts, pearl shell, boomerangs, weapons, various stone implements, string bags, gum cements, food and medical resources, wild tobacco and intellectual property.

Certain places were identified as established trade-fair sites. The most notable are the bunya feasts in south-east Queensland and the bogong moth feast sites in the south-eastern highlands (Namadgi National Park, ACT). Trade in an Aboriginal sense is based on relationships. Goods are traded from one community to the next.

Oenpelli in the Arhem Land region was a major trading centre, and goods were brought there along established trading routes (see Map 6) (Bourke *et al.* 1980:105). McBryde (1987) explains that along the various routes there were exchange centres, or in the schema of trading, 'marketplaces'. 'These markets, lying at the intersections of communication routes, were crucial in the ebb and flow of exchange transactions'

1a Two kinds of spears (eastern Djamalag people)
1b Nets, fishing lines, baler shells, etc. (northen Djamalag people)
2 Baskets, spears, spear throwers, stone knives, feathered string (Rom people)
3 Human hair twine for belts (Midjan people)
4 Mats and bags (Wurbu people)
5 European goods and bamboo spears (Mamurung people)
6 Stone spear heads and two kinds of red ochre (Njalaidj people (Bourke et al 1980:105).

Map 6 Map detailing movement of goods in the Arnhem Land region with Oenpelli, Northern Territory, as the trade centre.

(McBryde 1987:267). Markets were important because intellectual property and goods that were scarce in various regions were purchased that were then introduced into daily lives. McBryde's research indicates that Kopparamarra, Goyder's Lagoon, Birdsville, Bedourie and Boulia were business hubs (McBryde 1987:267). Isabel McBryde (1980) concludes that Flinders Ranges' ochre was traded into the Cooper Creek or Simpson Desert area in marketplaces, and would then travel to marketplaces at Goyder Lagoon or Boulia, and further to other marketplaces along the trade route (McBryde 1980:160).

A Wonkangurru Elder, Takaweejee (Crooked-Foot Peter), related that traders from 'Kooiannie, Dieri, Wonkonguru, Ngameni, and the Yaurorka' nations came into the area to trade for the red ochre (Horne & Aiston 1924:128–30). George Aiston worked at Lake Eyre as a mounted constable and storekeeper early in the twentieth century, and he describes one of these business hubs as a 'Mecca for clan groups' (Horne & Aiston 1924:128–30). The Wonkangurru people traded their flat grinding dishes, which came from the mines at Gagalbune (Mt Termination SA) and were used for grinding seeds and other foodstuff. These were traded as far as the Diamantina (McBryde 1987:267).

Trade routes were based on songlines: the story of Mindari the dog and the distribution of red ochre through trade provides evidence of this. At these commercial centres, intellectual property was deemed just as important. Trade in song, dance and visual art contributed to the social cultural fabric of all the nations who took part. 'Corroborees could involve hundreds of people and last for days. At such gatherings people performed rituals, settled disputes and arranged marriages. At night they shared stories both old and new through dance and song' (Australian National Museum 2004).

These trade fairs, where tangible and intangible property were traded, enriched the material and intellectual bank of knowledge of those who participated. Roth (1897), Spencer and Gillen (1912), and McCarthy (1939), all traced the path of a particular corroboree, but not through the perspective of trade. Corroborees can be simply about entertainment, they can be about morality, and have an emphasis on education; they can also introduce new technology. In this sense, they are a medium to present information; lines on a body, body ornaments, and colour of paint, the setting they are performed in, are all informative. Corroborees are used to convert intangible knowledge to a tangible form. Technical production makes corroborees a tradable commodity for 'its cultural complexity is deeply rooted in a past whose continuity exceeds that of most nations' (Mulvaney 1981:27).

McCarthy (1939) traced the movement of the Molonga corroboree and found its place of origin centred on the Diamantia River and Cooper Creek. The corroboree travelled to the Dieri, and across to the Western Australian border before returning to Central Australia (McCarthy 1939:84). Roth described the Molonga corroboree in Queensland in 1897, and Spencer and Gillen observed in 1904 that the Aranda (Arrernte) people also perform Molonga corroboree. However, there are several different names for this corroboree, and one of these is Tjitjingalla corroboree (Spencer and Gillen 1899:718). The Molonga corroboree was exchanged from north-west Queensland to the Great Australian Bight between 1893 to 1918, a distance of over 1,700 kilometres (Isaacs 1980:91–94). Anthropologists, such as A.W. Howitt in 1861, also noted that shields made from wood that did not grow in the region were bartered and that they came from great distances along the Cooper Creek. Walter Roth also referred to 'local markets' operating in Queensland (Roth [1897] 1984:264).

In South Australia, four major commerce routes intersect. One major route runs from the north-western peninsula to Adelaide, the second linked people of the upper Murray and into the Darling. The third linked people from the Coorong to the south-east commerce route where potatoes, radishes, yams and smoke-dried fish were distributed. The fourth exchange route ran along the river systems to commerce centres where 'intellectual property would be traded through ceremony, [and] art and songs were exchanged' (Berndt *et al.* 1993: 116–17). Generally at these intersections or cross roads, trade fairs would be established and various business activities would occur.

Alfred William Howitt (1882) attended an initiation ceremony while on fieldwork in the Shoalhaven River area of New South Wales. He saw a large number of Aboriginal nations attending the corroboree and also witnessed a trade in goods. This he describes as an Aboriginal 'market'. In one trade, goods were being haggled over by two men in an area that was set aside for trade. One of the men was trying to trade a complete set of corroboree ornaments, which comprised of 'one ngulia (fur string opossum belt), four burrian (men's kilts), and one gumbrun (nosepeg) (Howitt 1882 papers, 5). The trader negotiated for 'ten fighting warangun (boomerangs), ten gumma (grasstree spears), bembata (fighting shield), one gugerung/bundi (fighting club) and one wommera (spearthrower)' (Howitt 1882 papers, 5). He also witnessed women taking the opportunity to engage in trading of material culture such as opossum rugs, bags and digging sticks (Howitt 1882 papers, 5).

In 1880, Howitt also attended a trade market at Koppermana in South Australia, which he called 'one old trade centre'. Koppermana consists of two Aboriginal words: 'kapara', meaning hand, and 'mara', meaning root. Rose (1985) also explains, 'trade developed along the Cape York and Central trunk routes' along which were 'major gathering places (markets) where a type of haggling took place' (Rose 1985:34).

Just as 'all roads lead to Rome', so too is Koppermana the centre for trade, and the roads leading to it are mara, the root. Howitt acknowledged the language used at Koppermana comes from the Dieri Aboriginal nation (Howitt 1882 papers, 5). Howitt attended a marketplace at Cooper Creek, and while camped at a waterhole on what he calls Yantruwunta country, he interviewed a man about a shield. The man told him that 'the shield he traded for from a neighbour from Cooper Creek who got the clubs from a tribe further to the northeast' (Howitt 1882 papers 5). He also told Howitt that the Yantruwunta people traded 'stone grinding slabs, ochre from tribes to the south, skins from tribes in the south-east' (Howitt 1882 papers, 5). He also witnessed the trade of 'a portion of a large univalve shell', worn as a pendant, which came from tribes in the far north (Howitt 1882 papers, 5).

Walter Roth (1897) described several trade markets at Lake Nash, Austral Downs and Camooweal. The trading partners came from the Channel Country of 'Yaroinga tribe and the Workia tribe'. They traded in 'pearl shell, eagle-hawk feathers, stone-knives, large coolamons, human-hair belts, spears, hook and simple boomerangs, European knives, blankets, shirts, trousers, as well as the plant pituri, small coolamons, emu feathers' (Walter Roth 1897 in *AIA* issue 2, Queensland 1983:8). The nations around the Toko Ranges travelled up to Gordons Creek to a marketplace, using the Aboriginal road along Georgina River via Glenormiston. These people traded 'pituri, opossum-twine, blankets, bark ochre, boomerangs, stone-knives, human-hair belts', and had relations with the nations of Kalkadoon and people of the east toward the coast (Walter Roth 1897 in *AIA* issue 2, Queensland 1983:8).

During his investigation into Aboriginal trade, Roth attended what he calls a 'swapping ground', a marketplace, at Boulia in western Queensland. He witnessed the trade in opossum-hair and eagle-hawk feather ornaments, mother-of-pearl, and curiously barbed spears, which he noted were only made by one tribe in the Northern Territory, a distance of over 1,000 kilometres away (Walter Roth 1897 in *AIA* issue 2 Queensland 1983:8).

> Many people of both sexes gather at these markets, and so it is that ideas are interchanged, superstition and traditions are handed from district to district, new words and terms are picked up, and corrobborees are learnt and exchanged. Thus, tribes occupying territory at opposite extremes of north-west Queensland are brought into contact. (Walter Roth 1897 in AIA issue 2, Queensland 1983:8)

Rose (1985) also points out that Parachilna ochre was highly sought-after and is part of a mythological dog story string, and that the Dieri people were important middlemen in the trade of ochre collected from the Flinders Ranges in South Australia. They travelled south for the ochre and north for the trade in pituri (Rose 1985:35). Kopperamanna is situated in Dieri country and has been identified by researchers as an important market place (Rose 1985:35).

Letnic (2000) undertook an *Australian Geographic* funded expedition into the Simpson Desert for pituri. He located pituri bushes at Toko waterhole on the northern edge of the desert. Letnic and his team were following the explorer Hodgkinson, who followed Aboriginal paths to water. Letnic states that Toko was 'once a major distribution point for pituri where it would be traded for goods such as dugong-tusks from the Gulf of Carpentaria' (Letnic 2000:113). McConnell (1976) states that there was a 'trunk route' for pituri and that it begins at Bedourie and travelled to Birdsville, the Lower Diamantina, Goyders Lagoon, Mungeranie, Kopperamanna, where the pituri was distributed in many directions (McConnell 1976: 18).

Finally, Aiston (1937) also sighted a trading place where crowds would be waiting at 'Annandale on the Herbert to take [pituri], people would come from Birdsville, Bedourie, Urandangie, and down the Herbert (see Map 7). Others would be waiting to take pituri and other goods down the Diamantina to Goyder's Lagoon then into distant markets in the east and west' (Aiston 1937:373). He also witnessed a trading centre at Birdsville, where people 'would come in there from the overland telegraph line, Innamincka, Arrabury, Durham and Broken Hill' to purchase 'big lots' of pituri (Aiston 1933:376). Innamincka is recorded as being an Aboriginal trading centre. The name 'Innamincka' is formed by two Aboriginal words: 'yenie', meaning your and 'mincai', meaning shelter or home (Thallon 1967:311). The Yandruwantha, Yawarawarrka, Ngamini and Diyari (Dieri) people lived along Cooper Creek. Innamincka is

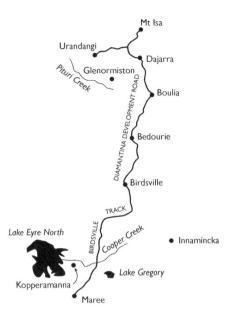

Map 7 Interpretation of information provided by Roth (1897), Aiston (1937), McConell (1976) and Rose (1985) detailing trading centres established along the Pituri Road.

surrounded by the Cooper Creek lake system, which is fed by monsoonal rainfall from central Queensland filters into the Cooper by way of the Barcoo, Thomson, and Wilson Rivers (*Innamincka Regional Reserve: Park Guide* July 2002).

Stone

> In south-eastern Australia, greenstone, a stone superior for the manufacture of axe heads, supports a vast exchange system. People came from hundreds of kilometres away to the quarries at Mt. William near Dayslesford, the only place in Australia that this valuable resource can be found. (Australian National Museum Canberra [2004] *The Importance of Trade*)

The Mount William quarry site is an Aboriginal site of national significance, and it is also of cultural significance to the Wurundjeri people for the greenstone, which is a metamorphic rock. The site covers several hectares and has been worked for thousands of years. The greenstone has been traded over many parts of Victoria, into New South Wales, and South Australia. 'Mount William axe-heads have been found up to 600 kilometres from the quarry' (Information Sheet, Aboriginal Affairs, Victoria).

Isabel McBryde investigated the trade of Victorian greenstone axes from the Mt William site near Lancefield, along the lines of distribution into New South Wales and South Australia, using anthropological information, museum collections and petrography. She found that these stone axeheads were traded into Cohuna in the Murray area, as well as Mt Camel Mungo Station east of the Darling, and north to Balranald in New South Wales (McBryde 1975:33).

Mick Leon describes finding this stone at Forster on the central coast of New South Wales: 'One day there was this Archo [archaeologist] looking at sites with me and I showed him a stone axehead at the site. His response after examining the stone was that the axe stone comes from a quarry in Victoria, Mt Williams' (Mick Leon, personal communication 2004). As it can be seen, 'Aboriginal people had organised networks of exchange that extended from one side of the continent to the other' (Australian National Museum [2004] *The Importance of Trade*).

The Kimberley region provides further evidence in the trade of stone for tools, where the 'making of spearheads from chalcedony, opalescent and similar stone' took place (Barlow 1979:2). The Kimberley mob's manufacturing technique made the spearhead a unique and highly sought-after product. Anthropologists, archaeologists, and museologists have traced stone distribution paths. For example, Micha (1970) linked the technique of the Wonkonguru (east of Lake Eyre) spearheads to the style of the spearheads from the Kimberley. He also stated that the Aranda, Kaitish, Unmatjera, Warramunga and Tjingilli nations in Central Australia were privileged recipients of these spearpoints from the Kimberley (Micha 1970:289).

Regional specialisation was a feature of tool component manufacture (Rose 1985). The people of the Victoria and Wickham Rivers of Western Australia added spearpoints to bamboo, which was traded into the community. This would then be traded further afield as a finished bamboo spear. People from this area also used iron to make spearpoints such as the 'shovel nose' (Rose 1985:26–27).

Isobel McBryde, from the pre-history department at the Australian National University, has found that stone axes found in the Simpson Desert area of Madlhu have the same silcrete and diorite (extremely hard material) as stone from the Cloncurry quarry. McBryde found that the stone axes from Cloncurry moved westward through the Mulligan River, and south-east into the desert country (personal communication 2004). Henry Page, from the Tjilpatha Land Claim Association, stated that, 'The stone axe, the blue metal type, and I don't think there is any blue metal around the desert here, so I think they traded with those axes' (Henry Page in *Aboriginal Land Tribunal Report* 1993:183).

Several important roads or communication routes are associated with the Dreamtime ancestors. The Dreamtime ancestors first travelled the country making all the songlines (trade routes/common ways), and linking totems and moieties across vast areas and national boundaries. Each of these routes is explained by ancestral myths of the 'Two Dog' (see Map 9), the 'Rainbow Serpent' (Central Australia), and Galaru (the Rainbow Serpent of the Kimberley). Further, the 'Two Snake' story (Western Queensland), Yamma-coona (Central Australia Western Queensland), the 'Seven Sisters' Dreaming from the Northern Territory, the Molongo correborree (South Australia and Central Australia) and 'Pigeon Dreaming' (see Map 11) all link Aboriginal communities across the landscape of Australia. These story lines were routes used to travel and communicate with other communities. These routes are marked below in the section on Trading Paths; they often followed the rivers, valleys, mountain range, and coastal belt.

The following section represents a combination of Mitchell, Gregory and Hodgkinson's surveys, as well as Buchanan's droving maps. Information has been taken from their journals and compared to the Aboriginal trading routes in Maps 19, 20 and 23.

Trading paths

In Aboriginal Australia, trading occurred across the breadth of the Australian continent and flowed from one nation to the next (Bourke *et al.* 1980:105). There are several important trade routes in Aboriginal Australia which are based on the movements of the Dreamtime ancestors (Bourke *et al.* 1980:106). Along these, storylines provided

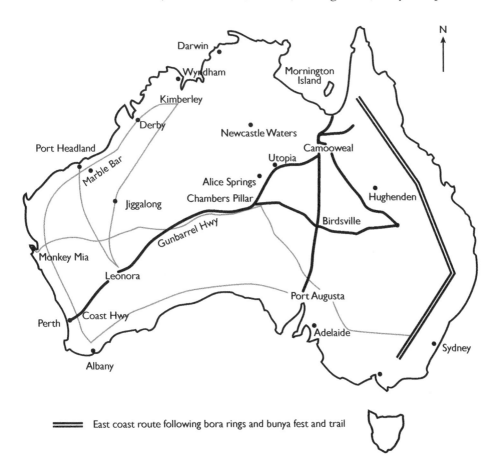

Map 8 The east coast route follows the national horse riding trail. Aboriginal people travelling to the Bunya Fest would follow this route, which is part of a chain of Bora rings/grounds along the Great Diving Range of the east coast.

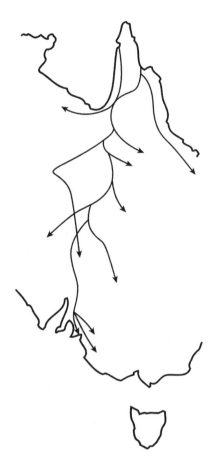

Map 9 Cape York to South Australia route.

chains of connection that linked Aboriginal nations across vast distances and across other Aboriginal nations' boundaries.

For example, the trade in pituri and stone axeheads is known to have occurred in the Queensland Channel Country. Alf Nathan told me that when trading parties moved through country, smoke signals along the path indicated the way to follow. 'The fires would be lit up on the high lookouts and would be kept burning until they concluded business. The fires would do two things: one would be to show the way and the other was to tell everyone that traders were coming' (Alf Nathan, personal communication April 2004).

The most important trade routes identified are:

1. *East coast route*: from the Torres Strait down the northeastern coast of Cape York and down the Great Diving Range into Victoria (McCarthy 1939:99, Rose 1985:13). Jardine followed this route in 1864 as did The Australian Bicentennial National Trails. The trade in bunya nuts flowed along the Great Dividing Range and the 3,000 kilometre route also incorporates the major bora grounds utilised for the Daramulan initiation rights (see Map 8) (Bourke *et al*. 1980:46).

Map 10 Kimberley to Eyre Peninsula route.

2. South eastern route: down the Murray–Darling basin to Port Augusta, following the river systems to the east coast (Harney 1950:44). Several stock routes follow this course and the most famous was Harry Redford who drove his stolen cattle from Cunnamulla to Adelaide. The major stock route that follows this track is the Darling route, which carried stock and people from south-western Queensland through New South Wales, Victoria and on to Adelaide. Major Mitchell also followed this route on his three explorations. Aboriginal people moved axe heads, twine, possum skins and other goods along the route (see Massola 1971:71 appendix 4).

3. Cape York to South Australia route: from the western coast of Cape York and across the top end to Normanton, following the inland river systems and connecting with the Murray–Darling catchment areas. The Birdsville Track lies along this route and has many storylines. For example: the Rainbow Serpent, Two Dog, Two Boys and Urumbula (McConnell 1976:74). The highway that runs through Parachilna to Port Augusta follows the path of the emu, and the railway line that heads north to Oodnadatta follows an Aboriginal road (McConnell 1976:74) (see Map 10). Leichhardt's 1844 survey took in the part of the trail that runs across the top end of Australia. Mitchell also followed part of this route in 1845, as did Gregory in 1855 when he surveyed from west to east. The Great Northern Road, the Channel Country, and the Gulf Road stock routes also follow this road.

4. **Kimberley to Eyre Peninsula route**: this Central Australian route (see Map

111

10) **has** three arteries in north-western Australia, which branch out from the Kimberley, and head south-west to the Warramanga people of Tennant Creek and onto the Barkly Highway to Mt Isa. Another branch connects the Victoria and Daly Rivers by way of the Buchanan Highway. Finally, the Kimberley connects to the east coast by a route that runs from Arnhem Land to Roper River by way of Victoria Highway. Two major trading routes converge in Arnhem Land: one runs from the west by way of Carpentaria Highway and the other from the east along the Hell Gate's track. The central Australian route also connects the Kimberley to the Eyre Peninsula through the totemic Wadi-Kudjara (two brothers, Kukuradi and Mumba) route that follows the Tanami Track and Stuart Highway (Bourke *et al.* 1980:47). In addition, the route from the Kimberley to south-western Australia later became the Canning Stock Route (McCarthy 1939:99; Rose 1985:13–18; Bourke *et al.* 1980:106). Leichhardt also travelled over one of these routes across the top end of Australia from east to west in 1844. In 1855 Gregory also travelled from west to east across the top end of Australia. Further several stock routes such as the Murranji stock route follow these paths (see Map 11).

5. *Kimberley to south-western Australia, and north-western route to Arnhem Land*: these connect to a major route heading south through the Central Desert (the Overland Telegraph Line) following the Rainbow Serpent (Bourke *et al.* 1980:46). The course then divides into two branches; the first from Alice Springs south-east to Lake Eyre following the Numbakulla Dreaming via the Oodnadatta Track, and the other south-west to Ooldea (Bourke *et al.* 1980:46). These two routes are also stock routes used for conveying cattle to the marketplaces on the coast (Harney 1950:46) (see Map 11).

6. **Pituri Road's central point is located in the Channel Country** and moves out over the Mulligan River and Pituri Creek to Rockhampton. Hodgkinson followed this route on his survey expedition in 1876 (Harney 1950:44; Barlow 1994). There are also several important stock routes that follow the southward flows of the Channel Country Rivers: one passes through Birdsville to the railhead at Marree, and the other twists east and crosses the lower edge of the Binditoota Plateau past Windorah and on to the Cooper to Quilpie or Charleville. The eastern route lay across the stony plains and rough range country and was used to connect to Brisbane markets via rail. The southern route follows the Diamantina toward the South Australian railhead, Marree. Marree was the terminus for the Adelaide markets (Duncan-Kemp 1961:16). The Birdsville route followed the course of the Diamantina River, the border fence at Birt's Hole and Andrawilla, then past Goyder Lagoon to Marree in South Australia (Duncan-Kemp 1961:19) (see Map 5).

Each of the trade routes identified above has been analysed in some detail, and constitute the beginnings of significant future research. However, it is in some ways misguided to discuss Aboriginal trade in a single region because the complex network of trading routes are holistic: the songlines and Dreaming also link trade goods and trade centres. In the Simpson Desert, for example, trade in ochres and pituri occurred over an area roughly covering 1,440,000 square kilometres – with the maximum distances being 3,000 kilometres in length (McConnell 1976:81).

Storylines

Each story or songline had several different storystrings attached to it and one story told at its beginning could (and often would) be different when it reached its destination. For example, the Two Dog story travels from Mornington Island to Burketown and down the Channel Country but it also crosses over the water from Mornington Island to Aurukun. At a place called Dingo Leach it travels down the western side of Cape York Peninsula in Queensland. Both stories converge near Camooweal and head down the Channel Country to Port Augusta. At the present time the Mornington Islander Dancers perform the 'Two Dog Story'; and in 2004 an Elder Narrimbi (Frank Watt) danced this story all over Queensland and during the week-long National Aboriginal Islander Day Observance Committee (NAIDOC) festival (May 2004). He performed it in Mount Isa, Gympie, and at the Cooroy Butter Factory on the Sunshine Coast in June 2004.

Deborah Rose (1987) highlights the route of the Two Dog story and illustrates it on a map as the 'Cape York–South Australia Route'. Aboriginal storystrings for the trade in pituri flow along the water systems of the Channel Country, the trade route that comes from the western side of Cape York Peninsula and follows the river system to Lake Eyre and on to Port Augusta in South Australia. Along the way the story disperses into other directions, for example, from Pituri Creek to Rockhampton following the inland rivers. Aboriginal artists perform songs and stories along the Pituri Road, and take in several trade centres or marketplaces (Rose 1985:14).

The red ochre in the Two Dog Dreaming story is the blood of the mythological ancestral emu, Kuringii, who was chased by two ancestral dingoes, Kilowilinna and Perilingunina from the Innaminka region. Kuringii was chased from Innaminka down the Cooper Creek to Mount Alick, where it changed into a mountain to fight the dingoes before turning and heading due east (the mountain is still a landmark for Aboriginal travellers and traders today). While in full flight, Kuringii met a man with a pack of dingoes at the foot of the Flinders Ranges. The leader of this pack of dingoes was called Thorijurra, a particularly ferocious dog. Following an epic battle, the dingoes killed Kuringii with the assistance of the man. After the battle, the man turned into a hill, which is the first hill at the fringe of the Flinders Ranges. The exhausted pack of dingoes sought a resting place and found a cave called Jerinna. As they rested, they died and turned into huge dolomite limestone boulders. Kilowilinna and Perilingunina, who had joined the battle with the pack of dingoes, were turned into two high peaks known by the European name of St Mary's Peaks. The blood of Kuringii became the sacred red ochre found at Parachilna Creek. The red ochre was collected and traded across the continent of Australia (McBryde 1980:92, Stevens 1994:31–35).

There are other versions of this Dreaming story. McConnell (1976) informs us of another which is about a dog that travels from Kopperamanna Dieri country. The 'dog chases some emus to Oorowilanie Parachilna where the dog turns himself into a hill, and the emus continue on to Spencer's Gulf' (McConnell 1976:68). The emus turn back to Parachilna and die where the red ochre is found (McConnell 1976:68). These Dreaming stories do change from location to location, but they all have the same theme of travel and trade for goods at some distant location. This story is also associated with the Mindiri emu ritual, and the people of the Yawarawarrka, Karangura, Diyari, Yarluyandi and Ngamini of the Simpson Desert region (Hercus 1990:158).

In the late 1990s, Ray Beamish (a Welsh-born white man) painted the Two Dog Dreaming story that he had heard from Aboriginal men at Utopia. He called the painting 'Storm in Atnangkere Country II', entered it in the 1996 Telstra National Aboriginal and Torres Strait Islander Art Award, and won. The Aboriginal community was outraged over cultural integrity and theft. The story was reported in all the major newspapers as an 'art scandal', and led many to question the originality and authenticity of Aboriginal art (McCulloch 1997:10; Nicholls 1997:44; Ryan 1997:17). And yet, Beamish's actions brought the Aboriginal tradition of storytelling and painting for meaning to the attention of the Australian public and highlighted how the Two Dog Story travels huge distances across the Australian landscape.

The Aboriginal conceptual landscape is criss-crossed with story or songlines that link nations across the continent. There is a complex series of symbolic motifs related to topographical features, which people learn through the unique story/songline trading system (Cowan 1992:79).

C.P. Mountford describes a song journey – Jarapiri the Great Snake – undertaken by two Walbiri men from Central Australia. One of the Walbiri men was being initiated and the other had a responsibility as a learned fellow to teach the stories so that the knowledge was kept alive in the community. The uninitiated man was taught the symbolic representations of the places they visited along the 160-kilometre route. This was done through body painting, song, sand drawings, and dance. Once the journey was completed the initiated took his place in the community to care for the country (Mountford in Cowan 1989:61–64).

Yoola and the Seven Sisters, told by Minyanderri (Pitjantjatjara nation) and recorded by Roland Robinson (1966:90–93), is a Dreamtime creation story which explains that after moulding the earth, the sisters travelled to the stars. The story is about travel, where to find water, and identifies geographical features they would encounter when travelling (Robinson 1966:90–93). Songlines are not merely conceptual lines across the Aboriginal landscape, just as boundaries are not merely conceptual lines in the European landscape. Just as boundaries may be policed, patrolled or repaired, so songlines are travelled and maintained, and acquire physical manifestations as routes of travel.

Aboriginal roads and tracks are maps; they are connections to country, they are about human movement, metaphor journeys, and the link between the spirituality of the self with the landscape. Aboriginal pathways are also about people, Dreaming stories and 'walkabout' – that is, the pace of life, the 'cadence of walking' (Reser *et al.* 2000:42).

When discussing Aboriginal paths, it is difficult to separate trade in material property and Aboriginal metaphysics and cosmology. Not knowing where to find water was fatal for people travelling on foot in the Channel Country. Dotted across this landscape are permanent mound springs or mikiri, fed by water that is pushed up from the underground artesian basin. These mound springs are important features recalled in song, stories, carvings, and drawings.

They are significant places and form part of the Dreaming tracks of the ancestral beings. These places are real geographical features and are reference points for travellers, so they have both a mythological and a practical significance. We can appreciate the innate power and energy of Aboriginal space more fully when the Dreaming is taken into account. To consider place through the Dreaming gives meaning to the inherent connectivity of contrasting roads and paths in North Queensland, the Great Sandy Desert, the Wet Tropics, the dry of Arnhem Land and the rugged Kimberley.

Song/story

Aboriginal story of place is important to the well-being of the country and also the well-being of Aboriginal communities. Rose states that 'Dreaming strings fix country and people, demarcating human and geographical identity. Some Dreamings belong to a particular locality while others travelled through many areas establishing connections between them' (Rose 1992:52–56). She explains that 'several different geographical regions and languages are brought into a relationship of joint responsibility as co-owning series' (Rose 1992:52–56). Each group creates a relationship based on a Dreaming story or songline.

> Each part of a beach, hill, water, creek, river or spring was sung in the song-map chants. And as people heard these songs they memorised the scenes and places. For the song-men are the oral map-makers of the tribe, and the wanderings of the culture heroes are the roads across the land. (Harney 1950:44)

As a story travelled over the landscape it brought together different languages and people; the story also varied according to the language and geographical location, but it retained the original theme. 'Each tribal group has only a part of the story, and to learn the whole myth one would need to trace it from its beginning through to its conclusion' (Alex Barlow 1979:5). In many respects the stories/songs relate to trade in intellectual property.

The Simpson Desert area is a song cycle that moves around the country of the Wangkangurru people and follows a chain of connections to other stories. The Two Men storyline moves out of the desert to instruct others to the east and south-west of the desert about the MaRaru corroboree and is celebrated in the form of a toa (Hercus 1987:64).

Songlines, as Isabel McBryde (2000) states, are 'associated exchange networks [and are] measured in thousands of kilometres. They are among the world's most extensive systems of human communication' (Isabel McBryde 2000:158). The ritual ceremonial journeying to trade along prescribed communication routes to collect goods and to learn new ideas was mapped for a traveller through song cycles, songlines and tangible objects.

It is interesting to follow some of these paths, and consider the associated Dreaming stories that are attached to the landscape. For example, a part of the Two Snakes story string from the Lake Eyre region was told to me by Tom Sullivan, an Elder at Dajarra, just south of Mount Isa. One of these snakes is an important Dreaming figure of the mob from Dajarra country.

> The Rainbow Serpent was chased here to Dajarra by a bird; this bird is a little brown bird about 20 cm long with white spots under its wings which comes out at night and chases insects. The bird has been identified as a nightjar. The Rainbow Serpent went from Dajarra to Woodul rockhole between Mistake bore, Pomegranate bore, and then straight down to Boulia. (Tom Sullivan, personal communication, 12 July 2002)

This story provides a chain of connection from the Victoria River in Western Australia, across the Northern Territory, down through Queensland and Lake Eyre to Port Augusta in South Australia. It relates to the trade in ochre and mentions most of the major trading ways. The stories are related to the tracks made by ancestral beings from the Dreaming, and are based on the movement of goods and major produce.

Isabel McBryde (2000) examined the trading expeditions to Pukardu Hill near Parachilna for red ochre. Her case study of long-distance exchange traced the song cycle of the Urmbula, and the main travels routes for over 900 kilometres. The song cycle belongs to the Dieri and Southern Aranda people. Urmbula is a song about the native cat, which links Amewara (Port Augusta, South Australia) to the Simpson Desert. She states that the 'Diyari, Yandruwantha, Wangkangarru and Wangkumara followed the actual path of the Dreamtime ancestral being' (McBryde 2000:157–58).

Yarralin peoples, who live around Victoria River Downs in the Northern Territory, told Deborah Bird Rose (1992) about a songline that she calls 'Dreaming strings'. 'Pigeon Dreaming' follows the Victoria River from the desert fringe to its coastal inlet. Two pigeons, a brother and sister, started at Buchanan Spring where they were speaking the Gurindji language (see Map 12). The brother was carrying a grinding stone, and as he did not have a hairbelt to tuck it in, he placed it on his head. As he travelled, he lost pieces of the stone, which are still visible as massive sandstone outcrops. Along the route from Buchanan Spring to Rifle Hole on the Victoria River, the pigeons spoke the Gurindji language. But from Wingkirani (another waterhole) to Mimosa Yard they spoke the Bilinara language. Near Camfield, in the Bilinara language area, they turned away from the river but were stopped from speaking the Mudbura language by other Dreamings. After speaking the Bilinara language they changed to Karangpurru and later again changed to Ngaliwuru (Rose 1992:52–56). Gregory followed this route in 1855 while surveying a route to the East Coast (see Maps 11 & 12).

Underneath the maps drawn by the early European surveyors' of Leichhardt, Mitchell, the Gregory brothers, the Jardine brothers and Hodgkinson, as well as the stockmen of that period, can be found Aboriginal story lines. For example, to follow the Dreaming story of the Yarralin people from Victoria River in Western Australia a chain of connection can be made. This story string, known as Pigeon Dreaming, links Aboriginal travellers along the Canning Stock Route to the people of the Yarralin nation located around the Victoria River region in the Northern Territory.

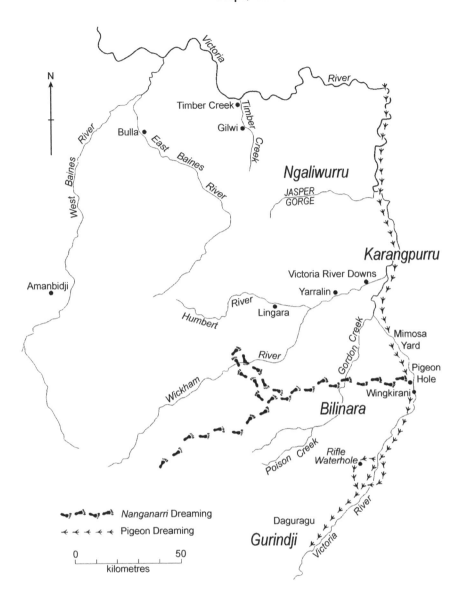

Map 11 Yarralin people's tracks of the Nanganarri and Pigeon Dreamings strings. Nanganarii Dreaming follows a track between Wickham River and Gordon Creek to Pigeon Hole. This Dreaming crosses both Wickham River and Gordon Creek. Pigeon Dreaming follows Victoria River. Gregory followed both of these Dreaming tracks on his survey of 1855–56. Reproduced by kind permission of Deborah Bird Rose.

The Gregory brothers spent several months in 1856 mapping this area. From here the story string moved west to east across the Top End of Australia. The Gregory brothers also followed this path along what is known as the Murranji Stock Route. The story string enters Queensland around Cloncurry and flows across to Ravenshoe or up the western coast of Cape York.

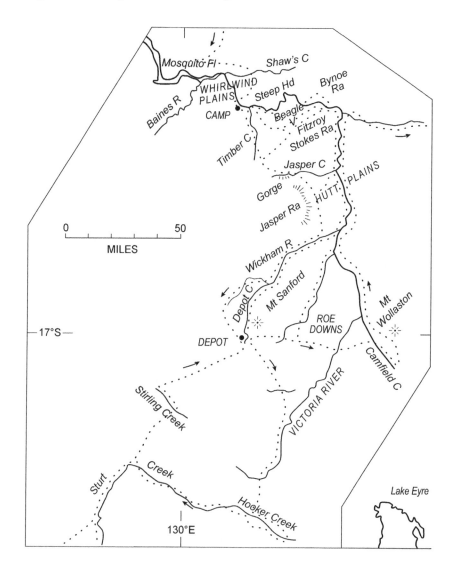

Map 12 Gregory's northern survey of 1855–56, in Birman and Bolton (1972). While surveying around Victoria River Gregory followed the Pigeon Dreaming track south along Victoria River where he encountered Wickham River which he followed and subsequently established a depot. At the point of the depot, Nanganarii Dreaming crosses the river and turns back to Victoria River to cross Gordon Creek. Gregory followed this Dreaming track during his survey.

Once the story string moves into Queensland, it takes on a regional variance of the Two Dogs Dreaming story. Interpretations of these story strings give meaning to the landscape and bring to life the movement of the ancestral beings of the Dreaming over the country. The stories are incorporated in song cycles and point to mythological sites, which are important water wells used by the ancestral beings. The Two Dog Dreaming story then travelled south to Birdsville.

Summary

It has always been believed that Aboriginal material possessions are relatively simple, but as demonstrated in this chapter these objects are functional for those who can 'read' them. Aboriginal ability to plot and assist long expeditions for the purposes of travel and trade has been largely unrecognised. When we consider the ritual learning styles and the recordings in song, drawings and etchings, we are able to determine how the Australian landscape is criss-crossed with songlines laid down in the Dreamtime: they are known as trading ways or Dreaming tracks. Explorers and stockmen also utilised these tracks, as we can see from their trails, diaries and maps of their wanderings. There are few surviving examples of Aboriginal navigational aids, very little documentation and even less available knowledge. It is difficult to collate data on Aboriginal trade

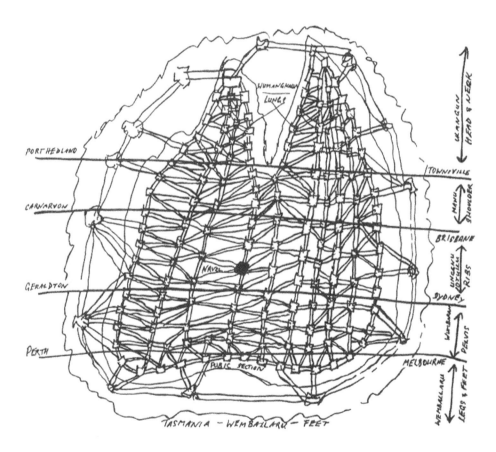

Map 13 David Mowaljarlai's (1993) map of trade routes and storylines linking Aboriginal nations across Australia. From David Mowaljarlai and Jutta Malnic, *Yorro yorro everything standing up alive: spirit of the Kimberley* (Perth: Magabala Books). Yorro Yorro is the story of the Wandjina creation spirits and their transformation into ancestor beings and eventually into human form. It is the story of Aboriginal creation and the renewal of nature and life. Reproduced by kind permission of Magabala books.

routes because of the Aboriginal silence on the subject of Dreaming tracks, as well as their still keenly felt stress of having been invaded and trying to survive the invasion.

Aboriginal people have a culture for travel and used directional aids that were well developed and diverse in their material forms, both in terms of subject matter and scale. Evidence of the trade routes in Aboriginal Australia indicates that Australia was a network of peoples 'economically integrated' by the Dreaming (Rose 1985:22). David Mowaljarlai (1993) detailed the interconnectedness of Aboriginal people in his map that linked Dreaming stories (see Map 13). Evidence suggests that the further cultural material was traded from point of origin, the more its use changed and its value increased; we have seen this in the case of the trade in baler shell (Rose: 1985:33). By interpreting Aboriginal knowledge of the landscape and learning about its secrets, Europeans assimilated Aboriginal knowledge of roads into their sphere of knowledge and mapped them on their charts, thereby creating text with which to read the landscape.

CHAPTER FIVE

To Travel Is To Learn

European exploration of Australia, and the Channel Country in particular, was made possible by Aboriginal trading paths and waterways. Without the assistance of Aboriginal people, exploration would have been much more difficult and time consuming. Once the survey of lands was completed and the old tracks of Aboriginal society annexed, so too was native title: on the mainland in Queensland by 1830, and in the Torres Strait by 1879 (Commonwealth Native Title Act 1993).

Surveyors quickly expanded European occupation and territories, and they coloured the map of Australia in their image. These people adopted a familiar pattern of action: they used Aboriginal trackers and guides, enlisted their cooperation and then usurped Aboriginal resources; this was a dynamic process that will now be explored in detail with reference to Queensland.

Mitchell, Leichhardt, Burke and Wills, Oxley, Landsborough, Kennedy, Jardine and McKinlay are historical actors from the European Australian cultural memory. All surveyed, plotted, and named the Aboriginal landscape for the purpose of owning it and to make it recognisable for their cultural group. Through their writing about their travels, we share their experiences and interpret their observations, and can reflect on the Aboriginal landscape.

Tindale records his observations of explorers and pioneers:

> Where such men were accompanied by aborigines with local knowledge, it is probable that to avoid transgression of the territories of others, for which the aborigines could be held responsible, pioneer whites were always steered along tribal boundaries and through neutral areas. Once these lines of European movement became established, they persisted. Anyone studying maps can find instances. For example, the boundary between Kitja and Malngin in north-western Australia is followed almost exactly from Hall's Creek to Wyndham and even when approaching Wyndham the track divides two tribal boundaries. (Tindale in Carter 1987:338)

A successful survey depended on the use of Aboriginal knowledge. Yuranigh, from the Aboriginal nation of Wiradjuri, travelled with Mitchell in 1836 and 1845. Leichhardt also took two Aboriginal trackers on his first survey to Port Essington in the Northern Territory on 1 October 1844: Charlie Fisher, a black tracker from the police force, and Harry Brown. Kennedy took Aboriginal guide Galmarra (Jacky Jacky) of the Dharug nation, from Jerry's Plains near Singleton in the Hunter Valley region of New South Wales. Galmarra was the sole survivor of a party of men and horses that travelled 2,254 kilometres from Rockingham Bay, North Queensland to Port Albany, Cape York. Two others had to be rescued from a base camp on 30 December 1848.

To explore Aboriginal trading ways it is necessary to follow several of the white historical characters that surveyed the Aboriginal space. All of these men have one thing in common: they chose to follow established Aboriginal paths. How do we know this? Because by reading and interpreting their sightings, and reviewing their accounts and actual records, we find Aboriginal villages, camping sites, cultivation sites, quarry sites, and road signage in the form of tree scarring and smoke signals.

Kennedy was not the only surveyor to perish in Aboriginal Queensland. Leichhardt (1 October 1844) and Burke and Wills (20 August 1860) did too, but what of the Aboriginal world in this collision of cultures? This chapter will first outline European exploration of South-east Queensland for the reason that this is where the official Australian diaries and records start. It will then identify Aboriginal historical actors and place-names, and transpose them into the landscape of Queensland.

South-east Queensland

John Oxley was a naval lieutenant who was appointed Surveyor General for New South Wales in 1812. He believed that a river flowed into an inland sea and that the Brisbane River might be the overflow of this sea (Fitzgerald 1982:61–65; McMinn 1970:85). Oxley was to help solve the riddle of the Murrumbidgee, Darling, and Murray River systems, which enabled graziers and herders to move into the areas he surveyed. This space came to be known by the Greek mythological term, Pandora's Pass. The illusory belief was that there was a pass over the seemingly impregnable mountain barrier of the Great Dividing Range, leading to a 'land of milk and honey'. This pass in particular has never become a major European road (*Australia's Heritage*, vol. 3, 1989:521–22; McMinn 1970:60).

In 1823 Oxley was ordered to an isolated part of the northern New South Wales coastline to find a suitable spot for a new penal settlement. He landed in the *Mermaid* at Point Skirmish, where he was greeted by Thomas Pamphlett (*Australia's Heritage*, 1989, vol. 3:521–22; Fitzgerald 1982:62–63). Oxley sailed in a whaleboat up the Brisbane River as far as Indooroopilly, which is an Aboriginal word for 'valley of leeches' (Watson, *Journal of the Royal Geographical Society of Australasia (Queensland)*, no. 30, vol. XLVIII:105). After this excursion he returned to Sydney to report to Governor Brisbane.

Oxley returned in the *Amity* and arrived at Redcliffe (Red Cliff Point) on 11 September 1824 with a well-equipped party; their task was to plant a colony of alien people, plants, animals, and values on Aboriginal soil – Ningy-Ningy country. Among that first contingent were Allan Cunningham, the royal botanist, as well as 29 convicts, 14 soldiers and their wives, and a Lieutenant Miller and his family. Miller was to be the first commandant of the settlement, which was officially proclaimed a penal settlement in August 1826, even though convicts had been sentenced to Queensland in mid-1825 (Finkel 1975:28–29).

The penal settlement was later relocated to Yugarabul (Brisbane River) and Mi-an-jin, the present site of Parliament House, in the vicinity of the Bonner Building on the Queensland University of Technology campus and the Botanic Gardens. Oxley and Cunningham surveyed the Brisbane River, and Cunningham named a species of pine after himself, *Araucaria cunninghamii*, the common name being Moreton Bay pine. Several logs of this pine were cut and sent back with the *Amity* to Sydney as dockyard material. The tree already had a name however; the Yugarabul people called it 'kur'an'. In June 1827 Cunningham left Sydney to unlock the mysteries of Pandora's Pass. Seven years after Oxley surveyed the area, Cunningham was to establish an overland route to Brisbane through the Kamilaroi lands, but squatters did not arrive until 13 years later.

On 27 May 1827 Cunningham reached the 29° parallel, on the border between New South Wales and Queensland. He stood on a high peak near present-day Warwick on 6 June 1827, with a 'most agreeable' view and named this landscape the Darling Downs. This whitefella artefact is marked on Kamilaroi lands. On his expeditions, Cunningham would take bags of seeds, and would plant peach or plum in places he thought were the best lands (*Australia's Heritage*, vol. 3, 1989:533–53). He saw very few Aboriginal people on his wanderings, which led him to remark 'the landscape was sparsely populated by Indians'. He was wrong. Raymond Evans suggests that over 3,000 Aboriginal people resided at that time in the Darling Downs area, and over 5,000 lived along the coastal belt of the Great Sandy Region (1992:8–10). It has been estimated that some 25 years after the start of the invasion, around 25,000 non-Aboriginal people lived in Queensland. The Aboriginal population was not counted. However, a nasty war was being waged by both sides (Finkel 1975:34–35).

Both Oxley and Cunningham found Aboriginal markings on trees, which led to the Liverpool Plains. While plotting these, Cunningham also described an Aboriginal campsite and village. At Warrah and Quirindi Creeks, 'we observed marks of the natives on the trees, also a few bark huts which had been recently occupied' (*Australia's Heritage*, vol. 3, 1989:533–53). Cunningham also noticed hatchet marks at a place he called Gwydir, which is recorded in a painting by the artist Govett around 1837, which he titled *Natives at a Grave*. The National Gallery of Australia Canberra has since accessioned this painting. Cunningham too observed several bark huts at the Macintyre River. In 1828 Cunningham led an expedition from Brisbane back to Cunningham's Gap and the Darling Downs area (McMinn 1970:88–91). Prior to these visits however, Cunningham made several mentions in his diaries of seeing stock drovers' camps on the Darling Downs.

It is presumed that the first Europeans to see the Brisbane River were the four ticket-of-leave convicts whose small boat was blown off-course while heading from Sydney to Wollongong, in the Illawarra area to the south, for a cargo of cedar (Finkel 1975:26–27). They were swept along the north coast by a violent storm, as far as Moreton Island, where they crossed over to the mainland to what is now known as Cleveland. Of the four men only three survived: John Finnegan, Thomas Pamphlett and Richard Parsons. The timbercutters made their way to Pumicestone Passage, where they were looked after by an Aboriginal chief, who is not named in any documents (Fitzgerald 1982:61–65).

Pamphlett lived with the Aboriginal mob from around Brisbane, and he and John Finnegan assisted Oxley in finding what was known about the Brisbane River by Aboriginal people of the region. 'Mr. Oxley and Mr. Stirling set out the following morning, taking Finnegan with them, in order to examine the river' (Riviere 1998:127). Both of these men lived with the Ngugi people of Moreton Island, the Ningy-Ningy people of Bribie Island, Nunukle people of Stradbroke Islands, Gubi Gubi people of the Noosa district, and the Turrbal people and Yugarabul-Jagarra people of Brisbane (*Australia's Heritage,* vol. 3, 1989:533–53; Fitzgerald 1982:61–65; Gray-Woods 1997:4–5).

Finnegan, Pamphlett, and Parsons travelled the region among salt-water people and provided first-hand accounts of the landscape and the people. In 1825 Finnegan observed that at one ceremonial, a gladiatorial event, the huts erected were 'so numerous I could hardly count them, each clan occupies their own designated residential area'. The site of this meeting was the present day Kippa-ring at Redcliffe. It is estimated that in 1825 there were over 120 bora grounds in the south Queensland region (Evans 1992:10–11).

The three cedar woodcutters went island hopping on well-defined watercrafts, and on the mainland they travelled on Aboriginal paths where 'the mangroves were so thick that we could not long keep the shore, but followed a native path' (Riviere 1998:117). While moving around the country they observed housing and local gatherings (Evans 1992:10–11). The three timbercutters landed on Aboriginal space, a space that only Aboriginal people occupied, but by 1859 the space was to become annexed from Aboriginal ownership.

Aboriginal nations along the Great Sandy Coast adopted the three shipwrecked timbercutters. These men were accepted by them, and taken on trips around the landscape; they were received into communities and shown the way. In turn the timbercutters showed the English invaders the Aboriginal communication paths they had learned about. When Oxley landed with all his cargo, he established a bridgehead for European occupation. Oxley found Pamphlett and then Finnegan, and heard their stories of a large river. His curiosity had to be satisfied, so he proceeded to look for the imagined river. With this objective in mind he looked for Yugarabul, and after entering the river, he rowed along the banks. Finnegan showed Oxley a creek from where they took a canoe; today this is known as Oxley Creek. Both Finnegan and Pamphlett rowed the stolen canoe up the Brisbane River for what Oxley estimated at approximately 20 miles. Oxley considered this as the largest river in New South Wales (Johnson 2001:198–201).

Finnegan, Pamphlett, and Parsons coloured the map and pointed to landmarks previously shown to them by local mobs. These landmarks were then used as navigational aids by the invaders. The three men travelled up the Brisbane River on foot and identified paths so that the surveyors could plot them on a map (Fairhall 1994:3). Kerkhove identifies some examples of where these paths were being used by Aboriginal people as well as the colonists:

> An Aboriginal pathway seemed to run from the sandy beach in South Brisbane between Grey and Stanley Streets out through Woolloongabba (roughly along Stanley Street). Here it became what is now Logan Road and Old Cleveland Roads . . . Early settlers remembered seeing Brisbane Aboriginals marching in hundreds along these, or saw them tracking along them in South Brisbane at night with a blazing torch in one hand. Another Aboriginal path went from sandy beach out along today's Montague Road. (Kerkhove 1985:4)

The first road cut into the landscape for white settlement in Brisbane was Russell Street, which connected to Stanley Street and then joined an Aboriginal path that travelled out to Woolloongabba. From there, the path led to Cleveland – the intended site for a new port, which is known as Old Cleveland Road. Logan Road is also an Aboriginal track that took Aboriginal people from Logan to Brisbane River (Brisbane City Council: Suburban Sites. Retrieved 20 August 2003). Reports indicate that Aboriginal people from the Brisbane area met at Pullen Pullen, Moggill Creek, and Mt. Elphinstone for ceremony and trade (Brisbane City Council: Suburban Sites. Retrieved 20 August 2003). From the mid-1890s, Colliver and Woolston (1978) plotted Aboriginal sites within the settlement area of Brisbane. A search of the Brisbane City library will easily identify similar historical maps that can be copied at little expense (see Map 15). Of interest in this particular map is the railway line, which connects Steele's map of Aboriginal paths and features the railway line north through the Sunshine Coast.

Steele's research on Aboriginal pathways highlights several Aboriginal roads that connect bora rings/grounds across the Brisbane greater area.

> A bora ring has survived near Sandy Creek at Camira, south of Goodna . . . The ring is about one kilometre east of the Old Logan Road . . . That road may well have followed an earlier track made by Aboriginals.
>
> The Old Northern Road from Brisbane via Cash's Crossing and Young's Crossing passed two kilometres west of Petrie. This road, marked out by Tom Petrie, probably followed an Aboriginal road (Steele: 1983:137 & 129). (see Map 18)

The convicts used Aboriginal paths that passed through West End and Highgate Hill towards forestry areas in order to log timber for the new colony (Finkel 1975; Fitzgerald 1982; Kerkhove 1985:4–5). Denis Cryle suggests that the Ningy-Ningy people and the mobs that lived in the mountains surrounding Brisbane Town were very aggressive and any gathering of large mobs was a source of alarm. He mentions that mobs, some of whom came from the Blackall Ranges to the north, would descend on Brisbane for ceremonial and bartering purposes (Cryle 1992:73).

Tom Petrie's father travelled with a group of Aboriginal people from Brisbane to the Bunya Mountains in the early 1840s:

> They travelled from Brisbane, a party of about 100, and camped the first night at what is now Enoggera. The third night they camped at Caboolture (a place of the

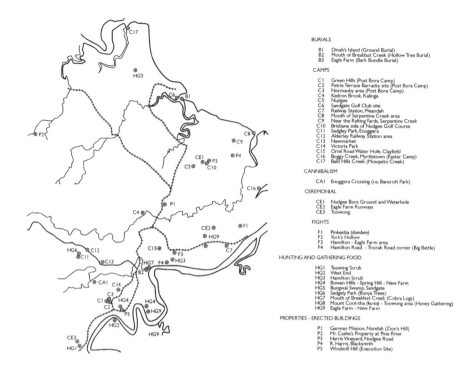

BURIALS

B1   Dinah's Island (Ground Burial)
B2   Mouth of Breakfast Creek (Hollow Tree Burial)
B3   Eagle Farm (Bark Bundle Burial)

CAMPS

C1   Green Hills (Post Bora Camp)
C2   Petrie Terrace Barracks site (Post Bora Camp)
C3   Normanby area (Post Bora Camp)
C4   Kedron Brook, Kalinga
C5   Nudgee
C6   Sandgate Golf Club site
C7   Railway Station, Meandah
C8   Mouth of Serpentine Creek area
C9   Near the Rafting Yards, Serpentine Creek
C10 Brisbane side of Nudgee Golf Course
C11 Sedgley Park, Enoggera
C12 Alderley Railway Station area
C13 Newmarket
C14 Victoria Park
C15 Oriel Road Water Hole, Clayfield
C16 Boggy Creek, Myrtletown (Easter Camp)
C17 Bald Hills Creek (Mosquito Creek)

CANNIBALISM

CA1 Enoggera Crossing (i.e. Bancroft Park)

CEREMONIAL

CE1 Nudgee Bora Ground and Waterhole
CE2 Eagle Farm Runways
CE3 Toowong

FIGHTS

F1   Pinkenba (dumben)
F2   York's Hollow
F3   Hamilton - Eagle Farm area
F4   Hamilton Road - Toorak Road corner (Big Battle)

HUNTING AND GATHERING FOOD

HG1 Toowing Scrub
HG2 West End
HG3 Hamilton Scrub
HG4 Bowen Hills - Spring Hill - New Farm
HG5 Bungwal Swamp, Sandgate
HG6 Sedgley Park (Bunya Trees)
HG7 Mouth of Breakfast Creek (Cobra Logs)
HG8 Mount Coot-tha (ku-ta) - Toowong area (Honey Gathering)
HG9 Eagle Farm - New Farm

PROPERTIES - ERECTED BUILDINGS

P1   German Mission, Nundah (Zion's Hill)
P2   Mr. Cashe's Property at Pine River
P3   Harris Vineyard, Nudgee Road
P4   R. Harris, Blacksmith
P5   Windmill Hill (Execution Site)

Map 14 Aboriginal cultural sites in the Brisbane area, Queensland; this is a Eurocentric map and without a legend is largely meaningless. However the map can be interpreted using the few reference points that are indicated using local knowledge. Located on the map of North Brisbane at C17 is Bald Hills Creek, C6 is Sandgate Golf Club site at the end of the Sandgate railway line (Mosquito Creek), and HG7 is the mouth of Breakfast Creek. Notice the other railway line, which is the line north to the Sunshine Coast. Both of these lines follow the major Aboriginal throughways for travelling north and south along the 'Bunya and Bora Ground', highways of the south-eastern route highlighted in Map 8.

carpet snake) and the next day started for the Glass-house Mountains. On the fourth day of this at about 4 pm the party arrived at Mooloolah . . . The party apparently arrived at the beginnings of the Blackall Ranges on the fifth day. Another day's travelling took them to where the tribes were all assembling from every part of the country. Some hailing from the Burnett, Wide Bay, Bundaberg, Mt. Perry, Gympie, Bribie, Fraser Island, Kilcoy, Mt. Brisbane. (Petrie, 1981:11–17)

At a place close to Mooloolaba and the connecting road to the Bruce Highway was another path that is now overlaid by old Gympie Road. Steele suggests that this is where there was a bora ring; it was also an important meeting place from where travellers would head off through Bald Knob to the bunya festival (Steele 1983:175). At Cooloola a path travels south from Double Island Point for 41 kilometres along the beach, where it then branches off at a waterhole known as Nemberthan. Here a path heads to Lake Cootharaba, and to a place called Wa-Wa where a bora ground is located. Travellers around this area used the beach to move around the Noosa Lakes to the Wide

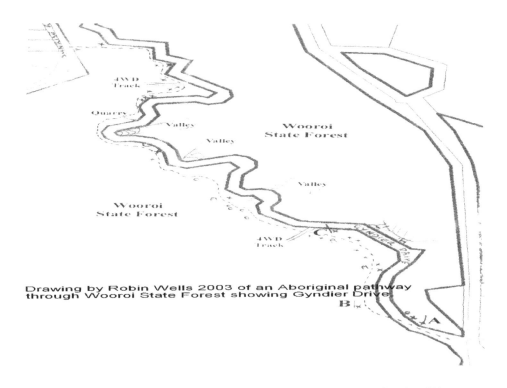

Map 15 Aboriginal Roads, Sunshine Coast, Queensland, based on maps by Gaiarbau (W. MacKenzie) cited in J. Steele (1983). Indicated on the map is a major Aboriginal road that heads north through the Glasshouse mountains and on to Gympie. From Wells 2003:28.

Bay area (Steele 1983:182–84). A path also leads over the mountains and across the range to a bora ring on the Conondale Range near Mt Langley, 10 kilometres from the Kilcoy–Jimna road. The Bellthorpe road overlays an Aboriginal path that takes travellers from Kilcoy to the Maryborough area; the path follows Sandy Creek and descends to the Mary River five kilometres from Conondale. This is a major route to Kenilworth from Kilcoy (see Map 16).

Robin Wells (2003), researcher of the Sunshine Coast Aboriginal people, identifies many Aboriginal roads that became overlaid by bitumen (see Map 15).

> Many of the Aboriginal pathways were widened and over time eventually evolved into European-style roads such as the Old Gympie Road, Tewantin-Cooroy Road. The North Coast Railway was built alongside the main Aboriginal pathway of the Sunshine Coast which went through Beerburrum, Landsborough, Nambour, Eumundi, Cooroy, Pomona and Cooran (Wells 2003:29, 30). (See Map 19)

While some Aboriginal people resisted Europeans, others assisted the settlers and provided valuable guidance for surveys of the country. In 1842 an escaped convict who lived with Aboriginal people and was accepted into Aboriginal communities as an

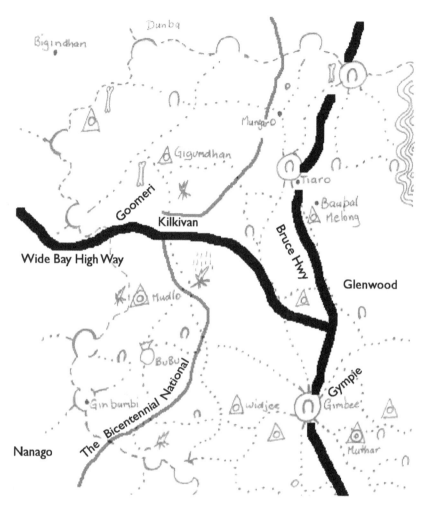

Map 16 Sunshine Coast, Queensland. Aboriginal paths with the Queensland railway line over the north–south path. In Steele (1984:5).

Aboriginal man was given the name of Durramboi (his English name was Jack Davis). He guided Joliffe, a shepherd with his flock and drays, along these paths from the Mary Valley to Tiaro (Steele 1983:210–30).

> Durramboi would have followed part of the Dreaming story strings of the Ibis people and the path they travelled from Mt Bauple to Urangan and to Fraser Island. The story is a tale about the Ibis people's theft of tomahawks; they were travelling from Mt Bauple to Urangan, where the maker of stone tomahawks caught the mob along the Mary River. Here he made them turn their dilly bags inside out; the tomahawks dropped into the river and made the island of Baddow. Along the journey of the Ibis, near Saltwater Creek (the Aboriginal name is Warrowngin), the present site of the Maryborough–Pialba road in the State Forest, is an important camping ground for

Figure 32 Gyndier Drive, Noosaville, Queensland, was used as a coach track. Photo: 1880.

travellers and is known as the Wongi Waterholes; wongi is an Aboriginal word for eugarie shell. (Steele 1983:235–36).

John Jones, a 71-year-old Elder from the Dalongabarra nation, took me to one of the paths at Noosaville that was used by his people. He reclaimed the road in 2002 and erected a sign stating that the path is of cultural heritage significance (see Figure 33). He said:

> The tracks were the easy way to reach the sea. The track wound from Dalongabarra country, some were trading ways and borders. Some tracks were within the tribal boundaries. This track is along the Tewantin Road (now Gyndier Drive) and led to Eumundi, the one below was the old Cobb & Co horse track. The paths were along resources such as water. We traded shell and pendants for ornaments the nautilus Shell. We traded shell, boomerangs and as the shell got traded inland it was worth more. We traded other shells and it was like money and be used like money. Mount Bauple was a landmark for us. (John Jones, personal communication 2004)

The track John Jones pointed out still exists in the Wooroi State Forest Noosa (see Figure 33). Gyndier Drive (see Figure 32 and Map 17) is a Dalongabarra traditional pathway.

The best-preserved bora ground close to Brisbane is located at Samford. Tom Petrie described this as having a well-defined path over a thousand metres long. Also along the path could be found images made from clay and grass, and designs incised in trees.

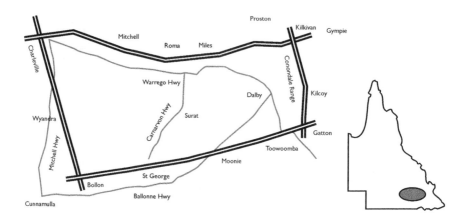

Map 17 Gyndier Drive. Reproduced by kind permission of Robin Wells.

Steele suggests that people from Ipswich, Cressbrook, Mount Brisbane, and Brisbane used this bora ground (Steele 1983:248–49).

Colleen Wall is the manager of the Aboriginal and Torres Strait Islander Arts Programs (Department of Arts Queensland) and is also a Kabi Kabi woman from Mt Bauple, Queensland. She shared with me her traditions of travelling and trading and also provided a map that she used as part of her Native Title application (see Map 18). The map details the internal traditional communication routes and bora grounds.

A songline from Noosa Cootharaba Lake runs through to Mt Bauple. It travels then through Jumpup and then onto Bam Bam Springs Many Peaks and Coalstoun Lakes.

It is a story of people who were starving and could not catch any fish; they could not reach a waterhole. Some of the waterholes along this storyway were created by a spirit man from Noosa.

Coalstoun Lake is a spiritual place and is west of Biggenden. Also linking this story is the Baddow Island, linked to five Bora grounds. The pathway ran from Many Peaks to Biggenden,

Figure 33 John Jones, an Elder from the Dalongabarra nation, reclaiming an Aboriginal path that runs along side Gyndier Drive. He stated "that the path is of cultural heritage significance". The road is located in the Wooroi State Forest of Noosaville, Queensland. Photo: John Jones, 2002.

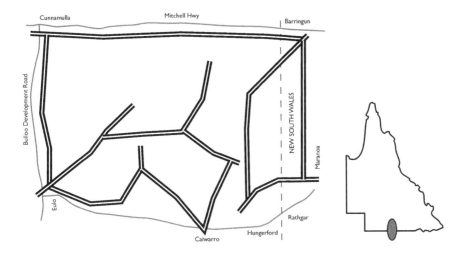

Map 18 Colleen Wall's detailed map of Kabi Kabi paths and cultural sites with Aboriginal names for places of significance. The map was used for a Native Title application. Detailed on the map are major road systems of the Sunshine Coast region, and the National Horse Trail. Gympie is in direct alignment with Gimbee. Colleen Wall, a Kabi Kabi woman, was in 2004 the Manager of the Aboriginal and Torres Strait Islander Arts Programs in the Department of Arts Queensland, and a practising artist.

Childers, Lowmead by way of Paradise Waterhole which is near Mount Perry. This is where the story track finished and went through Gurran. This track follows the waterholes.

Bunya nut festival was a time for trading. King Bombie is one of the areas which is the crossover between the Kabi and Waka mob, yeah! A trade gate. The other track goes from Marlborough to Bam Bam Springs – this is the coastal one. There is a gap in the range near Biggenden, which leads to Bundaberg. Part of the horse riding trails takes in these tracks. We traded axes, food and healing knowledge. When people came into my country they would wait at bora rings which were located at entry points into country. Songlines were along the water systems and along the course of the rivers were sites where people would sing and do ceremony. You know the Two Dog story – well it came into the Glasshouse Mountains from Arnhem Land. (Colleen Wall, personal communication 2004)

At Gatton, west from Brisbane, Steele inspected a gallery of rock engravings south of the town near a place called Black Duck Creek. He pointed out that there is 'an Aboriginal route over the Dividing Range to the Downs' (Steele 1983:154). Another major path led from the South Burnett to Mt Mowbullan – Dalby – to the Bunya Mountains. A significant Aboriginal camping site and bora ground is located along this track. Another major path, which is near Wengen Creek, led to Wengenville, a major camping and ceremonial site ('wengen' meaning old woman ghost) (Steele 1983:273–74).

Aboriginal Dreaming Paths and Trading Routes

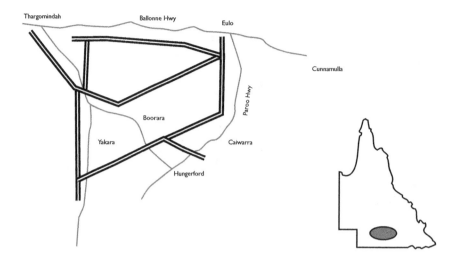

Map 19 Adapted from Bob Munn's story. Gunnggari peoples' trading path following the Warrego Highway between the western townships of Charleville to Chinchilla, and Balonne Highway between Cunnamulla and St George. The Moonie Highway between St George and Moonie follows the trading way to the Bunya Mountains and the Black Butt Range. Bob Munn is a Gungari person from south-western Queensland who was chairperson of the Queensland Aboriginal Consultative Committee for Education, and a member of the Aboriginal and Torres Strait Islander Advisory Board to the Queensland Government in 2000.

The Gunggari people of the Charleville region developed communication paths that were 700 kilometres in length, and linked people as far south as Bollon, and the nations of Waka Waka in the Bunya Mountains and Kabi Kabi in Kenilworth south eastern Queensland. Gunnggari people had well-established paths and utilised them to travel between Charleville and Chinchilla, as well as Cunnamulla and St George. Traders also travelled to the Bunya Mountains and onto the Black Butt Range (see Map 19).

The Kunja people also developed roads that linked them to other Aboriginal people and nations; along these roads can be found Aboriginal wells which are permanent watering holes (see Figure 34).

Another Aboriginal well can be found along Moonie Highway, 40 kilometres from St George, the waterhole is fenced and well signed (see Figure 34).

The Budjari nation of south-west Queensland also developed communication paths that linked them to other Aboriginal nations, but they also developed an internal road system that enables the Budjari people to move around their country. The major highways of Bulloo Developmental Road and the Paroo Hwy and several stock routes follow these paths. The Budjari people inhabited the lake systems, for example the Currawinga, Lake Numalla and Lake Wyara, which were permanent water systems. Map 21 details the Budjari paths (McKellar 1984:44).

As with the other Aboriginal nations in the south-western area of Queensland, the Kooma people developed internal communication tracks that assisted the movement of people around their country. The traditional paths of the Kooma people are located

Figure 34 Aboriginal well along the Moonie Highway near St George, Queensland. There are a series of these water wells dotted through the landscape that are used by Aboriginal travellers. Today they are maintained by Aboriginal CDEP workers. Photo: Dale Kerwin, 2003.

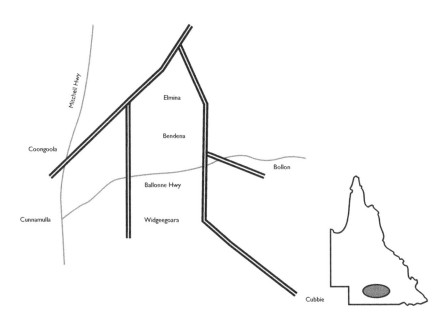

Map 20 Adapted from Hazel McKellar, *Matya – Mundu: A History of the Aboriginal People of the South West Queensland* (Cunnamulla Aboriginal Native Welfare Association, Cunnamulla, 1984), p. 13. Kunja peoples had well established paths which took that mob around the small townships, near Cunnamulla in south-western Queensland. Today the tracks are stock routes, and the major thoroughfares of the Mitchell Highway and Bulloo Development Road. Kunja peoples' paths also travel over the Queensland and New South Wales border.

133

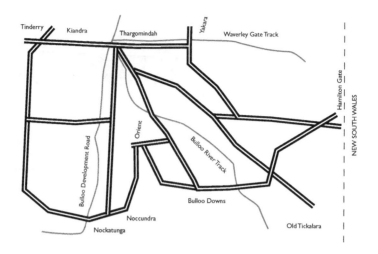

Map 21 Adapted from Hazel McKellar, *Matya – Mundu: A History of the Aboriginal People of the South West Queensland* (Cunnamulla Aboriginal Native Welfare Association, Cunnamulla, 1984), p. 44. Budjari peoples' paths in south-western Queensland between Cunnamulla and Thargominda. Bulloo Developmental Road, the Paroo Highway, and several stock routes follow these paths.

Map 22 Adapted from Hazel McKellar, *Matya – Mundu: A History of the Aboriginal People of the South West Queensland* (Cunnamulla Aboriginal Native Welfare Association, Cunnamulla, 1984), p. 56. The traditional paths of the Kooma people are located between the small townships of Coongoola and Bollon and travel south to Cubbie.

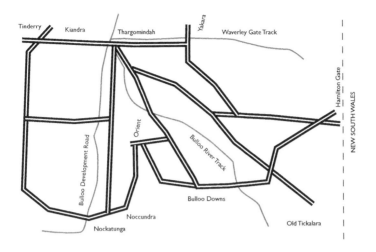

Map 23 Adapted from Hazel McKellar, *Matya – Mundu: A History of the Aboriginal People of the South West Queensland* (Cunnamulla Aboriginal Native Welfare Association, Cunnamulla, 1984), p. 56. Pathways of the Killilla people of the south-western corner of Queensland. The township of Thargomindah and Bulloo Track and Bulloo Developmental Road follow the Killilla peoples' paths which were used to stay clear of European settlement and avoid conflict.

between the small townships of Coongoola and Bollon and travel south to Cubbie. This is cattle and sheep grazing land; cotton is also grown in the area. Map 22 provides information on how extensive these tracks are (McKellar 1984:48).

Knowledge of Aboriginal paths in this region has been known since Mitchell's time, but today Aboriginal people and researchers are piecing them together for Native Title claims. 'There is evidence to suggest that the old road passing Goongannie springs is the track used by Aborigines when travelling south to join the people living around the head waters of the Warrego River' (Donovan 1976:4). The network of internal paths of the Kunja, Budjari, Kooma and Kullilla linked people to the major paths to the Gunggari nation and other major trading ways.

South-western Queensland corner: Mooraberrie (the Channel Country)

The Channel Country is bordered by the Simpson Desert to the west, the Grey Range to the north and the Isa Uplands Plains to the north-east. The Channel Country is a vast region of far horizons, distant low ranges, broad floodplains, red sand dunes and shimmering stony plains. In the main, the Channel Country lies in the arid zone of gidgees and open coolabah woodlands, lancewood, Normanton box, and spinifex.

The Channel Country is a land of rocky panorama and a sightline that is uninterrupted across vast distances of empty plains, except for sheep and dingo fences. The

135

region is channelled with watercourses, which provide the name for this region. Four major rivers flow at various times through this vast arid land: the Georgina, Diamantina, and Mulligan Rivers, and Cooper Creek. The Barcoo and Thomson Rivers, with their headwaters in central Queensland, feed Cooper Creek that flows into Lake Eyre – a course of more than 1,600 kilometres. All these rivers have long and deep waterholes that are known to never run dry, even in the most severe drought (Duncan-Kemp 1961:15). The Diamantina River is known as 'Kurrawoolben' or 'Kirrenderri' in local Aboriginal language, which means lonely or alone. It flows for more than 1,920 kilometres to empty into Lake Eyre. The Georgina River is known as 'Joordri', meaning gleaming belly. The Mulligan, where it meets the Georgina, is known as 'Noo-roon-dina', meaning unpredictable or moody one (Duncan-Kemp 1961:15).

The rivers of the Channel Country have numerous channels and tributaries and branches that criss-cross each other. These rivers are filled from the annual monsoonal rains in the headwaters of the catchment areas of the Gulf Country. In total, Cooper Creek, the Diamantina, Georgina and Mulligan Rivers cover a total area of about 96,000 square kilometres (Duncan-Kemp 1961:10).

The Channel Country is a harsh place, where the Min Min lights visit lonely travellers. Even today, only a few itinerant travellers can be found pulling their motorised homes loaded with camping equipment and supplies, following the long, desolate highways. The only distractions along this low flat land are the ubiquitous kites that circle and sprial over road kill. The Dreaming stories of the Channel Country people are derived from the creation period, when ancestral beings formed the landscape while travelling across the country. These events are remembered in song, dance, and drawings. The surveyors (and subsequently the stockmen) followed the Dreaming strings, watercourses, and Aboriginal traders.

The landscape is reminiscent of Albert Namatjira paintings, even though his paintings were not of this area. His watercolours of the Australian landscape speak of the Aboriginal Dreaming, where the song of Yamma-coona – the thread that binds all things – can be heard. It can be heard as a whisper sung across the landscape; it can be heard blowing though the trees, and skipping invisibly across billabongs forming little ripples. Richard Percy from the Kalkadoon Tribal Council at Mount Isa stated that Yamma-coona is the woman of the bush who alluringly sings a nameless tune (Richard Percy, personal communication, 10 July 2002).

In the Simpson Desert there is no permanent surface water, no rocky hills, and no creeks except the Lower Diamantina and the Kallakoopah. Researchers such as Norman Tindale in 1934, Luise Hercus in 1985, and Fatchen and Barker in 1979, have suggested Aboriginal peoples have occupied the Simpson Desert region for 6,000 years BP, which suggests that human occupation of the region began in the recent arid period (3000–6000 BP). On the other hand, Smith and Clark (1993), and Wasson (1983) put the figure at 14,000 BP following the dating of material from the fringes of the Strzlecki and Simpson Deserts. To live in this area and survive meant that having knowledge of how to find water was of extreme importance. Hercus (1987) mapped the mikiri (Aboriginal water wells) around the Simpson Desert region. She indicates that there were 21 wells which were an important resource to the Wangkangurru. These mikiri are also important Dreaming sites from where stories radiate out in all directions (Hercus 1987:67).

Mikiri are linked by a route across the desert that Hercus (1987) has drawn right across the Simpson Desert from Pandie Pandie on the Diamantina to Dalhousie Springs. She has also linked and connected the mikiri Puramanie to this route, and described it as 'a four and half day walk' (Hercus 1987:67). Kado Muir, an initiated man from Lenora in Western Australia, told me that his Dreaming is the Dingo Dreaming and that he has relations to people in the Dalhousie Springs area.

Several Aboriginal nations live in the Simpson Desert: the Aranda people occupy the western desert margins. The Karangura and Wangkamadla occupy the eastern fringes of the desert while their country boundary extended north; the Wangkangurru country extends from the central desert to the southern fringe in South Australia (Shephard 1992, Jones 1993). These story strings form the basis of social relationships and obligations to sites, country, and the Dreaming (Jones 1993:46). The Two Snake Dreaming, which is affiliated with the Two Dog story string, took W.O. Hodgkinson from Cloncurry through Dajarra down to Boulia.

Wangkangurru people lived in the desert and survived by managing their water wells, which are water soaks in the centre of low-lying depressions on gypseous flats between the sand dunes (Hamm 1993). The soaks appear when rainwater moves through sand and gets trapped in a depression formed in the clay. These would become permanent waterholes and the Wangkangurru would get water from these soaks by digging narrow shafts several metres into them. The Wangkangurru were traders; their life in the desert would have been difficult so they travelled long distances to trade. They traded with people from the Mount Isa region for stone axes, collected red ochre from Parachilna in the Flinders Ranges of South Australia, and also traded for baler shell from the Gulf of Carpentaria. They also traded for mussel shells from Aboriginal nations along the Manaroa River, which they used as jewellery. The Wangkangurru also traded for pituri from Aboriginal nations in western Queensland (Shephard 1992:64).

Hodgkinson (see penultimate section in this chapter), Mitchell and the Gregory brothers followed the Dreaming trails of the Channel Country. Aboriginal communication ways followed waterways, and consequently so did these surveyors. Thomas Mitchell and Gregory brothers will be discussed in more detail below.

The nomads and their penetration of the Aboriginal landscape

In the early 1800s, explorers were sent inland to look for new pastoral lands and to find a major waterway like the Amazon, or a major river system similar to those in Europe. Rumours were running rife in the colony. In 1831 a 25-year-old convict known as George the Barber (whose real name was George Clarke) escaped from a chain gang in the Bathurst area and lived with Aboriginal people. When he was captured he described a river 'Kindur' and claimed that he had twice reached the sea by this river. It was also rumoured that he saw hippopotamuses and orang-utans (Cannon 1987). The thought of finding an inland sea drove the imagination of explorers such as Sturt and Eyre. Mitchell on the other hand dreamed of a great inland river. He was inspired by George the Barber's reports and set out to find this great river (Carter 1987).

A need for fresh grazing lands found explorers being sent into the wilderness. The colony depended on good pastoral areas and water for the purposes of opening up new commercial interests. Explorers kept a continual lookout for Aboriginal campfires and smoke fires, because it suggested the country was good. John Oxley wrote of his exploration of the Lachlan Valley in 1817, 'The smoke of the native fires arising in every quarter distinctly marking that we were in country which afforded them ample means of substances' (Oxley in Reynolds 1990:5–17).

Mitchell noted that 'open plains and columns of smoke indicate a good country' (in Reynolds 1990:5–17). Leichhardt's guide pointed out fires along a range they were surveying, and the former commented that 'this was welcome intelligence, for we knew that their presence indicated the existence of a good country' (Reynolds 1990:10). Similarly, E.J. Eyre utilised the experiences of past explorers and wrote:

> The localities selected by Europeans, as best adapted for the purpose of cultivation or grazing, are those that would be equally valued above others, by the natives themselves, as places of resort, or districts in which they could most easily procure food. (in Reynolds 1990:5–17)

Reynolds notes that explorers used Aboriginal trading ways and that these were kept in good repair by fire and were well trodden. A.C. Gregory observed: 'a well-maintained path from which the loose stones had been cleared [and] piled in large heaps' (Reynolds 1990:5–17).

Reynolds describes that the paths 'linked wells, springs and other water sources, led to fords and mountain passes, and circumvented forests and other natural obstacles' (1990:5–17). Further, Burke and Wills on their return leg of their ill-fated trip to the Gulf of Carpentaria trekked into a bog and floundered. They stumbled across a hard, well-trodden path, which led them out of the bog and onto drinking water and yams. The yams were the replant from the annual harvesting of the yam by the local mob (Reynolds 1990:5–17).

While Aboriginal trading paths were important, so too was intelligence about the country for which they had designs. Like all peoples, Aboriginal people had intricate knowledge of the environment in which they lived. Eyre wrote:

> A great advantage on the part of the natives is the intimate knowledge they have of every nook and corner of the country they inhabit . . . they know the very rock where little water is most likely to be collected, the very hole where it is the longest retained, they fill their skins, thus obtaining a supply that lasts them many days. (in Reynolds 1990:5–17)

Dick Kimber comments on Queensland drover Ridley Williams, who drove cattle between 1883 and 1885 from the Georgina River across the Simpson Desert to Alice

Springs, along much the same route as the present-day Plenty Highway (in Kimber 1980:14–15).

None of the movement of explorers and stock drovers in this part of the Channel Country could have occurred without water being available, and knowing where to find it. It is easy to recognise the importance of having Aboriginal people as guides and scouts. Aboriginal people helped both explorers and stockmen survive the Australian bush by showing them the secrets of finding water and bush tucker. Aboriginal people had clearly learned the secrets of the desert country. Eyre wrote,

> any season of the year or any description of country does not yield him both animal and vegetable food . . . White men who borrow this knowledge usually survived: those who ignored it were often defeated in their attempts to penetrate the secrets of the huge continent. (in Cannon 1987:208–15)

Ludwig Leichhardt

Leichhardt was a botanist from Germany who was intent on becoming famous. As an explorer he wanted to 'explore the kernel of the Dark Continent' (Cannon 1987:208–15). Therefore, in 1844, he announced his intention to make a journey across northeastern Australia from Moreton Bay to Port Essington, on the Cobourg Peninsula. The exploration was a scientific and commercial expedition (Bolton 1972:11). On 1 October 1844, Leichhardt launched into the unknown to find an overland route from the Darling Downs to Port Essington in the Northern Territory.

The expedition received private funding, but relied on volunteers as Leichhardt had not received funds to pay wages. He estimated that the trip would take him six to seven months. The private interest groups that funded the expedition were also petitioning the Governor for squatters' rights to what they saw as 'their' lands. The resources Leichhardt managed to pull together were enough for 10 men, 17 horses and 16 bullocks, as well as dogs and supplies that he estimated would last for six months. The group included two Aboriginal men, Charlie Fisher and Harry Brown, who was also a black tracker and had worked for the police service. On 1 October Leichhardt left Jimbour Station, the northernmost station of the Darling Downs. The local mob called this spot Gimba, which means good pastures. The trip was to take Leichhardt and his men across 2,400 kilometres and took 14 months and 17 days. During his journey he described the Burdekin area as 'the most picturesque landscape we had yet met' (in Fitzgerald 1982:100; Bolton 1972; Turnbull 1983). He crossed the Plains of Promise in the Gulf and reached Port Essington on 17 December 1845. During this epic trip he passed through Jawoyn lands near Katherine Gorge, and Mataranka in the heart of Jawoyn lands. Burnum Burnum comments that Leichhardt wrote in his diary that the 'friendly locals led his party through a maze of swamps, waterholes and wetlands which extended beyond the reach of sight' (Burnum Burnum 1988:172).

Leichhardt began his survey around the Dalby area in south-east Queensland. He commented on the local mob's knowledge of bush tucker: 'they seemed to have tasted

Figure 35 Leichhardt blazed tree stump. Photo by Dale Kerwin 2002.

everything from the highest top of the bunya tree and the seaforthia and cabbage palm, to the grub, which lies in the rotten tree of the bush' (Fitzgerald 1982:20).

While surveying the Burdekin, Leichhardt met with what he called the Lotophagi people, which means lotus-eaters, and was shown a direct route that avoided the waterholes that slowed their trip down (Jensen and Barrett 1996:20–21, Fitzgerald 1982, McEwan 1985:268). At the end of his trip, Leichhardt was shown and guided over paths that led him to Victoria, the settlement at Port Essington, by the mob whose country surrounded the imperial outpost (Jensen and Barrett 1996:20–21; Fitzgerald 1982). The mob there provided the wandering expeditionaries with water and food.

Leichhardt is remembered because his was an epic overland trip. No other European had gone to Port Essington by any other means than boat. His expedition held out the promise of future land colonisation to the north. As a navigator his success was due more to good luck than good surveying, and he literally lived off the land. He was so obsessed with experimenting with bush tucker, that at times his men would become ill with stomach cramps and diarrhoea from eating some foodstuffs. The food he took with him lasted the whole trip, and unlike other exploring parties, Leichhardt's did not suffer from scurvy (Jensen and Barrett 1996:26–27; Fitzgerald 1982). Charlie and Harry Brown fed the travelling men with an assortment of bush tucker, which supplemented their provisions.

It has been reported that Charlie punched Leichhardt in the mouth and knocked out several teeth, possibly because Leichhardt had withheld food from him. Although Charlie supplied the travellers with bush tucker, Leichhardt would often not give Charlie and Harry Brown any of the tucker. It has also been noted that Leichhardt excluded both of the guides from the expedition over loyalty. They later rejoined the band of men, but Charlie discarded his white man's clothes and dressed in possum and kangaroo skins (Jensen and Barrett 1996; Fitzgerald 1982; McEwan 1985:264–65). McEwan also noted that when Leichhardt and his men would stumble on an Aboriginal village they would scare off the inhabitants and help themselves to their food and material possessions (McEwan 1985:267).

Leichhardt set out on a third expedition on 5 April 1848, with his two Aboriginal guides. He planned to travel from east to west across the interior of Australia. The whole crew and all the equipment was lost. They set out from Mount Abundance, Queensland with the objective of reaching the Swan River, Western Australia. Leichhardt. Seven men and 77 animals crossed the Condamine at a place called Tieryboo, an Aboriginal word for the wattle that grows along the banks of creeks, rivers, and billabongs in this area (Trebilco 2002:6). The whole caravan of men, horses and sheep disappeared without trace; not a shred of horse equipment, a piece of cloth, or material evidence was found.

Leichhardt, an ambitious botanist, travelled slowly, tasting and sampling what he surveyed and naming several species of flora and fauna. News of an itinerant white man building and planting on their country spread within Aboriginal nations. This quick awareness of white itinerants was evidenced during Kennedy's expedition during the same year (1848), as he was attacked constantly. At the time of Leichhardt's disappearance, Aboriginal nations were mobilising themselves against intrusions.

Thomas Mitchell highway to Carpentaria

In 1845, Surveyor-General Sir Thomas Mitchell was sponsored by the colonial government to find an overland route between Sydney and the head of the Gulf of Carpentaria. He pushed off into Aboriginal space, having calculated the point of no return in order to take sufficient provisions. He moved over the Aboriginal landscape until he received word of Leichhardt having reached Port Essington at which point he abandoned his survey, packed up his men and returned to Sydney before making a trip to Britain (Fitzgerald 1982).

Mitchell's survey was undertaken in five stages, and lasted fourteen months. During this survey he used words like the 'highway to Carpentaria', 'on the 'road' and the 'track'. The first stage was from Boree to Barwon, or the Darling River, at its junction with the Macquarie River. He knew this area well because he had surveyed it ten years previously, following which it became peopled and stocked with animals and things from Mitchell's own cultural background. The second segment of Mitchell's expedition was to the Narran and Balonne Rivers near St George in Queensland. When he had completed the third segment, he established his second depot on the Maranoa River. The fourth segment was south of Mt Douglas, being the northernmost point reached about 210 kilometres north of the Tropic of Capricorn. A third depot was established near Mount Salvator. The final stage was a survey of Mt Salvator, far to the west of Isisford near Charters Towers, from where he departed for Sydney (Baker 1997).

Yuranigh, a Wiradjuri man from the Molong area near Bathurst, accompanied Mitchell on several expeditions. Yuranigh was the chief guide for the survey of Queensland in 1845–46 from the Boree area of New South Wales to within 150 kilometres west of Mackay in Queensland. During this survey Yuranigh met one of his countrymen on 1 May 1846, between the present town of Mitchell and Surat – a distance of over 1,000 kilometres from his home (Mitchell 1848:142). In 1850

Yuranigh died and was buried in true Wiradjuri ceremonial style for important people. Five trees were incised with Yuranigh's clan design and totemic images and shapes, which are located at Gamboola Station, New South Wales. A year later, in 1851, Mitchell went to his friend's grave and re-cut the incision marks, deeper into the trees. He paid for the site to be kept clean and fenced the area off from animals and other destructive forces. Today the site is listed on the National Heritage registry. Only two of the five sacred trees survive and are still growing (Mulvaney 1989:85–86). According to Mitchell's notes it appears that Yuranigh's totem is the emu, because Mitchell noted that he would not eat the flesh of this bird for religious reasons (Mitchell 1848:317).

Aboriginal guides were rarely mentioned by name, in accordance with the European mentality of the era. At the start of Mitchell's expedition into the 'Interior of Tropical Australia' he did not mention any of the three Aboriginal guides accompanying the team of twenty-eight men. It was not until three weeks after the trip had started, that Mitchell mentioned Yuranigh. Throughout the rest of the journal Mitchell mentions Yuranigh more than ninety times (Mulvaney 1989:86–87). Mitchell also mentioned meeting with Aboriginal people over eighty times (Mitchell 1848), and receiving information from them several times. He also described following Aboriginal paths, and coming across camp sites and a number of shell middens. Each of these meetings will be discussed below, as the incidents indicate that Mitchell followed Aboriginal roads during his expedition.

Mitchell's feelings for Yuranigh, who travelled with him beyond the line of Capricorn, was summed up in his journal as: he 'has been my guide, companion, councillor and friend' (Mitchell 1848:414). The effect that Yuranigh had on Mitchell can be measured and gleaned from the Aboriginal place-names he mentions such as Mount Bindango in Queensland, the Culgoa River, and the Narran River. Two other Aboriginal guides accompanied Mitchell: Bultje, one of the guides had led him in an expedition to the lower part of the Darling ten years earlier. During that expedition Bultje led him to water on the Goobang Creek. Bultje also led Mitchell to the Bogan and in return for his services was rewarded with a tomahawk, a pipe and two ounces of tobacco (two figs). He joined Mitchell's men at Peak Hill in New South Wales and broke off from the troop at the Bogan four days later. The other Aboriginal guide was Piper, who had also assisted Mitchell in 1836; he joined this later expedition to Tropical Australia at Boree in New South Wales (Mitchell 1848:13–17; Baker 1997:148–52).

Mitchell also sought help from Aboriginal people along the journey. For example, at the cattle run of Derribong in New South Wales he sought the assistance of Dicky, a young Aboriginal boy of about 10 years of age who then stayed with Mitchell for the entire trip. Mitchell found Dicky's knowledge of the waterholes in the area to be extremely important. At a point near Mount Foster in New South Wales, Mitchell sought the help of another Aboriginal person, Yulliyally, who led them to the Barwon. Mitchell used Yuranigh to befriend Yulliyally and to retain his bush craft for the group. He stayed in their service for ten days, and was rewarded with a tomahawk, pipe tobacco and a shirt (Mitchell 1848:25–26, Baker 1997:158–60).

Mitchell also used two other Aboriginal guides to lead him to water in an area near the Narran River that was uncharted. These two men walked one hundred and thirteen kilometres (70 miles) and showed Mitchell where water and good grasses for his horses could be found. They followed the Narran into Queensland on his way to St George (Kooma country), where they found the well-used paths of the Ualarai people. At Angledoot Mitchell came across an Aboriginal village, with material culture such as duck and emu nets, and stone and iron tools, arranged around the huts. He noted that the tools were a mixture of traditional and introduced material, such as iron tied with cloth, and fixed with gum, a traditional method. Just north of the Queensland border Mitchell was looking for the Balonne River, which flows through Kooma country. Yuranigh interviewed a local to ascertain where this river was. Mitchell indicates that Yuranigh did not understand the local language but was able to confirm their present location (Mitchell 1848:106; Baker 1997:160).

After the Narran, Mitchell and his men encountered two Aboriginal men from the Kooma nation. One was an Elder; the other a youth who led them to the Balonnego River and the Barwango River (Barwan River), and into a large body of warriors from the Bigambul nation. Mitchell described this as 'a black phalanx of Aborigines amid the trees' (Mitchell 1848:109; Baker 1997:162).

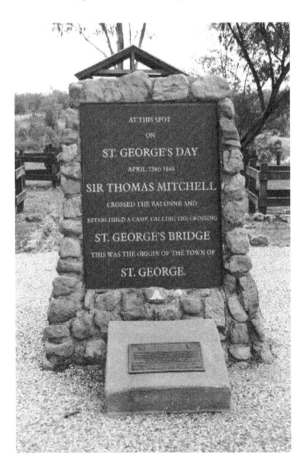

Figure 36 Mitchell's memorial, St George, Queensland. Photo: Dale Kerwin, 2004.

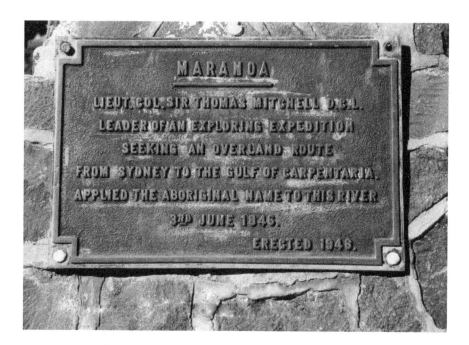

Figure 37 Mitchell's memorial at Mitchell Qld. Photo by Dale Kerwin 2004.

After meeting this large group of men Yuranigh would not go any further with the Elder and younger man (Mitchell 1848:109–10, Baker 1997:162). The Elder brought a number of his mob back to the camp and Yuranigh entered into a discourse with them. Mitchell and his men were camped on what the local mob called the Congo, on the Culgoa River near Dirranbandi (Mitchell 1848:109–11; Baker 1997:163). At this point Mitchell marked trees near his campsites with Roman numerals so other Europeans could follow his wandering and take up the Aboriginal space and make it theirs. The Culgoa was a branch of the Balonne River, which he followed to present-day Saint George, leaving half of his men with orders to follow his tracks in several weeks. Mitchell followed this river through Mandandanji country, passing several Aboriginal camping sites.

Mitchell's next encounter with Aboriginal people was at Cogoon River, now called Coogoon, near a lake called Turanimga and a hill the local mob called Toolumba, not far from Roma in Bidjara country (Baker 1997:165). Further north of Roma Mitchell encountered more men from the Mandandanji nation and they entered into a discussion, but he was unable to interpret what was said.

From the discussions he was able to fix four landmarks: the Bindango hill, the smaller Binyego hill, a creek called Tagando where he camped, and the Maranoa River (meaning 'human hand'). The men then travelled in a north-westerly direction until they reached the Maranoa River, where Mitchell made camp and waited for Kennedy to arrive with the rest of the supplies, equipment, and men (Mitchell 1848:142–45; Baker 1997:170–72).

Mitchell took another advance party of men and equipment up the Maranoa and left Kennedy in charge of the remaining men and equipment at this depot. He headed through the Nguri people's country and at one point made a horse charge against a warring party who were trying to move the invaders along. After this show of force, the local mobs stayed away from Mitchell and his men and strange animals until he reached Mt Gregory, where they encountered a group of Miyan or Bidjara people on the Belyando River. He travelled a little further up this river and decided to turn back at Mount Douglas, as this was not the river that he thought would lead to the Gulf of Carpentaria (Mitchell 1848:267–74; Baker 1997:174–75). Mitchell retreated south along the tracks he had made in the landscape with the hooves of the livestock and wagon wheels. He named the landscape by its geographical features and declared the areas uninhabited, even though he saw many foot scuffs in the dirt and firestick farmed land (Mitchell 1848:295).

As he was returning to his depot at Lake Salvator and the Pyramids, he saw a travelling band of Aboriginal men and women all carrying bags of goods (Baker 1997:176–77). Here at a place called Mt Pluto, Yuranigh interviewed an old woman who was mending some emu nets and he ascertained that the local word for water was narran. Mitchell observed that the mobs on the Narran River some 241 kilometres (150 miles) south also called water narran. This exchange took place at what the old women called Cunno; this river runs into the Warrego River (Mitchell 1848:313–16; Baker 1997:178). The Aboriginal words for the Warrego River mean crooked or winding, and Cunno Creek means a chain of ponds. Not far from this location is Cunnamulla, which in Aboriginal language means a long, deep stretch of water, with ulla meaning water (Baker 1997; The Historical Society 1969:9).

Around the Warrego district are the Aboriginal nations of Budjari on the Bulloo River and Thiralla on the Wilson River. Near Cooper Creek is the nation of Yantrawinta (Wangkumara), the Dieri of the lower part of Cooper Creek, and near the Paroo River the nation of Parundi (Barundji) west of Charleville. The nations of the Buntamurra (Kunia) and the nation of Barunga (Murwar) are near the border of New South Wales and the Northern Territory (The Historical Society 1969:147). In 1871, as a consequence of the invasion of Aboriginal space, over 300 Wangkumarra men, women and children were killed at Thargomindah homestead in retaliation for the murder of a white drover. The black troopers shot people as they ran from the police attack. Only a young boy survived, and told the tale as an old man. He told how his mother hid him under their hut, which was burned to the ground along with the rest of the huts in the village. The survivor was not identified in the records (in The Historical Society 1969:149).

When Mitchell was at the headwaters of the Barcoo, he named it the Victoria River. He thought the Barcoo (an Aboriginal word) was the great river that ran north to the Gulf and named it Victoria River, but did not realise that the Barcoo, which is its name now, empties itself into Lake Eyre. He observed some large huts of substantial structure, which were designed with a lean-to roof with rafters and thin square pieces of bark-like tiles fixed to it. This is believed to be a village of the Iningai nation. Mitchell considered this to be the Eldorado of Australia, the finest region. It was in fact the Barcoo, with its deep calm water as large as the Murray River and boundless plains covered with grass (Mitchell 1848:322). The area became famous during the shearers' strike of 1891 at Barcaldine in Queensland (Hoch 1986:14). Mitchell wrote that the land was unoccupied but did note that the ground on the banks of the Barcoo was littered with large mussel shells that made the ground white and appear covered with snow (Mitchell 1848:321). This is Kuungkari country. Here, in the middle of the continent, Mitchell found an iron tomahawk which appeared odd, as this country had not been surveyed by any white man (Mitchell 1848:325). The white hordes were breaking out of their colonial confines as people searched out land to squat on. Mitchell made camp near a large waterhole, which he named Yuranigh Ponds (Mitchell 1848:327). Then he returned with his men to Kennedy and to the depot that was known by the local mob as Mundi (Baker 1997).

Surveyors such as Mitchell built stockyards, fenced gardens and grew vegetables; in effect they created their own little Europe. 'A good stock-yard had been set; a store-house had also been built; a garden had been fenced in, and contained lettuce, radishes, melons, cucumbers' (Mitchell 1848:356). By the time Mitchell had reached St George, squatters were moving into the country. This was evidenced by horse tracks and information gained from some local women digging for food. Five white men and a group of Aboriginal guides made the tracks (Mitchell 1848:380). After travelling south, Mitchell camped at Snodgrass Lagoon at Waterloo Creek in New South Wales – the site of an 1838 massacre in which a large number of Kamilaroi people were killed (Baker 1997). Major Nunn, who led the troops, went on a murderous spree lasting four days, killing Aboriginal people as he met them (Elder 1988:63–71). At this site Mitchell considered his surveying expedition at an end, and handed command to Kennedy for the final stage back to Sydney.

Mitchell gained information from Aboriginal people during his survey to help him find water; to move his men over the best paths, and to find the best camping sites. The following records indicate that on nine occasions Mitchell relied upon Aboriginal knowledge:

19th December 1845. Bultje . . . informed me where the water was to be found; and how I should travel so as to fall in with my former route, by the least possible detour.

9th January 1846. These natives gave us also friendly hints that gentlemen should be careful of the spears of the natives of Nyingan, as many natives of Nyingan had been shot lately by white men from Wellington Valley.

27th January. I learnt from the natives that this creek also joined the Bogan . . . the natives point northward, they gave the name of Marra.

8th March. The natives maintained that the water in this extensive swamp came neither from the east nor west, but from the river directly before us, which came from the north-ward.

9th March. On my asking the natives where it went to, they pointed to the various narrow watercourses and the swamp as the final depositories of the water.

1st April. On our way the natives were very careful to point out how muddy hollows could best be avoided by our drays.

14th May. The old native pointed much to the north-west, frequently repeating the word Maranoa'.

10th August. The old man had intelligibly pointed out to Mr Brown the direction in which this river came, i.e. from the S.W.

19th October. Mr. Kennedy endeavoured to ascertain, through Dicky, the downward course of the river, and she seemed to express, and point also, that the river passed southerly into Balonne, which river she named, and even the Culgoa. (Mitchell 1848:13, 31, 45, 87, 89, 110, 162, 271, 357)

Information given to Mitchell assisted him to make use of Aboriginal paths that led him to water, or over ground low in vegetation that made pulling and carts easier, as the following journal entries attest:

21st December 1845, Guided by my old friend Bultje, we pursued a straight line through the forest to Currandong.

2nd March 1846, beyond the Barwan there at the Morella Ridges, to which the natives were in the habit of resorting at certain seasons, by a path of their own.

9th March, we had followed well-beaten paths of natives during the whole of this day's ride'.

25th March, crossing the Narran there, by a beaten track, beside a native fishing fence.

26th March, a small path along the river margin.

21st August, the track led us through hollows.

13th September, the extensive burning by the natives, a work of considerable labour, and performed in dry weather, left tracts in the open forest.

24th September, 'well beaten paths. (Mitchell 1848:15, 77, 90, 103, 104, 281, 306, 324)

During the survey, Mitchell also relied on sightings of smoke, as smoke generally indicated Aboriginal occupation of land, and so water would be in the vicinity. His journal of 1846 indicates that these sightings occurred on 26th January, 8th, 21st 30th May, 11th July, 3rd August, and 4th September. He witnessed 'a vast column of smoke . . . plainly to mark the further course of our river' (Mitchell 1848:216). Paths were also investigated and apparent by large numbers of footprints in the dirt. He recorded a number of these occurrences on 20th and 26th March, 11th July, 2nd and 12th August, and 3rd September (Mitchell 1848:98, 177, 229, 257, 273, 295).

Other information recorded in Mitchell's journal was the existence of shell middens used by Aboriginal people as signposts. Mitchell recorded these on the 8th July, 3rd August, 17th & 21st September (Mitchell 1848:225, 259, 313, 321). Mitchell also observed Aboriginal scarring on trees and followed them for some distances on 17th April and again on 20th June (Mitchell 1848:126, 206). As well as observing fires, following Aboriginal tracks and feet marks, he encountered Aboriginal communities on ten occasions: 6th, 25th, 27th March (Mitchell 1848:83, 103, 105), 30th April (Mitchell 1848:141), 16th, 17th, 29th May (Mitchell 1848:166, 169, 182), 8th July

(Mitchell 1848: 225), 21st September (Mitchell 1848: 319), and 2nd October (Mitchell 1848: 333).

Mitchell copied Aboriginal technology and applied it for European usage, and this included his patent of the water bag that was inspired by the Aboriginal kangaroo skin waterbag. The boomerang propeller was another Aboriginal-inspired invention Mitchell claimed (Baker 1997).

Mitchell's journals were a blueprint for occupation and assisted other travellers. As Mitchell surveyed, he used many Aboriginal names for the landscape, making it easier to get more information from the original owners of the land. He differentiated one part of the landscape from another by adopting the descriptive names of the local mob. Mitchell used Aboriginal names so that it became a spatially shared landscape. Furthermore he used Aboriginal names to describe the landscape more than any other explorer before or since. However, his descriptions of the landscape interpret places as uninhabited. He frequently writes that at various locations he did not encounter Aboriginal people but he does frequently mention seeing many footprints.

Mitchell had the habit of setting up depots and base camps under his second-in-command, Kennedy. Kennedy mentioned Aboriginal visitors frequently in his notes, without realising that Aboriginal people were shadowing his men continuously. The fast-moving horses were difficult to keep up with, but the slower-moving stock were easier to follow. This rendered the interior deceptively uninhabited. Mitchell took note of words used by the mobs out in the Channel Country that were similar to those commonly used around Sydney Town. One such word is 'yerraman', which is Aboriginal for horse (Mitchell 1848:270). Mitchell also records the word 'Murra' which he suggests is 'universally known to natives' and relates to water and anabranches; the word is derived from the hand (Mitchell 1848:56). On 11 September 1846, Mitchell interviewed an old woman near the present town of Tambo who used the word 'Narran'. He inferred from this that 'the migration of native tribes has been progressive from south to north' (Mitchell 1848:303). On 27 October, Yuranigh questioned a woman about the name of the river they were on, which was near the present town of Mitchell, and she answered him 'in his language the name of the river Maranoa' (Mitchell 1848:372).

As we have seen, Mitchell used Aboriginal guides extensively and followed Aboriginal roads and paths to Aboriginal communities and supplies of water. He owed his success to Aboriginal guides, and used Aboriginal place-names and landmarks to gain information. He also adapted Aboriginal intelligence for his own purposes – such as fires and scarred trees – to locate water.

Edmund Kennedy

Kennedy was placed in command of a survey expedition on 25 May 1848, with 12 other men, including the Aboriginal guide Galmarra. They travelled to Rockingham Bay near Cardwell, North Queensland, for an overland trip to Cape York. The point of departure was in the Djirbalngan and Wargamaygan countries. When he departed in the barque *Tam O'Shanter*, Kennedy stated that 'a viler looking country never looked me in the face before' (Fitzgerald 1982:101–102).

Kennedy was by now an experienced surveyor and in 1847 he took a small band of men to search for Mitchell's Victoria River, and so led this party to the northernmost point of Mitchell's survey. After finding Mitchell's river he followed it, but decided that this was Cooper Creek, which Charles Sturt described and named. It emptied into the desert country and did not flow either to the Gulf or across the continent. During this expedition he named the Thomson River, a large body of water similar in size to Mitchell's Victoria River (*Australia's Heritage*, vol. 5, 1989:841–45; McEwan 1985).

Kennedy knew that the Victoria was the river they had come across earlier with Mitchell; it dwindled into Lake Eyre. While camped on the banks of the Barcoo he was told its name by the traditional owners. The Victoria was then changed to the Barcoo (McEwan 1985:281). While surveying the Maranoa and Warrego Rivers, he described the Aboriginal landscape after it had been firestick farmed, with new grasses growing after the burn, 'like well advanced young fields of barley' (*Australia's Heritage*, vol. 5, 1989:842).

After this expedition was completed, Kennedy was asked to lead a party of 12 men, 27 horses and 100 sheep, and every bit of equipment that an expedition of this kind might require. His orders were to survey the east coast of Cape York Peninsula and take on new supplies once he reached the tip of Cape York, from a waiting ship at Albany Island (the northernmost government station in Queensland at that time). Then he was to survey the west coast of Cape York Peninsula and explore the rivers that flowed into the Gulf. The objective was to establish a route from the Gulf to the settled areas of the south of the country (Bolton 1972; McEwan 1985:281–82).

The trip started poorly on 24 May 1848; it took several days for the travellers to disembark at Cardwell because there was not a suitable landing site for the men and equipment (*Australia's Heritage*, vol. 5, 1989:841–45; McEwan 1985; Pike 1982). When Kennedy and his party left Cardwell they moved through the countries of Wargamy, Dyirbal, Yidiny, Djabugay, Kuku-Yalanji and the Guugu-Yimithirr language groups around Hope Vale (Bottoms 1999).

The Djabugay walking tracks went from Cairns into the surrounding ranges, and have been given the names of Smith's Track, Douglas Track and McDonald's Track (Reser *et al.* 2000:47). The mobs in North Queensland view themselves as Bama people, and belong to the rainforests of the east coast. Their Dreaming, or Bulurru, is recorded in stories related to place, storyplace. The mobs along this coast also have storywaters that relate to the travels of the ancestral beings along the coastal waters and coastal rivers:

Djimburra (walking tracks) cross the ranges throughout the Wet Tropics Bama Lands. Well-established djimburra were important for travel to access seasonal foods/resources, places and other Bama. They also linked the Storywaters, and often followed the path of these Stories, in line with associated customs – the way which their Gurra-Gurra (ancestors) had before them. With this in mind, one can appreciate that there were many major thoroughfares from the coast to the Tablelands. (Bottoms 1999:13)

The first part of Kennedy's survey covered the 'Atherton Tablelands and across Minbun bora ground. This track was approximately 26 miles in length and is now called Kenny road; it formed part of the Millaa Millaa track (Birtles 1967: file 19).

It was not long before sickness visited Kennedy and his party of men, as well as the failure of his introduced animals and equipment. This caravan of men and animals was travelling through the typical rainforests of the Tully area of Queensland. This region has Australia's highest rainfall, which slowed the party significantly. Kennedy had planned to take enough provisions to last eight months (McEwan 1985). The trip suffered one disaster after another: horses died, men stole food from the stores, and tropical disease afflicted them. The local mobs of the Kokowara, the Bakanambia, and the Mutumui attacked the party as it moved through their countries. Kennedy was almost killed early in the trip, but had been saved by a warning from Galmarra (*Australia's Heritage* vol. 5, 1989:844, McEwan 1985:285). He raised the alarm as a spear was thrown at Kennedy, and narrowly missed him. In the ensuing battle four Aboriginal men were shot (McEwan 1985:285).

During his travels, Kennedy was continually attacked by warring parties, which included the Lamalama people of the Princess Charlotte Bay area. The travelling group was again attacked by the Lamalama warriors who set fire to the grasses; they only just escaped with their lives by reaching a clearing (McEwan 1985:285).

On the way to Weymouth Bay, Kennedy and his men passed through the countries of the Kandju and the Kawadji. Kennedy made a depot at the mouth of the Pascoe River at Weymouth Bay, which is Umtaalnganu country. He left eight men there and one after another six of these men died; only two survived to tell the tale. Kennedy, Galmarra and three others made a dash for Port Albany, where Kennedy thought help was available. Kennedy left the three men near Shelburne Bay, Cape Grenville (Wuthathi country), two of them were very sick and one had accidentally shot himself. The three men were never seen again. This left Kennedy and Galmarra to travel the remaining distance for help with four horses, all of which died from being either trapped in bog or speared (Bolton 1972:13; Joy 1964:101–103; Pike1982).

When Kennedy and Galmarra were at Escape River and heading for Newcastle Bay, they were on Anggamundi and Yadhaiganna countries. This was basically a trap for the two travellers, as Kennedy was so weak that Galmarra was forced to carry him. Aboriginal warriors followed the two men and continued to harass them. On 13 December 1848, they attacked as dusk fell. Barbed spears fell on both of the men; Kennedy was hit in the back with a spear tipped with a barb of stingray, another hit him above the right knee, and yet another pierced his right side. Galmarra received a whack to his forehead from a spear, which cut him above the eye. When Galmarra went to fetch the saddlebags, the attackers came back and took Kennedy's possessions (McEwan 1985:286).

Galmarra had to carry his friend and the harassment continued until Kennedy was speared again, this time fatally. In his death throes, Kennedy told Galmarra to take his journals to the waiting ship. Galmarra dug a grave using a tomahawk, buried his friend and at nightfall waded into the river, which now has his English name Jacky Jacky, and swam for 13 days. He eluded the attacks of the warring party and reached the waiting *Ariel* on 23 December 1848. Along this flight he hid Kennedy's journal and notebooks (McEwan 1985:287). The journal has not yet been found and neither has Kennedy's grave. His notebooks were retrieved in May 1849; although damaged by weather they still provide some insight into this disaster (Pike 1982).

'Jacky Jacky' (Galmarra) became the darling of the colony until his painful death five years later from injuries he received when he fell into a fire and was badly burnt. Of the 13 men only Galmarra, Carron the botanist, and Goddard the convict survived the expedition (*Australia's Heritage*, vol. 5, 1989:844; McEwan 1985:287; Joy 1964:102).

There is little in the written record to determine whether Kennedy and his men followed Aboriginal paths. From all indications this band of men had to machete their way through the thick rainforest, which was covered with lawyer cane that dug thorns into their skin and ripped their clothing. There is no record of Kennedy naming any of the natural features on the Cardwell Range, which they scaled in the early stages of the trip. The river he crossed was the Tully. Carron named several species of flora after Kennedy and a species of grass after Galmarra. The road between Laura and Coen is now known as the Kennedy Road. Only Carron's written account of being stranded at Pascoe River survives as a record of this journey, and of the Aboriginal refusal to accept the occupation of their country. The most likely reason for the Kennedy's failure is that he was unable to secure the help of local Aboriginal people; he gained no information and was unable to secure the services of an interpreter. In the final analysis, Kennedy failed to gain intelligence as to the location of Aboriginal roads and paths.

The Gregory brothers

The young Gregory brothers moved from England and grew up with Aboriginal children on the edge of the frontier at Swan River in Western Australia, where they spent most of their time learning how to live off the land. These were first generation invaders; they were young boys growing up in a New World, where the old history was being written over and erased. They grew into bushmen, travelled with horses and guns, and moved over the landscape light and fast. The Gregory brothers were armed with the most modern weapons of that time – they were equipped with the Minie rifle that was used by the British in the Crimean War of 1854–55 (Gregory 1859:204; Birman1979:99).

In 1854, the Royal Geographical Society in London urged that an expedition be resourced for the purpose of travelling from the west coast of Australia to the shores of the east coast; they were also to search for Leichhardt who had been missing since 1848. However this objective was abandoned on orders received from London in early February 1855 (Birman 1997:1988). The British Government funded the survey and the New South Wales Government appointed Augustus Gregory leader of the expedition, which included his brother Henry along with 16 other men, 50 horses, 200 sheep and enough supplies and equipment to last two years (*Australia's Heritage*, vol. 6, 1989: 961–67). The group of men left Sydney on 18 July 1855 on the barque *Monarch* and the schooner *Tom Tough,* and sailed north, taking on livestock and provisions at Moreton Bay. From here they sailed up to the Torres Strait and west to Victoria River near the Northern Territory–Western Australian border (*Australia's Heritage*, vol. 6, 1989:961–67).

They set down at Treachery Bay, Point Pearce, at the mouth of the Victoria River on 24 November 1855. The livestock and supplies were unloaded at a point further up the river, where they made a base camp for six months. J.R. Elsey, surgeon and naturalist, was left in charge of the base camp and made friends with local Aboriginal men Drand and Deartijero, who assisted him in collecting zoological specimens (Birman

Figure 38 The boab tree, 2 July 1855. Gregory's base camp at Victoria River, Timber Creek, Northern Territory which is also an Aboriginal sacred site.

1979:140). Augustus Gregory undertook reconnaissance of the region to Sturt Creek – a preliminary preparation for his push into what was left of the Aboriginal space. They returned on 9 May 1856 after surveying 2,400 kilometres, and Gregory decided to leave most of his supplies and equipment at the depot that they had established before the major survey to Queensland (Birman 1979:88).

Gregory left camp on the Victoria River on 21 June at 10 a.m. with six other men, 27 packhorses, and five months' of provisions (Gregory 1859:79) to reach his goal at Port Curtis. Each man was equipped with a rifle, a horse pistol, powder and shot. They used these weapons when they encountered Aboriginal people. By 1855, European incursion had become more brutal, and encounters frequently ended in death (Birman 1979:145). Gregory's quest was to ride with supplies and equipment they could carry, and to travel 4,000 kilometres from west to east to reach Port Curtis on 16 December 1856 (*Australia's Heritage*, vol. 6, 1989:961–67; Pike 1982:57–58; Finkel 1975; Cannon 1987:212). Gregory's journal entries confirm that he followed Aboriginal paths (Gregory 1859). He reported that they encountered Aboriginal people on twenty-five occasions. The surveyors described five shell middens,

> February 15th. Followed a line of trees to the head of a small creek, this spot seemed to be much frequented by natives, and large quantities of mussel shells lay around their fires.
> July 14th. On the banks of which were large heaps of mussel shells at the camps of the blacks.
> August 5th. Large quantities of mussel shells lay at the old camping places of the blacks among the banks of the MacAthur River.
> August 21st, Camp LI. Large quantities of mica shells . . . on the banks of the river, in the camps of the natives. (Gregory 1859:51–97)

Further to the shell middens he reported and described an Aboriginal quarry,

> January 25th. Halted during the heat of the day at the spot the bed of the creek had been cut through the basal into sandstone exposing a line section of the junction of the two rocks . . . this altered sandstone and white quartz like rock are much used by the natives for the heads of their spears, during this day's journey great quantities of broken stones and imperfect spearheads were noticed on the banks of the creek. (Gregory 1859:44–45)

Like other surveyors Gregory scanned the horizon for signs of smoke from Aboriginal fires, which would indicate that water could be found in the area (Gregory 1859).

> February 19th. Surprised a native . . . several smokes have been observed . . . which show that water must exist.
> March 11th. Observed several fires along the creek . . . indicating that natives existed in that direction, and doubtless water.

July 2, Camp X. Observed the fires of a party of blacks who have camped at the waterhole . . . several heaps of mussel shells lay at interval on the banks of the creek.

July 10. In search of a sufficient supply of water . . . passed some blacks sitting at a fire.

25th July. Vast columns of smoke rise to the E. and SE (near Roper River) (Gregory 1859:52–89).

The surveyors also followed several Aboriginal paths

September 30th. Followed a native path to a creek.

March 20th. Observed a native line about 5 miles to the north . . . concluded that water existed at no great distance.

July 7th. Crossing the outward track, and at length came to a shallow water course. (Gregory 1859:15–83)

Gregory also described a line of Aboriginal scarred trees and an Aboriginal bora ground.

April 14th. Saw several native paintings.

August 14th, Camp XLV. Several trees near this pool of water had been marked by natives, the bark been removed and the wood painted yellow with brown spots at regular intervals, and vertical black-waved lines. (Gregory 1859:70–95)

These marked trees provided intelligence on where to locate water, and then it was not by chance that the surveyor came to several Aboriginal settlements,

December 1st. Many small stone huts had been erected . . . it is possible that these erections are used as temporary sepulchres.

May 14th. A small party of natives came to the camp this morning to barter.

July 6th. A fine water hole . . . a party of blacks were camped.

May 29. Mr Wilson brought a native in the boat from Stony Spit.

August 8, Camp XLI. Found some spears and water vessels . . . It is evident that they have been cutting instruments of iron and also stone.

August 13th, Camp XLIV. Found a fishing net neatly made of twisted bark, the mesh one and a half inch, the length about 30 feet. Some fishing spears showed the marks of iron tools having been used in their construction.

October 24th. On the banks of the creek we observed the marks of a recent camp of a large party of blacks, and a patch of ground was cleared of grass, and the surface scraped into ridges for a space of 30 yards long by 20 wide.

November 3rd, Camp CVIII. [At fine waterhole of the Suttor River] we saw some blacks, who decamped, and ran into the scrub.

November 13th. [At Peak Range] saw some blacks who pointed down the creek . . . where water can be found. (Gregory 1859: 30–126)

The men who went with the Gregory brothers were specialists in their field, and a reasonable amount of time was taken to record everything they encountered. These men could survey and analyse the landscape thoroughly and accurately.

Gregory successfully navigated around the landscape using other surveyors' records and descriptions of the east coast of Australia. He followed Leichhardt's 1844–45 trip east to west, as well as Mitchell's 1846 trip, and in 1858 undertook an expedition in search of Leichhardt. By following the Channel Country that fringes the Simpson Desert he was able to reach Adelaide (Birman 1979:188–90). By using Aboriginal paths, the information this crew of men gathered added a great deal to geographical knowledge, solving the great riddles of the inland sea, and the second inland river system (Bolton 1972:15, Birman and Bolton 1972:30).

As Cunningham had previously, Gregory encountered evidence of European incursion into the Aboriginal landscape at a point near Daly Waters. He found a deserted and overgrown European camp at Elsey Creek and spent the night there. Gregory observed that the trees were cut and marked by a metal axe and that there were the remains of a substantial hut that had been destroyed by fire (Birman and Bolton 1972:28; Birman 1979:146).

At Roper River in the Northern Territory, Gregory and his men were attacked and several Aboriginal warriors were shot. In a charge reminiscent of a horse infantry, Gregory and his men rode through the attack, firing as they went (*Australia's Heritage*, vol. 6 1989: 961–67, Pike 1982:57–58; Finkel 1975).

This itinerant band of men followed Leichhardt's tracks from Port Essington to Rockhampton and then on to Brisbane. Elsey, the surgeon who accompanied them, considered that they had 'steeple chased across the continent' (Birman 1979:155). Gregory and his men achieved the feat in six months: 'December 16th, reached Brisbane at 2 p.m.' (Gregory 1859:134), whereas Leichhardt the botanist had taken well over a year (Bolton 1972:15; Birman 1979:155).

The surveying work of Augustus and Henry Gregory involved travelling from west to east and later down through the Channel Country and on to Adelaide, Although they are not as well known as the other overlanders, they nevertheless accomplished these feats quickly and easily. The exploration from Victoria River to Port Curtis, near Rockhampton, took only four months. While moving south from the Dawson River Gregory made salient observations about Aboriginal trading paths in south-west Queensland. Aboriginal nations were linked by songlines along these paths such as the Two Dog. Gregory's surveying helped to complete the map of Australia: he coloured the blank areas and spaces on the map that were not known, thus confirming the unknown and rendering a European presence on the Aboriginal space.

Like other surveyors of the time, the Gregory brothers encountered the advancement of non-Aboriginal people such as stockmen and prospectors. They also travelled on Aboriginal paths. The Gregory brothers moved along sightlines that were overlaid on the Aboriginal paths, so they moved over known country. These areas had been sung and mapped and recorded by Aboriginal nations as a means of making sense of the landscape (*Australia's Heritage*, vol. 6, 1989: 961–967; Pike 1982:57–58).

The Jardine brothers

The Jardine brothers, Frank and Alick (Alec) were employed to run cattle to the settlement of Somerset (Pulu), at the tip of Cape York Peninsula which at that time was the most northern outpost of the Queensland Government. In May 1864 they set off from Rockhampton to Somerset (Pajinka), with eight other men, four of whom were Aboriginal (Finkel 1975:41–42; *Injinoo Handbook* 1995:5). These four Aboriginal men – Eulah, Peter, Sambo and Barney – were recruited from the districts of Rockhampton and Wide Bay and were police trackers. Typical of the chronicles of that period they were described as 'black boys' (Hiddins 1998). The Aboriginal scouts were to lead the droving team and to feed the party of men with food from the land (Hiddins 1998). This itinerant band of men collected provisions and stock along the way at Bowen, where they officially pushed into the Cape at Carpentaria Downs (Hiddins 1998:2).

Equipped with 42 horses and 250 cattle for the 2,000 kilometre trip, the Jardine brothers took a route up the west coast of the Cape York Peninsula; it had been surveyed by Leichhart as far as the Mitchell River in 1845, and by Kennedy as far as Escape River in 1848. This cattle drive took the brothers seven months and they travelled over much the same route as Kennedy. However, the Jardine brothers' departure point was 800 kilometres south of Kennedy's (Hiddins 1998:vi).

The Jardine brothers moved as a forward advance guard, scouting and finding the best tracks to use, and dispersing potential Aboriginal attacks.

> The natives at first stood up courageously, but either by accident or though fear, despair or stupidity they got huddled in a heap, in and at the margin of the water, when ten carbines poured volley after volley into them from all directions, killing and wounding with every shot . . . with about thirty being killed . . . Many more must have been wounded and probably drowned, for fifty nine rounds were counted as discharged. (in *Injinoo Handbook* 1995:5)

The men were well armed: the Aboriginal scouts were equipped with 'the ordinary double-barrelled police carbine and the whites with Terry's breech-loaders, and Tranter's revolvers' (Hiddins 1998:10), and they used these weapons to clear a path through the Aboriginal space. At a place on the Mitchell River known as Battle Camp, the two brothers were attacked by a large party of Kuku-Yalanji or Guugu-Yimidhirr warriors. They charged on their horses and ran down and killed 30 Aboriginal warriors. Once again, on the Nassau River, several Aboriginal warriors attacked Frank Jardine and he shot and killed another three men. At the same location, Gilbert (who had travelled with Leichhardt in the 1844–45 expedition) was killed by the local mob – the Kunjen warriors. The drovers aggressively attacked Aboriginal groups as they drove their cattle to the tip of the Cape (Hiddins 1998:vii).

In turn, Aboriginal nations on Cape York Peninsula took the opportunity to harass and attack the group as they moved cattle through their countries. On one occasion near Cape Keer-weer during a thunderstorm, a group of Wik warriors attacked the drovers and stampeded the cattle and horses; a number of the warriors were killed. The final attack by Aboriginal warriors who were defending their country happened at Cape Grenville, close to where the six men who Kennedy left were attacked. The Jardines repelled the attack and killed several warriors, taking their weapons as spoils of war (Hiddins 1998).

These drovers followed Aboriginal paths. For example, records indicate that they camped on an old black's camp at Sinclair Creek. Then again on 1 November the droving team camped on a stream, where 'they breakfasted off some opossums and rubbish they got out of a black's camp' (Hiddins 1998:22). Further along the path, while following a chain of ponds looking for a campsite, they encountered a 'mob of blacks' travelling (Hiddins 1998:35). Camp XLI was on a respectable waterhole, and Jardine named the creek 'Eulah Creek', in honour of the Aboriginal scout who led them there. Further along, the drovers camped at a creek for which they had learned the local name, and decided to record this as Belourgh, which is Aboriginal for the swamp mahogany. It was Christmas, and Frank Jardine blazed a tree with 'XMAS 1864'.

On 8 February, while driving deeper into the Cape, they recorded that 'an old black's camp was passed in which they found heaps of shells, turtle, and shark bones' (Hiddens 1998:85). The drovers also took to following the Aboriginal example of rubbing themselves with fat, which afforded them protection from mosquitoes and other biting insects that can be found on the Cape (Hiddins 1998:92).

Like other surveyors before them, the Jardine brothers used the skills of Aboriginal guides to find lost horses and cattle, and also to supplement their food supply so that their provisions would last the whole trip. They also followed Aboriginal communication paths, as can be seen by the number of Aboriginal villages they encountered on their foray into Aboriginal space. Further to this they encountered resistance from Aboriginal people along their tracks, in the shape of Aboriginal warriors who attacked them.

H.O. Hodgkinson

Hodgkinson travelled south from Cloncurry to Lake Coongi near Cooper Creek in South Australia in 1876 on his north-western expedition (see Map 24). He used two Aboriginal black trackers, Harry and Larry. There is no record of where these two were recruited, and they were probably assigned to the expedition. He traversed the Channel Country and recorded that he 'used Aboriginal paths to find water' on numerous occasions (Hodgkinson 1876:9–17). He also mentioned finding Aboriginal settlements, Aboriginal observation points, several Aboriginal paths, a bora ground, several smoke signals which are described below.

On nine separate occasions Hodgkinson recorded following Aboriginal paths and tracks to water. These are listed below.

December 13th. Noticed all tracks run to the solitary puddle we were so fortunate to find.

December 17th. I struck a well-beaten bush track, apparently used for bush timber

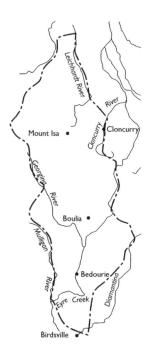

Map 24 W.O. Hodgkinson's north-western 1876 survey of the Channel Country. As adapted from the Queensland Depnartment of Natural Resources and Mines map of marine and inland explorers' routes. In Donovan 2002:49.

. . . finally upon a fine lagoon.

February 14th. The track was plain [and] unmistakable.

February 18th. I noticed numerous fresh native tracks.

February 19th, at Paltison Creek. Native fresh tracks, old camp and in the distance, smoke were numerous.

February 20th. Tracks of men, women and children were plainly visible in the sandy bed . . . Harry, the other boy ultimately found a native well.

February 21st. Very recent tracks of natives down the sandy creek.

February 22nd. Found blacks out hunting.

February 25th, at Swanwick River. Fresh native tracks. (Hodgkinson 1876:8–17)

As well as following Aboriginal paths, Hodgkinson also recorded an Aboriginal bora ground, Aboriginal observational points, and smoke signals on three separate occasions:

February 12th, at Malbon River. The blacks are busily firing the latter for wallabies.

February 29th. A warning smoke rose to the westward, I observed some form of communication . . . a large stone being placed in the form of bush with six other arranged in a semicircle on the ground beneath, three on each side of an opening left in the centre.

March 2nd. A whiff of smoke rise and instantaneously disappear . . . came upon a native camp near a splendid waterhole. (Hodgkinson 1876:9–19)

Also on three occasions, Hodgkinson records stumbling upon Aboriginal settlements;

December 2nd, at Black Gin Creek. A neat native Whirly . . . in an admirable position for a look-out.
December 3rd. The remains of a native camp.
December 4th. I struck a well-beaten bush track.
February 14th. An old native camp on the banks . . . tracks of the natives are more numerous, and their signal fires exhibit cognisance of our movements. (Hodgkinson 1876:8–14)

Hodgkinson also gained information from Aboriginal people while surveying and made diary entries to these contacts in the following records:

February 15th, at Macrossan River. Native seen . . . and Harry told me that he understood him to say that a large mob were camped close by. (Hodgkinson 1876:8–16)

Hodgkinson recorded Aboriginal trade routes on which there was a lively trade in pituri. He was informed of the trade in shells that came from the north-west. One of the interesting bits of information that Hodgkinson found was the place called Peecheringa, and it is presumed that this is where the pituri was grown (Hodgkinson 1876:214).

Hodgkinson surveyed and travelled Aboriginal trading routes and he recorded the movement of people along these common ways. He also noted that trade occurred along these paths. In later years, European commerce followed this movement of goods. Hodgkinson did a tour of the Channel Country, surveying from Cloncurry in the north to Cooper Creek in the south, before returning north to Cloncurry.

Stockmen and introduced beasts

Following the expeditions of the explorers, and in some cases leading the charge into the spatial geography of the new lands, were drovers and stockmen. It is estimated that there are over 72,000 kilometres of tracks used as stock routes which cover in excess of one million hectares in Queensland, along with associated camping and watering reserves (PestFact 1988:2).

The histories and exploits of the stockmen reveal that Aboriginal scouts usually went with them and doubled as stockmen. Aboriginal scouts interpreted the landscape and acted as emissaries when contact was made with other Aboriginal nations along the droving trails. The scouts would also round up stray cattle. David Hewitt suggests that Aboriginal people played a significant part in the early journeys through the north of Australia. Alfred Canning, who is remembered as the person who plotted the Canning Stock Route in Western Australia, used Aboriginal guides: Charlie, Gabbi, Bandicoot, Politician, Bungarra, Smiler, Sandow and Tommy Waldron (Hewitt 1980: 23). Canning was a cruel man who kept Aboriginal trackers in chains and would deprive them of sustenance for long periods. He would then release the unfortunates from the chains so they could direct Canning's team of cattle to water (Hewitt 1980).

Bruce Simpson surveyed the pioneering of the cattle industry in Australia, and comments on the resourcefulness and bushcrafts of Aboriginal stockmen. An Aboriginal scout worked for Nat (Nathaniel) Buchanan who led one of the most epic cattle drives in Australian history. Buchanan employed several Aboriginal stockmen. In 1860, Chucky and Tiger joined an expedition with Landsborough and Buchanan to the Thomson River. They travelled by way of creeks and rivers to Mount Douglas, across the Belyando to Lake Buchanan, to Torrens Creek and Towerhill Creek and the headwaters of the Thomson River, travelling as far south as Aramac (Buchanan 1997:8). Buchanan employed a number of Aboriginal trackers and stockhands and he named several of these men in his accounts (Cannon 1987; Barker 1966; Simpson 1996).

In 1861, an Aboriginal tracker who was with Buchanan and E.B. Cornish sighted fresh camel tracks near the Diamantina River in western Queensland, which they believed to belong to Burke and Wills' surveying party returning from the Cape. Buchanan and team had travelled from Bowen, on the coast, in search of new grazing land (Austin 1959:216; Buchanan 1997:13–14). None of the accounts gave a name to this tracker. In 1874, a feather footman, Birrianda from Belyando and the Dawson area, worked for Buchanan. Birrianda was employed as a black tracker; he was also notorious for attacking shepherds and was wanted for murder and killing stock. Birrianda obtained employment at Bowen Downs (Buchanan 1997:34–35). In 1876, Buchanan undertook a survey of the Gregory and Nicholson Rivers for better pastoral lands with an Aboriginal named Jimmy. The trip was over 480 kilometres, and Jimmy became a trusted friend. When Buchanan left Herbert Downs, Jimmy returned to his country at Normanton (Buchanan 1997:40–42). In 1878, Buchanan also made the first crossing of the Barkly Tablelands from the east to the Overland Telegraph Line in the Northern Territory near Powell Creek (Buchanan 1997:47).

In 1881, Buchanan drove twenty thousand head of cattle from Aramac to Glencoe, a distance of over 3,200 kilometres. He took several Aboriginal stock hands with him, but only names one, a fellow by the name of Spider, from Cunnamulla in Queensland. This column of men, horses, cattle, and gear were

Figure 39 A stock route positioned on an Aboriginal trading way. Located on the Moonie Highway and Bendee Road. Photo: Dale Kerwin, 2002.

strung out over a distance of 128 kilometres (Buchanan 1997:78–79). In his considerable travels over the Aboriginal landscape, Buchanan documented being led to water and following Aboriginal paths.

In 1886, Buchanan followed Aboriginal waterholes from Frew's Pond at Daly Waters to the Victoria River Downs area. This stock route is now called the Murranji Track, an Aboriginal word for frog. The purpose of this track was to establish a route to markets in Queensland and Kimberley goldfields. At Bucket Creek he employed local Aboriginal people to guide him along the Murranji Track to what is called Yellow Waterholes and the Murranji Waterhole. He drove his cattle and men to Top Springs and Wave Hill Station on the Victoria River. Following this, he went on to explore the headwaters of the Victoria River with George, an Aboriginal tracker. They followed Aboriginal paths that cut through the bends, making the trip shorter. In George's words, 'Good fella ground, can't miss 'em track'. Buchanan relied on George's tracking skills and on his ability to lead to water and to follow Aboriginal paths. George stayed with Buchanan for over 15 years and became a trusted friend (Buchanan 1997:114–15, 120–22).

In 1892, Buchanan drove one thousand cattle to the Murchison goldfields, a distance of 2,000 kilometres. This was to become known as the south-western Australian stock route. In his journals, Buchanan describes an Aboriginal cattle drover, Charlie Flannigan, who drove cattle along the same stock route from Richmond Downs in Queensland to the Northern Territory. In 1892 he killed a white drover and was sent to Fannie Bay jail in Darwin where he was executed. However, Charlie left a record of his life in the bush and droving cattle by being portrayed in a painting (Buchanan 1997:134, 138).

Buchanan, the lead drover and stockman of this epic trip, also pioneered Victoria River Downs, the Ord River station, and founded Wave Hill Station in the Northern Territory. The Wave Hill Station was the scene of an Aboriginal strike where the Gurindji people, led by Elder Vincent Lingiari, walked off the station to protest their living conditions – a battle that turned into one of the first claims for land rights. In 1975, nine years after the walk-off, Gough Whitlam handed the land back and it became the settlement of Daguragu Kalkaringi (Buchanan 1997:141).

In 1859, Buchanan also established a cattle and sheep station at Bowen Downs at Mount Cornish, Queensland, with Landsborough and established a stock route to Bowen, Queensland. (In 1861 William Landsborough was appointed head of an expedition to search for the ill-fated Burke and Wills expedition. He travelled from the Gulf of Carpentaria through central Queensland, naming the Gregory and Georgina rivers, onto Melbourne, in his search for the missing explorers. His search for the missing explorers last 16 months.)

Bowen Downs is famous for the largest cattle rustling in Australian history, with over one thousand head of cattle stolen from this property. Harry Redford, an expert drover and bushman, drove the stolen cattle to Adelaide in South Australia.

Harry Redford drove his stolen cattle down the Channel Country water system to Adelaide. Along this water system, when heavy rain fall it fills all the water holes and billabongs and provides plenty of feed and lush pastures to feed. Also along the Channel

Country there are native wells, such as the Artracoona native well, which rarely run dry and are used to water cattle. This water system encapsulates several Aboriginal Dreaming stories, including the Two Dog Dreaming and the Rainbow Serpent Dreaming stories. Harry Redford is fictionalised as Captain StarLight (Barker 1966: 40–45).

Buchanan followed Aboriginal Dreaming tracks across the length and breadth of Australia. He surveyed the track to Burketown from Bowen Downs, a distance of over 966 kilometres, and like other settlers of that time believed that the Gulf of Carpentaria would become the major port for the export of their wool and cattle. He made many long droving trips to stock properties in the Northern Territory and Western Australia. He drove 1,200 head of cattle from Queensland to Wave Hill Station in 1878. He departed from Aramac to Glencoe Station on the Daly River in the Northern Territory, and travelled a distance of over 2,250 kilometres. He is recorded as being the first to drive cattle from Burketown to Western Australia (Barker 1966:40–45). In 1881 he also drove 16,000 head of cattle from St George to Richmond Downs on the Flinders and collected a further 4,000 head of cattle to be taken overland to Glencoe, a distance of over 3,220 kilometres (Barker 1966:40–45). From Wave Hill, he surveyed stock routes so that he could drive cattle to reach markets and outlets. He established a stock route from Wave Hill to Newcastle Waters, where the overland Telegraph line stretched north and south, and on to the Georgina River in Queensland: a stock route still being used today (Barker 1966:40–45).

In 1896, the South Australian government gave Buchanan a grant of six camels and equipment for the purpose of establishing a stock route from the overland telegraph line to Lake Wells in Western Australia. Along the route, Buchanan hired a local Aboriginal tracker, Camel Jack, whom he chained at night to stop him from escaping. After being chained for a period of two weeks he freed Jack and paid him off with a waterbag, tucker, a tomahawk, and tobacco. However, Jack stayed with Buchanan and led him to several soaks, one of which was Welcome Water. The other water soak is known by its Aboriginal name, Kullga-ngunngunn. It 'had been excavated' and was 30 feet in diameter (Buchanan 1997:168). At the end of this survey Jack left Buchanan when they were near to his country at Tennant Creek.

In 1883 Buchanan, after establishing Richmond Downs in North Queensland, drove 4,000 head of cattle to the Ord River in Western Australia, a distance of 2,240 kilometres. In his quest to find lucrative outlets, he drove his beasts to the goldfields of Murchison in Western Australia to sell his animals. He pioneered stock routes from the Fitzroy River, in the West Kimberley, to the De Grey River, and from Roy Hill Fortescue River to Murchison. The latter stock route is about 3,000 kilometres and is known today as the Canning Stock Route (Barker 1966:40–45).

All of these main stock routes align with the major Aboriginal trading ways. Stock routes follow the water ways whether they are rivers, billabongs or soaks, because like people animals need water. In Western Australia the Canning Stock Route runs north to south and meets the Murranji Track at the Top End at Wyndham, Western Australia. The Murranji Track then heads down the Northern Territory main route south from Katherine, Mataranka, and to Newcastle Waters Station. The route splits

Figure 40 An Aboriginal path that is now a stock route located along the Diamantina Road near Winton. Photo by Dale Kerwin 2002.

into two, with one going south to Alice Springs and South Australia, and the other track into Queensland over the Barkly Tableland. It then travels south-east down the Georgina River to cross the Queensland border at Lake Nash and on to Camooweal and Dajarra. Before crossing the Northern Territory and Queensland border, the main route is joined by two feeder routes. The first came down from the western gulf, which joined the track at Anthony Lagoon; the second from Rockhampton Downs and Alroy. These joined to cross the border at Rankin for Camooweal or to continue south to Alice Springs (Simpson 1996: 91). Another important stock route is the Darling route, which takes stock and people from south-western Queensland through New South Wales, Victoria and on to Adelaide.

The Aboriginal stockmen's knowledge of the Australian bush made them indispensable members of any droving team. Aboriginal stockmen had a keen sense of direction, which made droving much easier. This was confirmed by a Royal Commission on 14 January 1908, which looked into Canning's treatment of Aboriginal people. An Executive Council found that if Aboriginal trackers were not used by explorers the exploring party would be in great danger, perhaps with tragic results (Hewitt 1980). It also found that stock routes were commonly established where water was available or could be found at a convenient distance, to enable the beasts to be watered and moved with less drama, and limiting the loss of stock when moved to markets.

CHAPTER SIX

Misrepresentation of the Grand Narrative – 'Walk Softly on the Landscape'

Surveyors cleared the Aboriginal landscape by rendering it in text; they replaced the Aboriginal text with their own form of communication. They also inscribed it with their own spatial representations (Carter 1987:50). It is clear from the foregoing analysis of surveyors' reports and journals that some, like Mitchell, described the landscape with the eye of an artist; in fact, they made the landscape picturesque:

> The hills overhanging outline. Some resembled gothic cathedrals in ruins; others forts; others masses were perforated, and being mixed and contrasted with the flowing outlines of evergreen woods, and having a fine stream in the foreground, gave a charming appearance to the whole country. (Carter 1987:237)

Carter points out that Mitchell's landscape was one in which the traveller, poet, colonist, and critic might feel equally at home. This was typical of the European attitude of that time; the Aboriginal landscape served an occupational purpose to a culture that regarded itself as a civilised society (Carter 1987:245). These nomadic overlanders came and went through the Aboriginal landscape – but on their heels came the squatters. This caught the Aboriginal within the boundaries of the white spatial taxonomic, and from then on forced Aboriginal society to the fringes of the newly-created boundaries (Carter 1987: 340).

The use of Aboriginal guides made it easier for the white surveyors to map and name the Aboriginal landscape. The Aboriginal landscape was created by firestick farming, thus presenting a balanced space that appealed to the eye of the European, and gave the squatter and pastoralist an advantage in terms of the exploitation of Aboriginal resources, thereby making the resources and landscape their own. The Aboriginal space came to be filled with European imagination. Private enterprise capitalised on the knowledge provided by surveyors; Europeans settlers moved into Aboriginal space and occupied it; these settlers then opened their own communication paths to move their introduced goods around the landscape.

In colouring the map of Australia, Europeans sketched it in their own image and brought with them things from their own household. The new Australians have only been here for a blink of the eye compared to the first Australians and the changes that they have wrought on the landscape in this short time are tremendous. Even the very sounds of Aboriginal Australia have changed. Where once the parrot screeched, and other fauna congregated, the space now reverberates with the sounds of the starling or the cane toad. These invaders are replacing the first inhabitants. Aboriginal Australia has seen the mass invasion of Aboriginal space by aliens that have imposed foreign laws over their laws, put people in chains, and committed genocide. They also displaced indigenous species of flora and fauna by bringing in their own, which have competed successfully against the old. And yet, despite all this, Aboriginal culture has survived and its survival incorporates cultural memory.

Typical reports from the chronicles of the nineteenth century include the notion that Aboriginal people were the aggressors; they were seen as thieves and outlaws, hanging around waiting for the opportunity to either steal or attack the colonists. The fact of the matter was that an invasion was taking place. The invaders were stealing, raping, and changing the face of the landscape. They felled trees, planted new species of food plants, and erected fences. Aboriginal people were merely defending their country, standing up for what they owned, and protecting what was theirs.

Notwithstanding, Aboriginal people assisted invaders such as Leichhardt, Mitchell, the Jardines, and Hodgkinson. These men used Aboriginal guides and paths to move through this space – the European means of charting and travel was not adequate for this landscape. All surveyors have commented that they saw Aboriginal travellers. However, more reports exist of the brutality of the exploitation endured by Aboriginal people at the hands of the invaders. Henry Reynolds, for example, calls the settlers 'cruel and inclement conquerors' (Reynolds 1990:232). Aboriginal trackers, scouts, and guides accompanied surveyors, troopers, and stockmen. These people aided and abetted the dispossession and renaming of Aboriginal Australia. Guided by their knowledge of the Dreaming strings, these Aboriginal scouts could read the landscape, knew the paths, and had a cultural appreciation of their own maps. These scouts could also parley with Aboriginal nations to elicit information (Willey 1979:200).

Reynolds suggests that these two themes of 'resistance and assistance', of 'confrontation and collaboration', have been woven into Australian history since the first European settlement was established at Sydney Town in New South Wales in 1788. It was evident that while Bungaree worked for the invaders, Pemulwuy fought them (Reynolds 1990:233; Willey 1979:201). Nonetheless, Aboriginal people remember the resistance leaders, as well as those who assisted the invaders, and who were subsequently immortalised by the new Australians.

The physical as well as the human geography of Australia has also changed. Aboriginal travellers moved along paths that later became highways that others now travel along. The surveyors, stockmen, pioneers, troopers, and settlers all moved over these highways to reach destinations. While in European terms these paths took and continue to take people to different places, from an Aboriginal point of view, time, space and distance link the Dreaming. This study has drawn attention to these aspects, but the map is still incomplete because the issues covered are as vast as the Australian continent. People now travel along Aboriginal highways and through Aboriginal space; they pass innumerable streets and any number of minor roads created by the ritual of travel, in this way acknowledging the social memory of that travel and movement of past explorers and people.

The concept of Aboriginal people as primitive and nomadic is erroneous given the many examples cited that show that Aboriginal settlements were numerous, and not simply regional oddities. The evidence presented also suggests that Aboriginal people were sedentary. Within Aboriginal communities there were people who specialised in certain activities and crafts, such as making and mending equipment. This level of specialisation released people from certain activities, such as food gathering. In addition, Aboriginal culture has been considered stagnant, lacking in economy, and food production. But the chapters herein have shown a different reality: many sources suggest that Aboriginal people were food producers, had a thriving economy, and were not dependent on the local wilderness for sustenance.

This nonsense viewpoint was not only applied to Aboriginal people; it was also projected onto the Aboriginal landscape. The representation of the landscape as natural and wild, has causes tensions between Aboriginals and Europeans. These misrepresentations distort perceptions and cloud our understanding of the true nature of Aboriginal people and culture. The examples detailed show that Aboriginal people had extensive, well-developed communication routes, which were used extensively for travel and trade. These criss-crossed the Australian continent and were central to the flow of culture. Furthermore, the trade routes were, and still are, thick with meaning and were fully mapped. Aboriginal people inhabited the entirety of the Australian continent and developed technologies to orientate and communicate with others over ancient trade routes.

For a long time, Aboriginal people have presented spatial awareness to non-Aboriginal people through the medium of art. Since colonisation, the arts have played a major role in promoting this form of cultural mapping. Social scientists have tried to map Aboriginal association to their country. However, since antiquity, Aboriginal people have been painting the landscape, drawing it, singing it, telling stories about it, dancing it, and performing ceremonies about it. Yet even though the tide of history is turning, Australian courts still do not recognise that these representations come from within Aboriginal culture. Instead, for native title deliberations, they still continue to look for white documentation to ownership of land. While cultural mapping does appear in native title applications, white history carries more weight in court. What this effectively means is that the courts do not understand Aboriginal people. The courts do not recognise Aboriginal religion, nor do they understand our laws. The result is that if we do not present this in a language the courts can understand they will not recognise our claims to ownership of land (native title) (Ritter 2000).

Before European invasion, Aboriginal people mapped spatial history and named geological formations so that they became directional devices. Places of significance were also named and these would be related or linked through stories and other material property. Dreaming stories created connections based on localised stories, and these intangible concepts were presented in a concrete way as signposts.

Before annexation from Aboriginal ownership in 1830, Aboriginal people in Queensland occupied and enjoyed this space through spiritual, cultural, and economic means. Aboriginal Australia became known by the European names and all geological formations were overwritten by the European names, such as Cape Keer-Weer,

Cooktown, and Glasshouse Mountains. Even Aboriginal great trading ways have been overwritten with names like the Stuart, Pacific, Hume and Leichhardt highways. These have become the great communication ways of European Australia. Many, if not all, of these arterial roads are built on remnant Aboriginal sites. The naming of landscape was based on the epistemological European imagination of place. This nomenclature was a means to overlay a geographical taxonomy on the landscape, based on European names. The outcome has increased European ownership concomitant with European culture and as a European artefact.

As a cultural landscape, Australia is now emblazoned with white fellow artefacts from the 'old land'. Burke and Wills were immortalised when their historical imagery was blazed on a tree at Cooper Creek. Gregory emblazoned his name on a boab tree when he began his travels from West Coast of Australia to the East Coast of Australia. Relics of these historical actors litter the landscape.

Figure 41 Burke and Wills' dig tree Nappa Murrie valorising their feats. But in actual fact their exploration trip was a disaster.

Aboriginal Dreaming Paths and Trading Routes

Aboriginal people have had to face the broader issues of cultural *terra nullius* emanating from government instrumentalities run and developed by unimaginative, non-Aboriginal bureaucrats and some sectors of academia. This bureaucratic culture is based on an entirely different spatial history. In the afterglow of Mabo (see p. xi), Aboriginal people sought the right to provide Aboriginal geographical taxonomy, and a project was initiated: the 1993 'National Indigenous Place-Names Project' funded by the Australian Institute of Aboriginal and Torres Strait Islander Studies. Completion stalled due to funding restraints, and the enormity of the task of locating and classifying names across the breadth of Australia.

Australia's topography creates a context for Aboriginal traders to travel and trade across the landscape by tracks and rivers. This book has brought together sources and information relating to Aboriginal land management practices, population density, and the spread of diseases through the Aboriginal landscape by Europeans along Aboriginal communication paths. The current research also compares and develops the argument that Aboriginal peoples had technology for map making and the production of orienteering devices, in the form of storystrings and songlines, which are prevalent in Aboriginal culture. Indeed, it has been demonstrated here that there is much Aboriginal knowledge on trade routes and associated market places, which are not inferior to the Silk Road or other ancient trade routes.

Finally, the ancestral spirits speak of ancient laws of the land, they speak also of customs and relationships to country based on totems. The exploitation of Aboriginal roads by stockmen to drive their beasts over the promised lands to rich markets involved following the Dreaming tracks created by the ancestral spirits. The Dreaming tracks have been part of the landscape since time immemorial and are a living memory to the ingenuity of Aboriginal people. They are also part of the collective memory of all Aboriginal people. Today some of these tracks are known as stock routes, and they link rural communities across the landscape and are inaccessible by modern conventional vehicles. These tracks are only used as stock routes when times are bad and droughts have depleted the land of fodder for introduced beasts; grazers will then move their beasts over the landscape in search of feed.

In common law the principle of 'public works' extinguishes native title. 'Public works' includes stock routes as well as public roads, railways, memorials, and bores (*Formile v Selpam* (1998) 152 ALR 294). These monuments of Australian cultural heritage (the stock routes, roads and railways) are also the monuments to Aboriginal ancestral spirits – the dreaming tracks and songlines. They are the heritage of Aboriginal people; they are part of the great tradition of 'walkabout' – when Aboriginal people walked softly on the landscape.

Native Title accords Aboriginal peoples rights and interests in lands and waters that Aboriginal and Torres Strait Islander peoples have under their traditional laws and customs – laws and customs that are recognised by the common law. These can be viewed as a bundle of rights for Aboriginal people's native title rights that protect against automatic extinguishment principles of Aboriginal land ownership in Australian law. These bundle of rights in native title:

- Recognise Traditional Owners Native Title rights;
- Provide for some basic principles about Traditional Owners Native Title rights in Australia;
- Allows governments ways in which to validate or make legal past acts such as leases which native title makes invalid; and
- Allows State governments to act in the future and yet still protect native title rights.
- Gives Traditional Owners compensation in one form or another in return for the loss of native title.
- Sets out conditions on future acts which may affect native title in land and waters;
- Contains a process for finding out who has native title and which people to compensate.

Figure 42 Water bore at Burketown Queensland, established in 1897. Original depth 2,304 feet. These water bores litter the landscape of the Channel Country. They are uncapped and millions of mega-litres a year flow into the sand of the desert country.

- Contains processes for government decision-making with respect to making whether to make future grants for mining leases.

Aboriginal people have rights to cultural heritage; stock routes belong to this category and fall within the bundle of rights for native title. There is no legal provision within Australian jurisprudence to extinguish the stock routes from the ambit of native title. However, Aboriginal people have not yet tested this through the Australian court system; and this will remain the case provided the goal posts do not get moved or new legislation changes the tenure. As advancements are made by Aboriginal people in the area of social and cultural policies, the Australian Government moves the goal posts or changes the laws to hinder these advancements. The win through the Australian court system for Mabo and Native Title rights generated much public debate for and against Aboriginal peoples rights to land. It also created hope amongst Aboriginal people that finally the fiction of *Terra Nullius* has been wiped from the Australian legal system. However, when the Howard Liberal government came to power in 1996 they moved to overturn the gains Aboriginal people had previously made through the courts. The Howard Government then changed the Commonwealth Native Title Act 1993 by amending it. The Government formulated a '10-Point Plan'; the resulting Native Title Act Amendment Bill 1997 was designed without the consent of, or consultation with, Aboriginal people. The Act resulted in wiping out many of the gains Aboriginal people made with the Act's provisions for outright extinguishment of native title in some instances. The amendments also conferred more rights to land for non-Aboriginal land interests and secured these gains for non Aboriginal property holders.

Bibliography

Aboriginal Affairs Victoria. (1999). Information Sheet Mount William Quarry Site.

Aboriginal Connections: The Jagara are the people of the Brisbane River Watershed. <http://www.brisbane-stories.powerup.com.au/maggil> (accessed 3 September 2004).

Aboriginal Land Clam to Simpson Desert National Park. Report of the Land Tribunal established under the Aboriginal Land Act 1991 to the Hon. Minister for Lands, December 1994. Auscript, Brisbane Queensland.

Aboriginal Land Tribunal Report (1993). 'In The Matter of Aboriginal Land Claims: To Simpson Desert National Park'. Auscript, Brisbane Queensland.

Aiston, George (1937). *The Aboriginal Narcotic Pitcheri. Oceania 7.*

Altman, J. C. (1987). *Hunter-Gatherers Today: An Australian economy in north Australia.* Australian Institution of Aboriginal Studies, Canberra.

Arts Division, Department of Premier, Economic and Trade Development (1991). *Queensland A State for the Arts: Report of the Arts Committee.* Queensland Government Press, Brisbane.

ATSIC, *Native Title Report July 1996–June 1997* (September 1997). *The Wik Case Aboriginal and Torres Strait Islander Social Justice Commissioner.* Report of the Aboriginal and Torres Strait Islander Social Justice Commissioner to the Attorney- General as required by section 209 of the Native Title Act 1993. J.S. McMillan Printing Group. Australia.

Auscript (1993). 'Land Claim to Simpson Desert National Park', *Aboriginal Land Tribunal Report.* Brisbane.

Austin, C. G. (1959). 'History of the South-West Corner of Queensland', in *The Royal Historical Society of Queensland: Special Journal to Mark the Centenary of Queensland 1859–1959,* vol. 6, no. 1. Smith & Paterson: Brisbane.

Australia's Heritage 1788–1988, vol. 1 (1989). 'The Continent Takes Shape'. Lansdowne Press, Sydney.

Australia's Heritage 1788–1988, vol. 1 (1989). 'The Long Search for the Great South Land'. Lansdowne Press, Sydney.

Australia's Heritage 1788–1988, vol. 1 (1989). 'Voyagers to a New Destiny'. Lansdowne Press, Sydney.

Australian Heritage 1788–1988, vol. 3 (1989). 'Birth of Brisbane Town'. Lansdowne Press, Sydney.

Australian Heritage 1788–1988, vol. 3 (1989). 'King's quest for new rivers'. Lansdowne Press, Sydney.

Australian Heritage 1788–1988, vol. 4 (1989). 'The river that never was'. Lansdowne Press, Sydney.

Australian Heritage 1788–1988, vol. 5 (1989). 'The last trek of Sir Thomas Mitchell'. Lansdowne Press, Sydney.

Australian Heritage 1788–1988, vol. 6 (1989). 'The Gregory trio could match any hazard'. Lansdowne Press, Sydney.

Australian InFo International. (1989). *Australian Aboriginal Culture,* Australian Government Publishing Service, Canberra.

Australian Natural Resources Atlas. <http://audit.ea.gov.au/mapping> (accessed 3/11/2004.

Baker, D.W.A. (1997). *The Civilised Surveyor: Thomas Mitchell and the Australian Aborigines.* Melbourne University Press, Melbourne, Victoria.

Baker, R.M. (1988). 'Yanyuma Canoe Making'. *Rec. S. Aust. Mus.* vol. 22, no. 2.

Bancroft, Joseph (1877). *Pituri.* Government Printer, Brisbane Queensland.

Barker, H.M. (1966). *Droving Days.* Morrison and Gibb Limited, London Great Britain.

Barlow, Alex (1979). *Trade in Aboriginal Australia.* Australian Institute of Aboriginal Islander Studies, Canberra.

Barlow, Alex (1994). *Aboriginal Technology: Trade.* Macmillan Education Australia Pty Ltd, South Melbourne, Victoria.

Bates, Daisy (1985). (ed.) Isobel White. *The Native Tribes of Western Australian,* National Library of Australia, Canberra.

Bell, Sharenne (1997). *Arts, Business, Culture: A research report on an indigenous cultural industry in Queensland.* Queensland Government Publishing Service, Brisbane.

Bellwood, P.S. (1989). *The Colonisation of the Pacific: Some current hypotheses.* In A.V.S. Hill and Serjeantson (eds), *The Colonisation of the Pacific: A genetic trail.* Clarendon, Oxford.

Benterrak, Krim (1984). *Reading Country.* Fremantle Arts Centre Press, Fremantle.

Berndt, R.M. and C.H. Berndt (1954). *Arnhem Land: Its History and Its People.* Longman, Cheshire.

Berndt, Ronald, Catherine Berndt and John Stanon (1993). *A World That Was: The Yaraldi of the Murray River and the Lakes, South Australia.* Melbourne University Press, Melbourne.

Bernstein, Douglas, Roy Edwards, Srull Thomas and Wicken Christopher (1992). *Psychology.* Houghton Mifflin Company, Boston.

Birman, Wendy W. and Geoffrey Bolton (1972). *Australian Explorers: Augustus Charles Gregory.* Oxford University Press, Melbourne.

Birman, Wendy (1979). *Gregory of Rainworth: A Man in his Time.* University of Western Australia Press, Perth.

Birtles, Terry G. (1967). *A Survey of Land use and Settlement and Society in Atherton – Evelyn District, North Queensland 1880–1914.* Eacham Shire Council, Malanda.

Blainey, Geoffrey (1975). *Triumph of the Nomads: A History of Ancient Australia.* Macmillan, Melbourne.

Bolton, G.C. (1972). *A Thousand Miles Away: A history of North Queensland to 1920.* Australian National University Press, Canberra.

Bottoms Timothy (1999). *Djabugay Country: An Aboriginal History of Tropical North Queensland.* Allen and Unwin, St Leonards.

Bourke Colin, Colin Johnson and Isobel White (1980). *Before the Invasion: Aboriginal Life to 1788.* Oxford University Press, Melbourne.

Braidwood, Robert J. (1975). *Prehistoric Men.* Scott, Foresman, Glenview.

Brandl, C.G. (1972). *The Symbolism of the North-western Australian Zig-zag Design,* Oceania, vol. 42, no. 3.

Brisbane City Council: Suburban Sites. Retrieved 20 August 2003 from <http://www.bris-bites.com/suburbView.asp>.

Broome, Richard (1984). *Aboriginal Australians: Black Response to White Dominance 1788–1980.* George Allen & Unwin, Sydney.

Brown, Anne (1990). *Aborigines in the Environment,* Victorian Archaeological Survey Department of Conservation and Environment, Melbourne.

Buchanan, Bobbie (1997). *In the Tracks of Old Bluey: The Life Story of Nat Buchanan.* Central Queensland University Press, Rockhampton.

Bunya Mountains National Park: Visitor Information Sheet (2000). Queensland Environmental Protection Agency, Brisbane.

Burnum, Burnum (1988). (ed.) David Stewart. *Burnum Burnum Aboriginal Australia: A Traveller's Guide*. Angus & Robertson Publishers, North Ryde.

Burra, Laksar (2003). *Spirits of the Night Sky*. J.B. Books, Marleston.

Butlin, Noel (1983). *Our Original Aggression: Aboriginal Populations of Southeast Australia 1788–1850*. George Allen & Unwin, Sydney.

Butlin, N.G. (1984). 'Macassans and Aboriginal Smallpox', and 'The '1789 and '1829 Epidemics', *Working Papers in Economic History*, no. 22. Australian National University, Canberra Australia.

Butlin, N.G. (1993). *Economics and the Dreamtime: A Hypothetical History*. Cambridge University Press, Cambridge.

Butterworths (1997). *Australian Legal Dictionary*. Butterworths, Sydney.

Cairns, Hugh (2003). *Dark Sparklers: A Yidumduma's Wardaman Aboriginal Astronomy Northern Australia*. Australian Institute of Aboriginal and Torres Strait Islander Studies Press, Canberra.

Campbell, Judy (1985). 'Smallpox in Aboriginal Australia', *Historical Studies*, vol. 21, no. 84, pp. 280–350.

Cannon, Michael (1987). *The Exploration of Australia: From first sea voyages to satellite discoveries*. Reader's Digest, Surrey Hills.

Gardner, William (1854). 'Boundaries of the Blacks', cited in Paul Carter (1987), *The Road to Botany Bay: An essay in spatial history*. Faber and Faber, London.

Carnegie, David W. (1982). *Spinifex and Sand*. Hesperian Press, Victoria Park, Perth.

Carter, Paul (1987). *The Road to Botany Bay: An essay in spatial history*. Faber and Faber, London.

Cartwright, Frederick (1973). *Disease and History*. Fletcher & Son Ltd, Norwich, Great Britain.

Clendinnen, Inga (1993). *Aztecs: An interpretation*. Cambridge University Press, Melbourne.

Cleverly, John and Dennis Phillips (1987). *Visions of childhood: Influential models from Locke to Spock*. Allen & Unwin, Sydney.

Colliver, F. S. (1970). 'A Survey of monuments and antiquities in Queensland', in *Aboriginal Antiquities in Australia: Their Nature and Preservation*, (ed.) F.D. McCarthy. *Prehistory and Material Culture*, Australian Studies no. 22, Series no. 3. Australian Institute of Aboriginal Studies, Canberra.

Colliver, F.S. and F. P. Woolston (1978). *Aboriginals in the Brisbane Area: Eight Aspects of Brisbane History*. Library Board of Queensland, Brisbane.

Council for Aboriginal Reconciliation (1994). *Valuing Cultures: Recognising Indigenous Cultures as a Valued Part of Australian Heritage*. Australian Government Publishing Service, Canberra.

Country of Australia: The Land and People (1989). Reader's Digest, Sydney, NSW.

Courier Mail (1997). 'Art Scandal', 15 November.

Cowan, James G. (1989). *Mysteries of the Dream-Time: The spiritual life of Australian Aborigines*. Prism Press, London.

Cowan, James G. (1992). *The Aboriginal Tradition*. Element Books, London.

Critchett, Jan (1990). *A 'distant field of murder': Western District Frontiers 1834–1848*. Melbourne University Press, Melbourne Victoria.

Cryle, Denis (1992). 'Snakes in the grass: The press and race relations at Moreton Bay 1846–47', in *Brisbane: The Aboriginal Presence 1824–1860*, (ed.) Rod Fisher, Brisbane Historical Group, Papers no. 11. Brisbane History Group, Brisbane.

Daes, Erica-Irene (1997). *Protection of the Heritage of Indigenous Peoples*: Study Series 10. United Nations, New York.

Dalton, George (1971). *Economic Anthropology and Development: Essays on tribal and peasant economies*. Basic Books, New York.

Davidson, D. S, (1933). 'Australian Netting and Basketry Techniques, *Journal of the Polynesian Society*, vol. 42, pp. 257–99.

Davidson, D.S. (1935). 'The chronology of Australian watercraft', *Journal of the Polynesian Society*, vol. 44, pp. 140–75.

Davidson, D.S. (1937). 'Transport and Receptacles in Aboriginal Australia', *Journal of the Polynesian Society*, vol. 46, pp. 175–205.

Dawson, James (1981). *Australian Aborigines: The Languages and Customs of Several Tribes of Aborigines in the Western District of Victoria, Australia*.[1881] Australian Institute of Aboriginal Studies, Canberra.

Dayton, Leigh (2001). 'A genetic quirk discovery in the DNA of ancient Mungo Man could set off a new debate about human origins'. *The Australian*, January 9.

Dayton, Leigh (2001). 'Mungo Man: the last of it kind'. *The Australian*, January 9.

Department of Communications and the Arts (1994). *Creative Nation: Commonwealth Cultural Policy.* Australian Government Publishing Service, Canberra.

Department of the Arts, Sport, the Environment and Territories *The Role of the Commonwealth in Australia's Cultural Development*: A Discussion Paper (1992). Australian Government Publishing Service, Canberra.

Diamond, Jared (1998). *Guns, Germs and Steel: A short history of everybody for the last 13,000.00 Years*. Random House, Sydney NSW.

Dodson, Michael (1994). *Cultural Rights and Educational Responsibilities*, University of New England Press, Armidale.

Dodson, P. (1976). *Report of the Third Annual Queensland Conference of the Aboriginal and Islander Catholic Council of Australia*, January 1976.

Donovan, Val. (2002). *The Reality of the Dark History: From contact and conflict to cultural recognition*. Platypus Graphics, Brisbane.

Donovan, Val and Colleen Wall (eds.). (2004). *Making Connections: A journey along Central Australian Aboriginal trading routes*. Queensland Government, Arts Queensland, Brisbane.

Donovan, H. L. (1976). *The Aborigines of the Nogoa Basin: An Ethnohistorical Archaeological Approach*. University of Queensland Press, Brisbane.

Duncan-Kemp, A.E. (1961). *Our Channel Country: Man and nature in south-west Queensland*. Angus and Robertson, Sydney.

Dunphy, Myles (1986). *Myles Dunphy: Selective writings*. Ballagirin, Sydney.

Edwards, Rodney. H. (ed.), (1998). *The Romance and the Reality: A Guide to Managing Queensland's Stock Routes*. Queensland Department of Natural Resources, Brisbane.

Edwards, W.H. (ed.), (1987). *Traditional Aboriginal Society: A reader*. The Macmillan Company of Australia Pty Ltd. South Melbourne, Victoria Australia.

Edwards.W.H. (1988). *An Introduction to Aboriginal Societies*. Social Science Press. Wentworth Falls, Sydney, NSW.

Elder, Bruce (1988). *Blood on the Wattle: Massacres and Maltreatment of Australian Aborigines since 1788*. National Book Distributors and Publishers, Sydney.

Elisseeff, Vadime (ed.), (2000). 'Approaches Old and New to the Silk Roads', in *The Silk Roads: Highways of Culture and Commerce*. UNESCO, New York.

Elkin, A.P. (1934). 'Cult totemism and mythology in north-eastern South Australia'. *Oceania*, vol. 5. no. 2, pp. 160–93.

Ellis, Jean A. (1994). *Australia's Aboriginal Heritage*. Collins, Victoria.

Ethnography of the South-East of Queensland with special reference to Brisbane and District, a pamphlet.

Evans, Raymond (1992). 'The mogwi take mi-an-jin: Race relations and the Moreton Bay penal settlement 1824–42', in *Brisbane: The Aboriginal Presence 1824–1860*, (ed.), Rod Fisher Brisbane Historical Group, Papers no. 11. BHG, Brisbane.

Evans, Raymond. (2003). 'Dance to the Music of Time', *The Courier Mail*, 25 October.

Fairhall, Patricia (1994). *Ningi Ningi our First Inhabitants*. Redcliffe Historical Society, Brisbane.

Fatchen, T.J. and S. Barker (1979). 'Gradients in the distribution of plant species in the southern Simpson Desert'. *Australian Journal of Botany*, vol. 27, pp. 643–56.

Federal Department of the Environment, Sport and Territories (1996). *The National Strategy for the Conservation of Australia's Biological Diversity*. Australian Government Publishing Service, Canberra.

Finkel, George (1975). *Queensland 1824–1900*. Thomas Nelson (Australia) Limited Melbourne.

Fisher, Rod (1992), (ed.) *Brisbane: The Aboriginal Presence 1824–1860*, Brisbane History Group Papers no.11. Brisbane.

Fitzgerald, Ross (1982). *From the Dreaming to 1915: A History of Queensland*. University of Queensland Press, Brisbane.

Flannery, Tim (2000), (ed.). *Terra Australis: Mathew Flinder's circumnavigation of Australia*. Text Publishers, Melbourne Victoria.

Flannery, Tim (1998), (ed.). *The Explorers*. Text Publishing Company, Melbourne Victoria.

Flannery, Tim (1996), (ed) *Watkin Tench 1788*. The Publishing Company, Melbourne Victoria.

Flannery, Tim (1994). *The Future Eaters: An ecological history of the Australasian lands and people*. Reed New Holland, Sydney.

Flood, J. (1990). *The Riches of Ancient Australia: A Journey into Prehistory*. University of Queensland Press, Brisbane.

Flood, J. (1995). *Archaeology of the Dreamtime: The Story of Prehistoric Australia and its People*, Angus & Robertson, Sydney.

Flood, J. (1997). *Rock Art of the Dreamtime: Images of Ancient Australia*. HarperCollins Publishers, Sydney, NSW, Australia.

Forde, Daryl C. (1968). *Habitat, Economy and Society*. Methuen, London.

Fourmile, Henrietta. (1989). 'Who owns the past? Aborigines as captives of the archives', (in) *Aboriginal History*, vol. 13, nos. 1–2, pp. 1–9.

Ganter, Regina. (2006). *Mixed Relations: Asian-Aboriginal contact in North Australia*. University of Western Australia Press, Crawley Western Australia.

Ganter, Regina. (1999). 'Letters From Mapoon: Colonising Aboriginal gender'. *Australian Historical Studies*, vol. 30, no. 113.

Gardiner-Garden, John (1994). *Mabo Papers, "Aboriginality and Aboriginal rights in Australia"*. Australian Government Publishing Service, Canberra.

Geertz, Clifford (1973). *The Interpretation of Cultures: Selected essays*. Basic Books, New York.

Gilbert, Kevin (1989). (poem) *The New True Anthem*.

Gill, Sam. D. (1998). *Story Tracking: Texts, Stories, & Histories in Central Australia*. Oxford University Press, New York.

Gonzales, Ray. (2004). *The Geography of the Silk Road*. <http://www.humboldt.edu/~geog309i/ideas/raysilk.html> (accessed 5 March 2004).

Gostin, Olga. (2001). 'Accessing the Dreaming: Indigenous Students Response to Mungo

National Park', in *Working on Country: Contemporary Indigenous Management of Australia's Lands and Coastal Regions*. Oxford University Press, Melbourne.

Gray-Woods, Doris (1997). *With Compass Chain and Courage*. The Queensland Women's Historical Association, Miegunyah, Bowen Hills, Queensland.

'Greenslopes Aboriginal History'. <http://www.brisbites.com/suburbView.asp> (accessed 4 December 2003).

Gregory, A.C. (1859). *Journals of Australian Expedition*.

Grenville, Kate (1988). *Joan Makes History*. University of Queensland Press, Brisbane.

Griffiths, Tom (1996). *The Antiquarian Imagination in Australia*. Cambridge University Press, Melbourne.

Groom, A. (1950). *I Saw a Strange Land*. Angus & Robertson, Sydney.

Hamm, Giles (1993). *An Archaeological Survey of the Simpson Desert National Park: Aboriginal Historical Affiliations to Land*. A Report to the Tjilpatha Association. Giles Consultant Archaeologist.

Haralambos M. and R.M. Heald (1980). *Sociology: Themes and Perspectives*. University Tutorial Press, London.

Haran, Brady (2002). 'How the night sky came alive in Aboriginal lore'. *The Adelaide Advertiser*, 22 April, p. 4.

Hardy, M.E. (1969). *West of the Darling*. Jacaranda Press, Brisbane

Harney, W. E. (1950). 'Roads and Trade', in *Walkabout*, vol. 16, no. 5, pp. 43–45.

Hart, Victor. (1998). *Mapping Aboriginality and Aboriginal Landscapes: A Schematic Approach to Indigenous Landscape Knowledge*. University of Queensland Press, Brisbane.

Healy, C. (1997). *From the Ruins of Colonialism: History as Social Memory*. Cambridge University Press, Melbourne.

Hercus, L.A. (1987). 'Just One Toa', *South Australian Museum Records* 20, pp. 59–69.

Hercus, L.A. (1990). 'Aboriginal People', in M. J. Tyler, C. R. Twidale, M. Davies and C. B. Wells (eds.), *Natural History of the North East Desert*, Royal Society of South Australia Inc.

Hewitt, David (1980). *Brief History of the Canning Stock Route*. D. Hewitt, Perth Western Australia.

Hiddins, Les. (1998). *The Complete Jardine Expedition Journals*. Corkwood Press, Adelaide.

Hill, Marji. (1981). 'Untrammelled Art: Travelling Exhibition of Aboriginal Art', in *From Earlier Fleets –11 Hemisphere: An Aboriginal Anthology 1981*. Ruskin Press, Melbourne Victoria.

Hoch, Isabel (1986). *Barcaldine 1846–1986*. Barcaldine Shire Council, Barcaldine.

Hodgkinson, W.O. (1876). *Diary of the North Western Expedition, Votes and Proceedings of the Legislative Assembly*. Brisbane: Government Printers, Queensland.

Holmes, Sandra Le Brun (1992). *Yirawala Painter of the Dreaming*. Hodder & Stoughton, Rydalmere, NSW.

Horne, G. and G. Aiston (1924). *Savage life in Central Australia*. Allen & Unwin, London.

Howitt, Alfred William. (1882). *Notes on some trade centres*. Papers, Box 6, folder 3, AIATSIS. Canberra.

Humphrys, Ray (1999). 'Boni-Bonyi: Life and Legends of the Bunya Mountains', *Wyndham Observer*, Nanango.

Hunter, Rosemary (1996). *Aboriginal histories, Australian histories, and the law*, in The Age of *MABO History, Aborigines and Australia*, edited by Bain Attwood. Allen & Unwin, St Leonards, NSW.

Injinoo Land Council (1995). 'Injinoo Handbook: Welcome to Our Traditional Lands – Injinoo Language Names and Rock Art Figures'. *Torres News*, Thursday Island.

Innamincka Regional Reserve: Park Guide (July 2002). South Australian Government, Adelaide S.A.

Isaacs, Jennifer (1980). *Australian Dreaming: 40,000 Years of Aboriginal History*. Lansdowne Press, Sydney.

Isaacs, Jennifer (ed.). (1980). *Australia's Living Heritage: 40,000 Years of Aboriginal History*. Lansdowne Press, Sydney.

Jacaranda Atlas (1999). 5th (edn.) John Wiley, and Sons Australia, Ltd. Milton, Queensland Australia.

Jensen, Jo and Barrett Peta (1996). *Australian Explorers Ludwig Leichhardt*. Future Horizons Publishing, Brisbane.

Johnson, Richard (2001). *The Search for the Inland Sea: John Oxley the Explorer, 1783–1828*. Melbourne University Press, Victoria, Australia .

Johnston, Harvey and Cleland J. Burton (1933). 'The History of the Aboriginal Narcotic, Pituri', *Oceania*, vol. 4, no. 2, 3; [201]-223, [268] 289.

Jones, Phillip (1993). *Simpson Desert National Park: Land Claim*. A Report to the Tjilpatha Association (unpublished work).

Jones, Philip and Sutton, Peter (1986). *Art and Land: Aboriginal Sculptures of the Lake Eyre Region*. South Australian Museum and Wake Press, Adelaide South Australia.

Jordan, Jill (1996). *Report on Cherbourg Cultural Mapping Project*. Undertaken by the Local Government Association of Queensland for Cherbourg Aboriginal Council.

Joy, William (1964). *The Explorers*. Shakespeare Head Press, Sydney.

Keesing, Roger M. (1981). *Cultural Anthropology: A Contemporary Perspective*. Holt, Rinehart and Winston, New York.

Kerkhove, Ray (1985). *West End to Woolloongabba: The Early Aboriginal History of the District*. Foundation of Aboriginal and Island Research and Action, Brisbane.

Kerwin, Dale (1998). *Whose Rights? Aboriginal Peoples Rights for Intangible and Tangible Intellectual Property*. M.Phil., Faculty of Humanities, Griffith University, Brisbane.

Kimber, Dick (1980). 'Kangaroo Skin Water-bags: Some Early Notes on Manufacture and use in Central Australia', *Australian Institute of Aboriginal Studies Newsletter*, N.S., 14.

King, Robert J. (1986). Eora and English at Port Jackson: A Spanish View, *Aboriginal History*, vol. 10. no. 1. pp. 46–58. Australian National University, Canberra.

King-Boyes, M.J.E. (1977). *Patterns of Aboriginal Culture: Then and Now*. McGraw-Hill Book Company, Sydney.

Knapp, Vincent (1989). *Disease and its Impact on Modern European History*. Edwin Mellen Press, New York.

Lack, Clem (1966). *The Pale Invader and the Dark Avenger: The Story of the Aboriginal Tribes of Queensland*. Royal Historical Society of Queensland, Brisbane.

Latz, Peter (1995). *Bushfires & Bushtucker: Aboriginal Plant Use in Central Australia*. IAD Press, Alice Springs.

Lawlor, Robert (1991). *Voices of the First Day Awakening in the Aboriginal Dreaming*. Inner Traditions, Rochester, Vermont, New York.

Leichhardt, Ludwig (1847). *Journal of an overland expedition in Australia from Moreton Bay to Port Essington, a distance of upwards of 3000 miles, during the years, 1844–1845*. Facsimile edition (1964). London: T and W Boone, Libraries Board of South Australia, Adelaide.

Leopold, Aldo (1921), (ed.) Nash 1991, in *Wilderness and the American Mind*, 3rd edn. Yale University Press, New Haven.

Lethbridge, H.O. (1934). *Aboriginal Songs: Melodies, Rhythm and Words Truly and Authentically Aboriginal*. Allan & and Company Imperial Edition no. 420, Sydney.

Letnic, Mike. (2000). 'Along the Pituri Track', in *Australian Geographic, April–June* 2000, no. 58. pp. 104–13. Australian Geographic, Terrey Hills.

Lindsey, David (1890). *Explorations in the Northern Territory of South Australia. Proceedings of the Royal Geographical Society of Australia*. South Australian Branch, vol. 2, no. 1, pp. 1–16.

Logan, Jack Robert (1915). The Exploration of Cape York Peninsula, 1606–1915. *Australian Historical Society*.vol. iii, part v, pp.182–225.

Long, J.P.M. (1970). *Aboriginal Settlements: A Survey of Institutional Communities in Eastern Australia*. Australian National University Press, Canberra.

Low, Tim (1987). 'Pituri: Tracing the Trade Routes of an Indigenous Intoxicant', *Australian Natural History*, vol. 22, no. 6, pp. 257–60. The Australian Museum Trust. Sydney.

Low, Tim (1988). *Wild Food Plants of Australia*. Angus & Robertson, Sydney.

Low, Tim (1990). *Bush Medicine: A Pharmacopoeia of Natural Remedies*. Angus and Robertson, Sydney.

Mackellar Dorothea. (poem) *My Country*.

MacKnight, C.C. (1976). *The Voyage to Marege: Macassan Trepangers in North Australia*, Melbourne University Press, Melbourne.

Marika, Banduk (1992). *Bunjilaka Gallery:* 'Knowing Country', 2004, Melbourne Museum, Melbourne Victoria.

Marika, Wandjuk (1980). (Forward). Cited in Jennifer Isaacs, *Australian Dreaming 40,000 Years of Aboriginal History*. Lansdowne Press, Sydney.

Marika, Wandjuk (1974). In A.M. Moyle , *Songs from the Northern Territory*. Australian Institute of Aboriginal Studies, Canberra.

Marika, Wandjuk (1976). 'Aboriginal Copyright', *Art and Australia*, vol. 13, no. 3, pp. 242–44.

Massola, Aldo (1971). *The Aborigines of South-Eastern Australia: As they were*. Heinemann Publisher, Melbourne Victoria.

Mattingley, C. (ed.), (1988). 'Nungars telling their story of the invasion', *Survival in Our Own Land: 'Aboriginal' experiences in 'South Australia' since* 1836'. Wakefield Press, Adelaide.

McBryde, Isabel (1975). *Trade and Technology in South-East Australian prehistory*. AIAS Newsletter no. 3. Australian Institute of Aboriginal Studies, Canberra.

McBryde, Isabel (1980). 'Travellers in storied landscapes: a case study in exchange and heritage', *Aboriginal History*, vol. 24, pp.152–74. Australian National University Press, Canberra.

McBryde, Isabel (1987). 'Goods from another Country: Exchange Networks and the People of the Lake Eyre Basin', in *Australians to 1788*, D.J. Mulvaney and J.P. White (eds.), Fairfax, Syme and Weldon, Sydney.

McBryde, Isabel (2000). 'Travellers in storied landscapes: A case study in exchanges and heritage', *Aboriginal History*, vol. 24, Aboriginal History Inc. ANU printing, Canberra Australia.

McCarthy, Frederick David (1939). *Trade in Aboriginal Australia, and Trade Relationship with Torres Strait, New Guinea, and Malaya*. Government Press, Sydney.

McConnell, Anne (1976). *Aboriginal Trade in Australia* (A dissertation submitted for an MA), Department of Prehistory and Anthropology, ANU, Canberra.

McConvell, Patrick and Nicholas Thieberger (2000). A Report: *The State of Indigenous Languages in Australia*, Australia Institute of Aboriginal and Torres Strait Islander Studies, Canberra.

McCulloch, S. (1997). 'Art scandal a black cloud over Utopia', *The Australian*, 24 November.

McEwan, Marcia (1985). *Great Australian Explorers*. Bay Books, Sydney.

McKellar, Hazel (1984). *Matya – Mundu: A History of the Aboriginal people of the South West Queensland.* Cunnamulla Aboriginal Native Welfare Association, Cunnamulla.

McKnight, Tom L. (1977). *The Long Paddock: Australia's Travelling Stock Routes.* University of New England, Department of Geography, New South Wales.

McMinn, W.G. (1970). *Allan Cunningham: Botanist and Explorer.* Melbourne University Press, Carlton, Victoria.

Mercer, Colin (1997). *Australian Studies Images of Australia.* Faculty of Humanities, Griffith University Queensland.

Meston, E. A. (1955). 'Mestonian Flashes' in *Gummins & Campbell's.*

Micha, Franz J. (1970). 'Trade and change in Australian Aboriginal culture', in A.R. Pilling and R.A. Waterman (eds), *Diprotodon to detribalization.* Michigan State University Press East, Lansing.

Minyanderri-Pitjantjatjara (1966). Cited in Roland Robinson (trans.), *Minyanderri: Aboriginal Myths and Legends.* Sun Books, Melbourne.

Mitchell, T.L. (1836). *Three Expeditions into the Interior of Eastern Australia*, 2 vols, London.

Mitchell, T.L. (1846). *Journal of Exploration Expedition to Tropical Australia*, Manuscript in Mitchell Library, Sydney.

Mitchell, T.L. (1846). *Journal of Exploration Expedition to Tropical Australia*, Field Sketchbook, C66, reel 192, Mitchell Library, Sydney.

Mitchell, T.L. (1848). *Journal of an Expedition into the Interior of Tropical Australia in Search of a Route from Sydney to the Gulf of Carpentaria.* Facsimile edition 1999. Longman, London.

Moorehead, Alan (1963). *Cooper's Creek: The classic account of the Burke and Wills expedition across Australia.* Phoenix Press, London.

Morphy, H. (1972). *A reanalysis of the toas of the Lake Eyre tribes of Central Australia: an examination of their form and function.* M.Phil. Thesis, London University.

Morrish, Ivor (1978). *The Sociology of Education: An Introduction.* George Allen & Unwin, London.

Mountford, Charles P. (1976). *Nomads of the Australian Desert.* Rigby, Adelaide.

Mowaljarlai, David and Malnic, Jutta (1993). *Yorro yorro everything standing up alive: spirit of the Kimberley.* Magabala Books, Perth.

Moyle, A.M. (1974). *Songs from the Northern Territory.* Australian Institute of Aboriginal Studies, Canberra.

Mullins, Barbara (1988). *Aboriginal Lore: A pictorial review of ancient Aboriginal life, ritual and culture, as recorded in the marks they left on the land.* Shepp Books, Sydney.

Mulvaney, J. and J. Kamminga (1999). *Prehistory of Australia*, Allen & Unwin, Sydney.

Mulvaney, D.J. (1989). *Encounters in Place: Outsiders and Aboriginal Australians 1606–1985.* Queensland University Press, Brisbane.

Mulvaney, D.J., and White, J.P. (eds) (1987). *Goods from another Country: exchange networks and people of the Lake Eyre Basin Australians to 1788.* Fairfax, Syme and Weldon, Sydney.

Mulvaney, John (1976). 'The chain of connection', in N. Peterson (ed.), *Tribes and Boundaries.* AITSIS, Canberra.

Mulvaney, John (1975). *The Prehistory of Australia*, 2nd en., Penguin, Harmondsworth.

Mulvaney, John (1979). 'Thirty years for thirty thousand plus', in *Hemisphere – An Aboriginal Anthology 1981.* Ruskin Press, Melbourne.

Mumbulla Percy (1966). Robinson Roland. *Aboriginal Myths and Legends.* Sun Books, Melbourne.

Munn, Bob (2003). *Our Past Our Future: A Native Title Land Claim Report.*

Munn, Nancy (1970). 'The Transformation of Subjects into Objects in Walbiri and

Pitjantjatjara Myth', in *Australian Aboriginal Anthropology*, (ed.) R. Berndt. University of Western Australia Press, Perth.

Murphy, Lyndon (1996). *Reconstructing the Indigenous Australia: The Politics of Non-recognition*. University of Queensland Press, Brisbane.

Murphy, Lyndon (June 2000). *Who's Afraid of the Dark?: Australia's Administration in Aboriginal Affairs*. University of Queensland Press, Brisbane.

Myers, Fred and R. Edwards (eds.), (1987) *Always Ask: Resource Use and Land Ownership among Pintupi Aborigines of the Australian Western Desert* in *Traditional Aboriginal Society: A Reader*. Macmillan, Sydney.

Nash, Roderick (1982). *Wilderness and the American Mind*, 3rd edn., New Haven Publisher London.

Neate, Graeme (1989). 'Power, Policy, Politics and Persuasion: Protecting Aboriginal Cultural Heritage under Federal Laws', in *Environment and Planning Law Journal*. September, pp. 214–48.

Northern Land Council (1994). *Proceeding of the Ecopolicities IX Conference*. NLC, Darwin.

Northern Territory Government (2000). *Nitmiluk National Park: Jawoyn Country- Jawoyn Law Information Sheet*. Jawoyn Association and Parks and Wildlife Commission of the Northern Territory, Katherine.

O'Dwyer, Erin (2002). 'More embrace their heritage', *The Courier Mail*, 18 June.

Oliver, Douglas L. (1989). *Oceania: The Native Cultures of Australia and the Pacific Islands*, vol. 1, pp. 501–528. University of Hawaii Press, Honolulu.

Page, Henry (1993). *Aboriginal Land Tribunal Report: In the matters of Aboriginal Land claims to Simpson Desert National Park*. Australian Government Publishing Service, Brisbane.

PestFact an information Bulletin for the Queensland Rural Lands Protection Board (November 1988). 'The Stock Routes of Queensland'. Rural Lands Board, Brisbane.

Peterson, N. (1981). 'Art of the Desert', in *Aboriginal Australia*, Australian Gallery Directors Council, Sydney Australia.

Peterson, Nicolas and Lampert, Ronald (1985). 'A Central Australian Ochre Mine', *Records of the Australian Museum*, vol. 37, no. 1.

Petrie, C.C. (1981). *Australian Classics: Tom Petrie's Reminiscences of Early Queensland*. Lloyd O'Neil, Melbourne.

Pike, Granville (1982). *Queensland Frontier*. Pinevale Publications, Mareeba, North Queensland.

Queensland Government (1994). *Royal Commission into Aboriginal Deaths in Custody: Queensland Government Progress Report on Implement*. Government Printers, Brisbane.

Queensland Government (1998).*Queensland Aboriginal and Torres Strait Islander Economic Development Strategy*. Queensland Government, Brisbane.

Queensland Government (1999). *Innovation – Queensland Future: discussion paper*. Department of State Development, Brisbane.

Radcliffe, A.R. (1937). 'Correspondence', *The Times*, London, 15 December. Cited in W.E.H. Stanner and D. Barwick (1979). 'Not by Eastern Windows Only: Anthropological Advice to Australian Governments in 1938', *Aboriginal History*, vol. 3, nos. 1–2, pp. 37–61.

Radio National (2000). *Along the Pituri Trail*. Australian Broadcasting Corporation, 9 January.

Read, Peter (2000). *Belonging: Australians, Place and Aboriginal Ownership*. Cambridge University Press, Melbourne.

Reader's Digest (1989) *Country Australia: The Land and the People*. Reader's Digest, Surrey Hills.

Reese, Lew [1920s] (1930s). *Correspondence with J.B. Cleland*. AA60, South Australian Museum Anthropology Archives, Adelaide.

Reser, Joseph, Joan Bentrupperbaumer and Sandra Pannell (2000). 'Highway Construction(s) and World Heritage Values: Roads Taken and Roads Forsaken', in *Cultural Landscape of the Wet Tropics of North Queensland and the Antipodean Imaginary*. James Cook University Press, Townsville.

Reynolds, Henry (1972). *Aborigines and Settlers: Problems in Australian History*. Cassell Australia Limited, Melbourne.

Reynolds, Henry (1978). 'Before the Instant of Contact: Some Evidence from Nineteenth-Century Queensland', *Aboriginal History*, vol. 2.1, pp. 63–69. The Australia National University Press, Canberra.

Reynolds, Henry (1990). *With the White People: The crucial role of Aborigines in the exploration of the continent*. Penguin Books, Sydney.

Reynolds, Henry (1996). *Aboriginal Sovereignty: Three Nations, One Australia?* Allen & Unwin, Sydney.

Ritter, David (2000). *The Weltgericht of Yorta Yorta: Die Weltgeschichte Ist Das Weltgericht*. Unpublished paper.

Riviere, Marc Serge (1998). *Discovery of the Brisbane River, 1823 Oxley, Uniacke and Pamphlet 175 Years in Retrospect*. Royal Historical Society of Queensland, Brisbane.

Robertson, 'Drawing of an eel trap', dated 30 April 1841, displayed at *Bunjilaka Gallery*, Melbourne Museum.

Robinson, C. and N. Manunggurity (2001). 'Sustainable Balance: A Yolngu Framework for Cross-cultural Collaborative Management', in *Working on Country: Contemporary Indigenous Management of Australia's Lands and Coastal Regions*. Oxford University Press, Melbourne.

Robinson, Fergus and Barry York (1977). *The Black Resistance: An introduction to the history of the Aborigines' struggle against British Colonialism*. Widescope International Publishers, Melbourne.

Robinson, Joan (1983). *Economic Philosophy*. Pelican Books Australia Ltd, Melbourne.

Robinson, Roland (trans.), (1966). *Minyanderri: Aboriginal Myths and Legends*. Sun Books, Melbourne.

Rose, Deborah Bird (1985). *Aboriginal Trade: Research Brief Prepared for Network*. AIATSIS, Canberra.

Rose, Deborah Bird (1992). *Dingo Makes Us Human: Life and land in an Aboriginal Australian culture*. Cambridge University Press, Melbourne.

Rosser, Bill (1990). *Up Rode the Troopers: The Black Police in Queensland*. University of Queensland Press, Brisbane

Roth, W.E. (1897). 'The Queensland Aborigines', *Aboriginal Studies Series*, vols. 1, 2 & 3, no. 2, Facsimile edition 1984. Hesperian Press, Perth.

Roth, Walter (1897). *Ethnological Studies among the North-West-Central Queensland Aborigines*. Government Printers, Brisbane.

Roth, Walter [1897] (1983). 'Trade, Travel and Barter', in *One Week in Gympie. Department of Aboriginal and Islander Advancement: Cultural Series* issue 2.

Sahlins, Marshall (1972). *Stone Age Economics*. Aldine & Atherton, Chicago.

Saunders, M. (2002). 'Blacks in move to cities', *The Australian*, 27 June.

Schmidt, Annette (1990). *The Loss of Australia's Aboriginal Language Heritage*. The Institute Report Series, Aboriginal Studies Press, Canberra.

Schreiber Hermann (1962). *Merchants, Pilgrims and Highwaymen: A History of Roads Through the Ages*. Putnam, New York.

Serle, Geoffrey (1973). *From Deserts the Prophets Come: The Creative Spirit in Australia 1788–1972*. William Heinemann, Melbourne.

Sharing The Vision: A Framework for Cultural Development (1993). Australia Capitol Territory Cultural Council, Darwin.

Shephard, Mark (1992). *The Simpson Desert: Natural and Human Endeavour*. Royal Geographical Society of Australasia, Adelaide.

Simpson, Bruce (1996). *Packhorse Drover*. Australian Broadcasting Corporation Publisher, Sydney.

Smyth, R, Brough (1878). *The Aborigines of Victoria with Notes Relating to the Habits of the Natives of other parts of Australia and Tasmania*, vol. 2, George Robertson, Melbourne.

Smith, M.A. and P. Clark (1993). 'Radio-carbon dates for prehistoric occupation of the Simpson Desert', *Records of the South Australian Museum*, vol. 26, no. 2, pp. 121–27.

South Australian Government (2002). *Innamincka Regional Reserve: Park Guide*. Department for Environment and Heritage, Adelaide.

Spencer, W. and Gillen, F. (1899). *The Native Tribes of Central Australia*. Macmillan, London.

Spencer, W.and Gillen, F. (1912). *Across Australia*. Macmillan, London.

Stanner, W. (1968). 'After the Dreaming: Black and White Australians: An Anthropologist's View'. *The Boyer Lectures*, Australian Broadcasting Commission, Sydney.

Stanner, W. (1979). *White Man got no Dreaming: Essays 1939–1973*. Australian National University Press, Canberra Australia.

Stanner, W.E.H. and D. Barwick (1979). 'Not by Eastern Windows Only: Anthropological Advice to Australian Governments in 1938', *Aboriginal History*, vol. 3, nos. 1–2, pp. 37–61.

Steele, J.G. (1983). *Aboriginal Pathways: in Southeast Queensland and the Richmond River*. University of Queensland Press, Brisbane.

Stevens, Christine (1994). *White Man's Dreaming: Killalpaninna Mission 1866–1915*. Oxford University Press, Melbourne.

Swain, Toney (1993). *A Place for Strangers: Towards a history of Aboriginal being*. Cambridge University Press, Melbourne.

Taplin, G. [1879] (1967), (ed.). *The Folklore, Manners, Customs, and Languages of the South Australian Aborigines*. Johnson Reprint, Government Printers, Adelaide.

Taylor, N. (1966). *Plant Drugs that Changed the World*. Jarrold and Sons, Norwich.

The Warrego and South West Queensland Historical Society (1969). 'The History and Other Subjects Relating to Cunnamulla and District', a collection of papers, vol. 1.

Tench, Watkin [1789] (1996), (ed.) Flannery Tim. *Watkin Tench 1788*. The Text Publishing Company, Melbourne.

Terry, Michael (1974). *War of the Warramullas*. Rigby Limited, Melbourne.

Thallon, Keith (1967). 'Return to Cooper's Creek: In the Tracks of Burke and Wills and Their Predecessors', *The Royal Historical Society of Queensland*, vol. VIII, no. II.

The National Estate in 1981: A Report of the Australian Heritage Commission (1982). Australian Government Publishing Service, Canberra.

The Wotowurung: Aborigines in the Ballarat District Victoria, a pamphlet.

Thomson, D. F. (1957). 'Some watercraft of the Australian Aborigines', in *Walkabout*, vols. 19–20.

Thomson, Donald (1957). In *Bunjilaka Gallery: Journey of the Great Snake* (2004). Melbourne Museum. Melbourne, Victoria.

Thompson, Patrick (1989), (ed). *Myles Dunphy, The Father of Australian Wilderness*, Ballagrin, Sydney.

Thorne, Allan and Phil Macumber, Phil. (1972). 'Discoveries of Late Pleistocene Man at Kow Swamp Australian', *Nature*, vol. 238, no. 5363, pp. 316–19.

Toohey, J. (1979). 'Land Claim by Warlpiri and kartangarurru-Kurintji', cited in Graeme Neate (1989). 'Power, Policy, Politics and Persuasion: Protecting Aboriginal Cultural Heritage under Federal Laws', in *Environment and Planning Law Journal*. September, pp. 214–48.

Thrower, Norman J. W. (1996). *Maps & Civilization: Cartography in Culture and Society*. University of Chicago Press, Chicago.

Tibbett, Kevin (2002). 'Archaeological analysis of stone axe exchange networks in the Lake Eyre Basin during the mid- to late Holocene', in *Australian Archaeology*, no. 55, pp. 22–29. Flinders University Press, Adelaide.

Tindale Norman. B. (1987). 'The Wanderings of Tjirbruki: A Tale of the Kaurna People of Adelaide'. *Records of the South Australian Museum*, vol. 20, pp. 5–13. South Australian Museum, Adelaide.

Tindale, N. B. (1934a). *Diamantina Journal*.

Tonkinson, R. (1978). *The Mardudjara Aborigines: Living the Dreaming in Australian Desert*. Holt, Rinehart and Winston, New York.

Trebilco, Murielle (2002). *Wagon Wheels along the Wambo*. Wambo Historical Society, Queensland.

Turnbull, David (1989). *Maps are Territories, Science is an Atlas: Portfolio of exhibits*. Deakin University Press, Geelong.

Turnbull, Henry (1983). *Leichhardt's Second Journey: A First-Hand Account*. Halstead Press, Sydney.

UNESCO (1983). *Australian Aboriginal Culture*, Australian National Commission for UNESCO, Australian Government Publishing Service, Canberra.

Urry, James (1978). 'Old Questions: New Answers? Some Thoughts on the Origin and Antiquity of Man in Australia', *Aboriginal History*, vol. 2, nos. 1–2, pp. 149–66. Australian National University Press, Canberra.

Wambo Shire Council (2000). *Lake Broadwater Conservation Park: Information Sheet*. Wambo.

Warner, W. Lloyd (1969). *A Black Civilization: A Study of an Australian Tribe*. Harper and Row, New York.

Wasson, R. J. (1983). 'Dune sediment types, sand colour, sediment provenance and hydrology in the Strzelecki-Simpson Desert dunefields, Australia', in M.E. Brookfield and T.S. Ahlbrandt (eds), *Eolian Sediments and Processes*. Elsevier Science Publishers, Amsterdam.

Watson, F. J. (n.d.). 'Vocabularies of Four Representative Tribes of South Eastern Queensland: with Grammatical Notes there of and some Notes on Manners and Customs', *Journal of the Royal Geographical Society of Australia (Queensland)*, no. 34, vol. 58, pp. 1–114.

Watson, Pamela (n.d.). *Journal of the Royal Geographical Society of Australasia (Queensland)* vol. XLVIII, no. 30, p. 105.

Watson, P. *The use of Mulligan River Pituri. Occasional Papers in Anthropology.*, no. 10. University of Queensland Press, Brisbane.

Watson, Pamela (1983). *This Precious Foliage: A Study of the Aboriginal Psycho-active Drug Pituri. Oceania Monograph*, no. 26, pp. 1–56. University of Sydney, Sydney.

Wells, Robin A. (2003). *In Tracks of a Rinbow: Indigenous Culture and Legends of the Sunshine Coast*. Gullirae Books, Sunshine Beach, Queensland.

Willey, Keith (1979). *When the Sky Fell Down: The Destruction of the Tribes of Sydney Region 1788–1850s*. William Collins, Sydney.

Williams, Elizabeth (1984). 'Documentation and Archaeological Investigation of an Aboriginal Village Site in South Western Victoria', in *Aboriginal History*, vol. 8, nos. 1–2, pp. 173–88. Australian National University Press, Canberra.

Williams, Nancy M. (1987). *Two Laws: managing disputes in contemporary Aboriginal community.* Australian Institute of Aboriginal Studies, Canberra.

Willmot, Eric (1987). *Pemulwuy: The Rainbow Warrior.* Weldons, Sydney.

Wilson, Lindsay (1988). *Thathilgaw Emeret Lu: A Handbook of Torres Strait Islands Material Culture.* Education Queensland, Brisbane.

Yallop, Colin (1982). *The Language Library: Australian Aboriginal Languages.* Thetford Press, Thetford.

Younger, R.M. (1975). *Australia! Australia! The Pioneer Years: A Pictorial History.* Rigby, Adelaide.

Yunupingu, Galarrwuy (1997). An address to the Australian Arts Board, in Colin Mercer, *Australian Studies Images of Australia.* Faculty of Humanities Griffith University Queensland.

Personal Communications

Cheebalum (Uncle Bob Anderson), (20 July 2004), aged 75, a Nugi man from Mulgumpin (Moreton Island), Honorary Doctorate.

Coghill, Shane (October 1999) from Kroompul nation, Stradbroke Island.

Crombie, Jim (7 May 2004), a traditional owner from the Wangkangurru nation, Birdsville.

Crombie, Linda (6 May 2004), an Elder and a traditional owner from the Wangkangurru nation, Birdsville.

George, Tommy Senior (1990), a Kuku Tappan Elder, Laura, far north Queensland

Hurley, Ron (May 2000), from the Gareng Gareng nation, Queensland, a practising artist.

James, Alison (Parker) (6 May 2004), aged 72, a traditional owner and Elder from the Pitta Pitta nation, Boulia.

Jones, John (9 April 2004), aged 71, a traditional owner and an Elder from the Dalongabarra nation, Fraser Island.

Lee, Brett (1 June 2004), aged 30, an Aboriginal Ranger, Katherine, Northern Territory.

Leon, Mick (16 July 2004), a Goorie from the Worimi nation, Forster, NSW, and a cultural heritage manager/archaeologist.

MacNarra, Shirly (12 May 2004), a practising artist from Mount Isa.

McKellar, Danny (30 April 2004), an Aboriginal Ranger at Currawinya National Park in south-western Queensland.

Muir, Kado (21 June 2004), totem Dingo, an anthropologist and traditional owner from Leonora in Western Australia who represented the Greens at the Federal Election in 2004.

Munn, Bob (October 2002), a Gungari person from south-western Queensland who was chairperson of the Queensland Aboriginal Consultative Committee for Education, and a member of the Aboriginal and Torres Strait Islander Advisory Board to the Queensland Government in 2000.

Nannup, Noel (15 June 2004), a Wajuk man from the Bibbulmun nation, who received an Honorary Doctorate from Western Australian University.

Nathan, Alf (18 May 2004), aged 73, an Elder and traditional owner from the Pitta Pitta nation, born 60 miles (100 kms) outside of Georgina Yarrie (meaning all small hills), Pituri Creek, Glenormiston

Percey, Richard (10 July 2002), Kalkadoon Tribal Council Limited Cultural Keeping Place, Mount Isa, Queensland.

Renshaw, Barry (24 July 2002), Northern Territory Sacred Sites Authority.

Rowlands, Don and Lynn (5 May 2004) Park Managers, Simpson Desert National Park.

Smith, Dick (Robert) (15 May 2004,) aged 72, born at Beagle Bay Western Australia, and now resides at Tennant Creek, Northern Territory. A stockman in his youth, he drove horses across the Murranji Stock Route.

Sullivan,Tom (July 2002), an Elder at Dajarra, north-west Queensland.

Tarrago, Isabel (7 April 2004), aged 53, totem Dingo, a senior Aboriginal women from Arrente nation, a senior manager in the Aboriginal and Torres Strait Islander Cultural Heritage Branch, Queensland Department of Natural Resources Mines and Energy.

Wall, Colleen (10 April 2004), a Kabi Kabi woman, the Manager of the Aboriginal and Torres Strait Islander Arts Programs in the Department of Arts Queensland, a practising artist.

Wharton, Jim (30 April 2004), aged 64, an Elder from the Kooma nation, Cunnamulla, his totem is Dunble murri, and in his youth he was a stockman.

Yanna, Murrandoo (28 May 2004), aged 31 from the Gananggalida nation, Mungubie, (Burketown, north Queensland).

Collecting Institutions

Australian National Museum (2004). *Aboriginal Gallery: Cultural Exchange*, 'Macassans have visited north-eastern Arnhem Land over the last 400 years'. Canberra, ACT.

Australian National Museum (2004). *Aboriginal Gallery: Trading Goods and Culture: Crossing Boundaries*. Canberra, ACT

Australian National Museum (2004). *Aboriginal Gallery: The Importance of Trade*. Canberra, ACT.

Australian National Museum (2004). *Aboriginal Gallery: The Glimmer of Fires in the Night*. Canberra, ACT.

Australian National Museum (2004). *Aboriginal Gallery: Elders*. Canberra, ACT.

Melbourne Museum (2004). *Bunjilaka Gallery:* 'Journey of the Great Snake'. Melbourne, Victoria.

Melbourne Museum (2004). *Bunjilaka Gallery:* 'possum/kangaroo skin cloak'. Melbourne, Victoria.

Koori Heritage Trust (2004). 'Possum/kangaroo skin cloak'. Melbourne, Victoria.

Newspaper articles

'Art scandal', *Courier Mail,* 15 November 1997, p. 5.

Dayton, L. 'DNA clue to man's origin: How Mungo Man has shaken the human family tree', *The Australian*, 9 January, 2001 cover page, pp. 8–9 & editorial p. 16.

Dayton, Leigh. 'Prehistory pin-up boy', *The Australian*, 20 February 2003, p. 15.

Bowler, Jim. 'Mungo dates out of kilter: The claimed age of 62,000 years for Mungo Man is too old, *The Australian*, 10 January 2001, p. 19.

Harris, Trudy. 'In the eye of the evolutionary storm: Extinct gene gives debate a new life', *The Australian*, 10 January 2001, cover page.

McCulloch, Susan. 'Separated couple paint up a storm: Black art scandal unfolds', *The Australian*, 15 November 1997, p.10.

McCulloch, Susan. 'White man claims credit for prize-winning Aboriginal painting Revealed: Black art scandal', *The Australian*, 15 November 1997, p. 1.

McCulloch, Susan. 'Chance to start again with a clean canvas', *The Australian,* 15 November 1997, p. 5.

McCulloch, Susan. 'Artist retreats from authenticity storm', *The Australian*, 18 November 1997, p. 3.

McCulloch, Susan. 'Art scandal a black cloud over Utopia', *The Australian*, 24 November 1997, p. 4.

Nicholls, Christine. 'Kathleen Petyarre's message', *The Advertiser*, 19 November 1997, p. 44.

Ryan, Chris. 'Storm in the desert', *The Sydney Morning Herald*, 18 November 1997, p. 17.

Vince, Gaia. 'Aboriginal ancestry descends into robust debate', *The Australian*, 10 January 2001, p. 4.

Conferences

Creating Culture: The new growth industries (1994). Conference papers, Australian Government Publishing Services, Canberra.

Ecopolicities IX Conference Resolution (1994), organised by the Northern Land Council in Darwin Australia.

Index

Printed and bound by CPI Group (UK) Ltd, Croydon, CR0 4YY

23/04/2025

14660995-0001